# BANKING
## ON SOCIAL JUSTICE

I0491298

# BANKING
## ON SOCIAL JUSTICE

V John Devaraj

# Notion Press

Old No. 38, New No. 6
McNichols Road, Chetpet
Chennai - 600 031

First Published by Notion Press 2016
Copyright © V John Devaraj 2016
All Rights Reserved.

ISBN 978-1-945497-44-5

This book has been published with all efforts taken to make the material error-free after the consent of the author. However, the author and the publisher do not assume and hereby disclaim any liability to any party for any loss, damage, or disruption caused by errors or omissions, whether such errors or omissions result from negligence, accident, or any other cause.

No part of this book may be used, reproduced in any manner whatsoever without written permission from the author, except in the case of brief quotations embodied in critical articles and reviews.

TO
THE COMMON CITIZEN

BY
A COMMON CITIZEN

# CONTENTS

# PREFACE

This work is, in a way, an inspired response to the following verses from the Bible, St. Matthew, 25:35-40 in as much as they exhort the readers to be mindful of social justice and recognition of the basic needs of every human individual living in the contemporary, highly materialistic world:

"I was hungry and you fed me; I was thirst and you gave me water; I was a stranger and you invited me into your homes; naked and you clothed me; sick and in prison; and you visited me."

Then, these righteous ones will reply, "Sir, when did we ever see you hungry and feed you? or thirsty and give you anything to drink? or a stranger, and help you? or naked, and clothe you? When did we ever see you sick or in prison, and visit you?"

And the King shall answer them, "When you did it to my brother, you were doing it to me."

The above verses set forth the principle that the Creator of the Universe identified with those who were deprived and oppressed. Although the passage refers to past events, the truth applies today.

This book attempts to connect the themes of social welfare and banking activities in India. The Indian banking system has attempted to reach the common citizens to improve the quality of life by widening and deepening its activities to attain ultimately economic growth or development with justice in tune with the national objectives. Particularly, after nationalization, the role of banks has been considered pivotal for the process of economic development. The Reserve Bank of India (RBI), in the light of the above, formulated branch licensing policies, the lead bank scheme and other innovative programmes to be implemented in coordination with the State Governments.

Over the last four decades, the banking system has shown phenomenal growth in numbers in every region of the country. Whether this realized growth has promoted avenues to fulfill the basic needs of the common citizen is the central theme of the present study.

The empirical study has been carried out using published data on banking and other relevant variables at the national, state and district levels. The period covered is from 1950. Attempt was also made to distinguish the features, if any, for the post-nationalization period. Wherever applicable and based on the uniformity of data availability, analysis has been carried out to bring about micro level aspects. Future studies may bring out better findings, using technology.

Use of some simple statistical techniques and a simplified design of regression analysis have yielded varied results. Subject to the limitations of the analysis and the data, findings have been presented. There is a vicious circle in the mechanism of credit versus deposit creation.

The book contains six chapters. They are followed by an annexure containing Tables and historical data to enable the common citizen for analyses.

The responsibility for the contents of the book, facts, opinions, conclusions, etc. is entirely that of the author.

# ACKNOWLEDGEMENTS

The study was originally carried out under the guidance of revered teacher Prof. Dr. Ranganath Bharadwaj, Professor of Econometrics and Director of the Department of Economics, University of Bombay (Mumbai). He shaped my thoughts and I am grateful to him for his patience and affection. Thanks are due to the Senior Executives of the Reserve Bank of India (RBI) who permitted this author with the mandatory 'No objection Certificate' to pursue research work at the Mumbai University and on successful completion of the study again granted requisite permission to publish the same. Thanks are also due to the University of Bombay (Mumbai) to publish the work. I express my gratitude to the Indian Council of Social Science Research (ICSSR), New Delhi for the grant sanctioned for undertaking the study. Thanks are also due to the Publishers in its present form *viz.* M/s Notion Press, Chennai.

My profound thanks are due to Mr. Krishna Raj, Dr. A. Ramanathan (Professor at the Indian Institute of Technology, Bombay, (Mumbai) and Senior Executives of the RBI.

I express my inexplicable gratitude to my wife Caroline - a Pianist and a music Guide - for her devotion, tolerance, sacrifice, monumental understanding, extreme patience and silent support. Her love is a gift and without her help my study would not have been published. To my daughters Ms. Grace Shoba Merilyn and Ms. Adeline Lily for their technological help amidst their respective official routine, my son-in-law Mr. Sunil Mani and my grandson Shane Stanford Sunil for having been a source of immense joy and delight. To my father-in-law Mr. Thomas Durairaj Sell, former Manager at Economic and Political Weekly (EPW), my brothers Dr. V. Sam Sahayam and Mr. V. Selvin Devadhas and sister Mrs. Alice Aruldhas for their constant concern and affection. Finally, to all those persons whose names I might have inadvertently omitted I am deeply grateful.

Mumbai,

27-05-2016

V. JOHN DEVARAJ

# ABBREVIATIONS USED

AFI – Alliance for Financial Inclusion

AICC – All - India Congress Committee

ARC – Asset Reconstruction Company

ASHA – Accredited Social Health Activists

ASSOCHAM – The Associated Chambers of Commerce of India

ATM – Automated Teller Machine

BBB – Banks Board Bureau

BC/BF – Banking Correspondent/Banking Facilitator

BCP – Brach Credit Plan

BLBC – Block-Level Bankers Committee

CD ratio – Credit-Deposit ratio

CSS – Centrally Sponsored Schemes

CV – Coefficient of variation

DCC – District Consultative Committee

DCP – District Credit Plan

DLRC – District Level Review Committee

DRI – Differential Rate of Interest

EPW – Economic and Political Weekly

EXIM – Export – Import

FDI – Foreign Direct Investment

FIP – Financial Inclusion Plan

FIR – Financial Intermediation Ratio

FRB – Federal Reserve Bank

FSS – Farmers' Service Societies

GBS – Gross Budgetary Support

GDP – Gross Domestic Product

GNP – Gross National Product

HC – High Court

IBH – International Book House

ICT – Information and Communication Technology

ICRA – International Credit Rating Agency

ICSSR – Indian Council of Social Science Research

IDBI – Industrial Bank of India

IMF – International Monetary Fund

IRDP – Integrated Rural Development Programme

IT – Income Tax

JLB – Joint Liability Group

KM – Kilo Meter

LBS –Lead Bank Scheme

LDM – Lead District Manager

M – Mean

$M_1/M_2$ – Money Supply

MAP – Monitorable Action Plan

MIS – Management Information System

MLA – Member of Legislative Assembly

MP – Member of Parliament

MSE – Micro and Small Enterprise

NABARD – National Bank for Agriculture and Rural Development

NBER – National Bureau of Economic Research

NCT – National Capital Territory

NGO – Non-Governmental Organization

NHB – National Housing Bank

NPA – Non-Performing Asset

NREGP – National Rural Employment Guarantee Programme

NRLM – National Rural Livelihood Mission

NSSO – National Sample Survey Organization

NSWRCA – New South Wales Research Center Australia

PACs – Primary Agricultural Credit Societies

PCPNDT – Pre-Conception Pre-Natal Diagnostic Techniques Act, 1994

PDS – Public Distribution System

PLP – Potential Linked Credit Plan

PMO – Prime Minister's Office

PMJDY – Pradhan Mantri Jan Dhan Yojana

PRI – Panchayati Raj Institution

RBI – Reserve Bank of India

RBSC – Rare Books and Special Collection

RCC – Regional Consultative Committee

RGGVY – Rajiv Gandhi Grameen Vidutikaran Yojana

RRB – Regional Rural Bank

RTI – Right to Information

SAA – Service Area Approach

SD – Standard Deviation

SEEUY – Self-Employment Scheme for Educated Unemployed Youth

SEPUP – Self-Employment Programme for the Urban Poor

SIDBI – Small Industries Development Bank of India

SHG – Self-Help Group

SGSY – Swarnajayanti Gram Swarozgar Yojana

SJSRY – Swarna Jayanti Shahari Rozgar Yojana

SLBC – State Level Bankers Committee

SRMS – Scheme for Rehabilitation of Manual Scavengers

SSC – Special Sub-Committee

SSC – Special Sub-Centre

TOI – The Times of India

TRYSEM – Training of Rural Youth for Self-Employment

UCO – United Commercial

URL – Uniform Resource Locator

U.S.A. – United States of America

# INTRODUCTION

Social justice has been accorded top priority in the Constitution of India. Great emphasis has also been laid on the prevention of concentration of wealth and economic power. Growth with justice was also at the core of the Five-Year Plans. The banking system in India has been assigned a significant role to achieve this objective by widening and deepening its activities at the micro level.

The nationalization of the Reserve Bank of India (RBI) in 1948 paved the way for the linkage between central banking functions and the socio-economic objectives of the Government. Besides Indian banks are the prime movers in the process of development with social justice.

The Reserve Bank of India, through its branch licensing policies, has attempted to bring about rapid socio-economic development of different sectors of the economy by letting commercial banks into areas where orthodox banks fear to tread.

In 1954, the Indian Parliament declared that the broad objective of economic policy was to achieve a socialistic pattern of society. Following the reorganization of the princely states, state-associated banks were brought under the control of the State Bank of India during the period 1956-59, as suggested by the All-India Rural Credit Survey Committee in 1954.

The ideal of democratic socialism was accepted as per the resolutions of the All-India Congress Committee (AICC) session in Bhubaneswar in 1962. In 1967, at the AICC session, there was a resolution regarding social control over banks which ultimately led to the nationalization of major banks in 1969.

One of the study groups constituted by the National Credit Council headed by Prof. D.R. Gadgil recommended adoption of an area approach to evolve schemes for the proper growth of banking and credit structure. Based on its recommendations, the Reserve Bank of India formulated the Lead Bank Scheme (LBS) in 1969 under which all districts were allotted to commercial for opening branches, conducting surveys and assisting the overall development of the district concerned.

Providing adequate bank credit to priority sectors and neglected sections was one of the objectives of nationalization of banks. Banks, therefore, formulated district credit plans and annual action plans as part of development process.

These plans were intended to ultimately improve the quality of life of all citizens. Lead banks were required to lead each district through formulation of suitable schemes in consultation with the local administration. It was, thus, assumed that the system would thereby improve the hitherto neglected rural sector.

Therefore, under the service area approach, each bank branch in the rural and semi-urban areas of the entire country was allotted a designated service area of about 15 to 25 villages in the neighborhood.

Rural branches were allowed to utilize one day in a week under 'non-banking working day' scheme devoting banking services connected with deposit mobilization and recovery of advances. Lead Bank Scheme is administered by the Reserve Bank of India.

Prudent planning of branch expansion, it was thought, would lead to the establishment of forward and backward linkages which in turn, induce multiplier effect initiating accelerated growth process in various sectors and regions, increasing the level of output, employment and income and thereby growth of the economy with distributive justice. Experience of a few countries confirms that commercial banks have aided in their economic development at a certain stage.

Economic growth requires a high level of savings and investment. Capital formation is a determinant of growth of output. It also demands profound structural changes in various sectors and positive changes among various sections. The banking system plays its role in the economy as a catalyst to bring about increased output and income to aid capital formation through economic activities. Given the urgent need to expand national output at a stable pace, the need for efficient utilization of capital stock and infrastructure to induce manufacturing activities also assumes special importance.

The Reserve Bank of India monitors branch expansion, credit deployment and money creation by banks to serve the broader public interests. The Banking Regulation Act, 1949 has been amended from time to time to meet the credit needs of India - a developing economy.

Extension of the monetized sector to widen the banking habits, narrowing down of disparities between the supply of and the demand for funds, lending at reasonable cost to priority sectors and development of adequate institutional machinery for meeting the credit requirements of industry and agriculture are important aspects of the Reserve Bank of India's promotional role.

The period since 1951 has been eventful for the commercial banks in India as mobilisers of savings and purveyors of credit. Since the nationalization of major Indian banks in 1969, the Reserve Bank of India has reoriented the banking policy as an active instrument of development and for securing a progressive reduction in inequalities in income, concentration of economic power and regional disparities in banking facilities.

The objectives of geographical expansion of banks in India have always focused at attaining the goals of promotion of monetization and monetary integration of the economy; filling in the gaps in the financial infrastructure; meeting the credit needs of all sectors of the economy and above all in extending support to the planning authority in efficient and productive deployment of investible funds so as to maximize economic growth and social justice. Therefore, the branch licensing policies have been designed, *inter alia*, as a tool for reducing inter-regional disparities in development and deployment of credit.

There were 2,857 bank branches in 1946. At the time of nationalization of major commercial banks in 1969, there were 8,262 bank branches and the average population served by a bank branch was 65,000. At present there are more than 1,30, 500 bank branches of scheduled commercial banks and the average population served by a bank branch has been reduced to 10,000.

According to the current policy, every village in India with a population of 5,000 and above will have a physical bank branch by March 2017. There are 18,760 villages with a total population of over 13 crore and many of them do not have a bank branch. Banks are using banking correspondents and business facilitators to meet rural targets set by the RBI and the Union Government. How far the geographical expansion of commercial banks has aided economic development to benefit the common citizen of India is the aim of this Study.

The present work, thus, seeks to examine and evaluate some of the crucial aspects related to development of banking sector in India. The study, in particular, attempts to unravel various aspects relating to the implications of development banking for socio-economic perspectives. The first Chapter, *inter alia*, deals with the following sections: the conceptual, definitional and theoretical framework, the problem formulation, objectives of the Study in detail, the methodology adopted and the chapter contents.

## Section – I: Conceptual, Definitional and Theoretical Framework:

Money supply *(RBI (1977), "Report of the Second Working Group on Money Supply in India: Concepts, Compilation and Analysis")* in India consists of currency with the public, demand and time deposits with the banks and other deposits with the Reserve Bank of India (RBI). Money is, thus, a social phenomenon and many of its current features depend on what people think it is. For instance, Milton Friedman *(Friedman, M. (1971) "A Theoretical Framework for Monetary Analysis" NBER)* emphasized the store of value function of money. Other definitions of money supply were evolved to underline importance of banks and economic activities.

A bank mobilizes the savings of the community in the form of deposits and deploys these to productive activities and also creates assets to generate income and thus, secondary deposits. While an individual bank acts on the basis that loans are advanced out of its deposits, the entire banking system partially acts on the basis of that loans and advances also constitute the basis for additional deposits. The banking system, thus, transmits the monetary policy.

The study assumes that the number of bank branches established across our country have performed this basic function.

Deposits which result directly from the lending and investing activities of an individual commercial bank are termed 'derivative' *(Keynes, J.M. (1930), "A Treatise on Money," Harcourt Brace & Co. Vol.I, Chapter II)* or secondary deposits which are distinguished from primary deposits which result from the actual placement of cash or its equivalent. Derivative deposits create additional bank credit. Primary deposits do not create credit. Hence, increases in total supply of money in an economy come about primarily as a result of lending and investing activities of the banking system in the form of derivative deposits.

The growth of productive activities of various industries and sectors hinges on allocation of investment funds or bank credit. Banks provide capital which is a means of diverting the factors of production to new uses *(Schumpeter, J.A.(1949), "The Theory of Economic Development," Harvard University, Massachusetts, p.122)*. The flow of capital into various segments is a facet of the provision of finance and capital formation in the country.

As banks play their role as catalysts, it was hoped that industrialization would bring about social transformation, social equality, higher levels of employment, more equitable distribution of income and well-balanced regional development *(Meier, G.M. (1976), "Leading Issues in Economic Development," Oxford University Press, New York, p.659)*.

Banks, indeed, in a few countries–developed as well as developing countries- have participated in economic development at a certain stage *(Arumugam, P (1989), "Banking Systems of the World," Skylark Publications, New Delhi)* and continue to do so. The success of banking activities largely depends on the geographical as well as population coverage. The concept of branch banking particularly seeks to attain these aspects.

As there are overwhelming factors in favour of the branch banking, many countries have opted for it. In the United States of America, Japan, Malaysia, Germany, Australia, Finland, Italy, Kenya and Austria, for instance, the branch network has been instrumental in development.

The Reserve Bank of India, through its branch licensing policies, has helped rapid development of different sectors of the economy by letting banks into areas where orthodox banks would have feared to tread. Micro-operations of banks through branch network have wide-ranging effects on the micro-economy and social welfare. Prudent planning of branch expansion, it was thought, would lead to forward and backward linkages, thereby inducing the multiplier effect.

In order to evaluate success stories of development and branch banking, it is indeed, useful to place various facets and features of economic development ('development' as a term) in its proper perspective.

Development means people- the preparation and activation of people-is the cause of economic and social development *(Leopold Laufer, (1967) "Israel and the Developing Countries; New Approaches to Co-operation," Twentieth Century Fund, New York, p.69).*

Development is the fuller utilization of a country's resources, including human resources to maximize economic growth and advancement of the welfare of the community so as to ensure fair and equitable distribution of benefits of such growth. While dealing with human development, Nobel laureate Amartya Sen, *inter alia,* emphasizes educational rights, gender equality, healthcare, social security and land reforms.

Economic growth or development ought to be tied down to the maximization of productivity of commodities, such as the green revolution, hydro-electric projects, roads, heavy industry, manufacturing activities, etc. *(Goel,D.1986)," Development: Some Analytical Remarks" in 'Development: Socio-Cultural Dimensions" (ed), S.L. Sharma, p.234).* According to the United Nations, 'the ultimate purpose of development is to provide increasing opportunities to all people for a better life; it is essential to bring about a more equitable distribution of income and wealth for promoting both social justice and efficiency of production; to raise substantially the level of employment, to achieve a greater degree of income security, to expand and improve facilities for education, health, nutrition, housing and social welfare, and to safeguard the environment. Thus, qualitative and structural change in the society must go hand in hand with economic growth and existing disparities-regional, sectoral and social-should be substantially reduced. These objectives are both determining factors and end results of development. They should, therefore, be viewed as integrated parts of the same dynamic process *(United Nations (1975), "Poverty, Unemployment and Development Policy: A Case Study of Selected Issues with Reference to Kerala, United, New York, p.iv).*

The objective of economic development is not only a steady rise in gross national product, per capita income, real output and general standard of living, but also a high physical quality of life. The physical quality of life will be high when the marginal social marginal productivity of wealth is high.

The Directive Principles of State Policy require the State to direct its policy in such a manner as to secure the distribution of ownership and control of the material resources of the community, to ensure that the operation of the economic system does not result in the concentration of wealth and means of production to common detriment. In other words, the State shall promote the welfare of the people through an equitable social order. The directive principles also commit the State to narrowing inequalities in income. The State has to eliminate inequalities in status; facilities and opportunities not only among individuals, but also amongst groups of people residing in different areas engaged indifferent occupations

(*Article 38.2*). National development objectives, therefore, relate not only to a rate of growth, but also to distribution of resources.

Since independence, the thrust of banking activities has been on social control schemes. The nationalization of the Reserve Bank of India in 1948 paved the way for the linkage between central banking functions and the socio-economic objectives of the Government. Branch licensing policies were evolved to 'meet progressively and serve better developmental needs of the economy in conformity with the national policy objectives' (*See Preamble to the Banking Companies Acquisition and Transfer of Undertakings), (Nationalisation Act) Act, 1969*).

The Reserve Bank of India sought to meet through geographical expansion of banks the goals of monetization and monetary integration of the economy, filling in the gaps in the financial infrastructure, meeting the sectoral credit needs and above all, in supporting the planning authority in its efforts towards efficient and productive deployment of investible funds so as to maximize growth with stability and social justice (*Reserve Bank of India, 1983), "Functions and Working," pp.7-8*).

The branch licensing policy of the RBI formulated over the years has also been greatly influenced by the Lead Bank Scheme in striving for planned extension of banking facilities to bring about greater regional balance.

The existing Indian banks have been classified into scheduled banks and non-scheduled banks. All scheduled commercial banks together account for more than 99 per cent of total banking business.

(*Scheduled banks are those included in the Second Schedule to the Reserve Bank of India Act, 1934. They, inter alia, satisfy the RBI that their affairs are not conducted in a manner detrimental to the interest of depositors. Scheduled banks are required to maintain a certain amount of reserves with the RBI; they, in turn, enjoy the facility of financial accommodation and remittance facilities at concessional rates from the RBI*)

(*Non-Scheduled banks are those not included in the second schedule to the RBI Act, 1934*) There were 4 non-scheduled banks as at end- December, 2015.

All scheduled banks are expected to accelerate development and, thus, make a significant impact on the problem of poverty and unemployment and to bring about progressive reduction of disparities between the rich and the poor sections and between the relatively advanced and backward areas of the country (*See Text of the Statement made by the Prime Minister in Parliament, "The Banker," July, 1969 p.366*).

Central banks in underdeveloped countries are regarded as engines of economic growth (*Basu, S.K., (1967)."Central Banking In The Emerging Countries," Asia Publishing House, Bombay, p.180*). Sections 17 and 18 of the Reserve Bank of India Act, 1934 relate to advances by the RBI in general and advances to banks against any security as it may consider sufficient. The Indian commercial banks are also structured to control the commanding heights (*Vaish, M.C., (1984), "Modern Banking," RBSC Publishers, Jaipur, p.192*) of the economy in accordance with the accepted maxim of growth with justice. Growth based on equity is a valid alternative for reformation (*Gunnar Myrdal, (1969), "Economic Theory and Underdeveloped Regions"*) which warrants increase in marginal social productivity.

## Section – II: Problem Formulation

Due to rapid and massive branch expansion since nationalization, banks have grown into large institutions with their branch network spread far and wide. The number of branches of scheduled commercial banks rose from 8,262 in June 1969 to 1, 30,482 as on March 31, 2015. As a result, the average population served by a bank branch declined from 65,000 in June 1969 to 10,000 in March 2015.

The branches have been performing both traditional and innovative banking functions in achieving socio-economic objectives. There has been a marked shift in the deployment of bank credit in favour of a few preferred sectors and sections of the society. The bank branches have also been participating in poverty-alleviation programmes pursued by the Government.

The main aim of the present study is to find out how far the geographical expansion of Indian commercial banks has aided economic growth (development) with justice. Though numerous studies have been undertaken earlier on banking development and its relevance in the economy, these did not touch the grass root level. The present study has gone deeper and has made a micro (geographical) analysis of the relationship between the banking variables as well as the real sectors of the economy. Inter-regional disparities have also been examined closely. Based on the authentic published data, the District-wise position is presented as **Annexure –I.**

## Section – III: Objectives

The major objectives of the study are:

(i)   To examine whether the widening and deepening of banking facilities have benefitted the common citizen at the grassroots level;

(ii)  To analyze whether the geographical expansion of Indian banks has provided stimulus to sectoral growth;

(iii) To measure how far the lead banks have helped in district-level development;

(iv)  To examine the role of banks in the uplifting of the weaker sections of the society;

(v)   To analyze whether the Indian banking system has reduced the inter-regional disparities;

(vi)  To examine whether there has been any structural change in the pattern of Indian banking system during the post-nationalization period;

(vii) To assess the part played by geographical expansion of banks in increased access to banking services; and

(viii) To enable further research on the subject by common citizens.

## Section – IV: Methodology

The methodology adopted is based on available literature. In view of paucity of certain data such as end-use of funds, customer service and complaints and security arrangements in bank branches primary information was sought through discussions with the bank branch managers, customers, trade unionists and social scientists.

Data collected since 1950-51 on the number of bank branches, aggregate deposits, aggregate credit, national income, gross savings, and bank credit to agriculture, agricultural production, bank credit to industry, industrial production, etc. on all –India basis were subjected to empirical analysis separately for the (i) pre-nationalization period (i.e. from 1950-51 to 1968-69), (ii) post-nationazation period (i.e. from 1969-70 to 1987-88) and (iii) the entire plan period (i.e. from 1950-51 to 1987-88).

Tests also covered from 1970-71 to 1986-87, 12 major states of the Indian Union for which relevant data were available. The States are: (i) Andhra Pradesh, (ii) Bihar, (iii) Gujarat, (iv) Karnataka, (v) Kerala,

(vi) Madhya Pradesh, (vii) Maharashtra, (viii) Punjab, (ix) Rajasthan, (x) Tamil Nadu, (xi) Uttar Pradesh and (xii) West Bengal. Districts also have been surveyed.

The techniques used in the various analyses of the study to enable a common citizen/readers to understand are as under:

I. Simple tools of analyses of quantitative data such as:

(a) Computation of percentages, coefficient of variation and correlation coefficients for selected intervals and for the whole period.

(b) Chow's 'F' value was calculated to justify division of the plan period under study into pre and post-nationalization periods.

II. Multiple regression analyses using time series data to identify the behavior of variables representing socio-economic aspects with reference to banking indicators.

## Sources of Data

For the purpose of this study, secondary data on all scheduled commercial banks were taken from various Government of India and Reserve Bank of India publications, Central Statistical Organization, Planning Commission and census reports. As there was paucity of data, primary information was sought to be gleaned through discussions with branch managers of commercial banks, customers of banks, editors of journals, trade unionists and social scientists.

Chapter - 1: Introduction

This chapter explains the role of money and banking in economic growth with distributive justice.

Chapter - 2: Money, Credit and Economic Development – Issues and Evidences.

This chapter presents a brief survey of a few theoretical and empirical studies in the field of banking development.

Chapter - 3: Banking Development in India – A Historic Perspective

This chapter deals with the evolution of branch banking in India. It traces the Indian experience of widening and deepening of bank branches from its origin. Branch licensing policies pursued up to 2016 are also presented.

Chapter - 4: Development Indicators and The Progression

This chapter points out the level of structural transformation achieved at the national, state and district level in terms of certain common socio-economic indicators. It looks into the implications for growth and social justice in India and directions for further research.

Chapter - 5: Branch Banking - Empirical Evidence

This chapter presents a model consisting of banking and economic variables. It is an attempt to capture the effects of financial intermediation attempted in India by widening and deepening of bank branches. The model has been subjected to empirical analyses.

Chapter - 6: Conclusion

This chapter summarizes the main conclusions of the entire study.

CHAPTER

# 2

# MONEY, CREDIT AND ECONOMIC DEVELOPMENT – ISSUES AND EVIDENCES

Economists have expressed divergent views on the efficacy of banking system in widening and deepening monetization and monetary integration in economic development. Joseph A. Schumpeter *(Schumpeter, J.A. (1923) 'The Theory of economic development," Cambridge)*, the first modern economist to study the relationship, regarded banking system as one of the two key agents (the other being entrepreneurship) in the whole process of development. Alexander Gerschenkron *(Quoted in A.C. Shah, (1974), "Banking for Economic Growth," Journal of the Indian Institute of Bankers, vol.45, No.1 (Jan-March), p.33)* looked at banks as substitutes for deficiencies in the original accumulation of liquid wealth, in moderately backward economies.

In the word of Sayers *(Sayers, R.S.(1967)," Modern Banking," Oxford University Press, p.218)* banks and other financial intermediaries perform the useful service of 'mobilizing savings', making available to those who will use them for adding to the real capital equipment of the economy. The primary reasons are:

(i) Commercial banks are the only institutions in the economy with the ability to create money in the form of demand deposits,

(ii) Commercial banks are the primary financial institutions responsible for administering the payment mechanism,

(iii) Commercial banks remain the focal point though monetary policy is implemented by the central bank of the country,

(iv) Commercial banks affect all sectors of the economy because of their broad lending powers and consequently have an impact on economic growth;

(v) Commercial banks are generally more heavily regulated than other financial institutions *(Roger, D. Rutz, (1979), "Commercial Banking Structure and Economic Growth in United States:, University of Chicago, pp.107-108)*.

Opening new branches in an unbanked area is the right way to attract bank customers and deposits. In other words, there is a correlation between the rate of growth of deposits and the rate of growth of new branches *(Karkal, Gopal, (1977), "Perspective in Indian Banking," Popular Prakashan, Bombay, pp.68-69)*. Banks mediate between the ultimate borrowers who are the investors and the ultimate borrowers who are the investors and the ultimate lenders who are the savers in the community.

These institutions provide lenders with financial assets which are liquid and less risky. The first step in the mobilization of deposits and in disbursement of credit is to create necessary financial infrastructure facilities by establishing more branches (*Kannan, R. (1987), "Banking Development and Regional Disparities," The Indian Economic Journal, Vol. 35, No.2, p.59*).

The principal policy objective after nationalization of major commercial banks was to bring about an equitable distribution of bank funds in accordance with certain broad sectoral and regional priorities (*Ghosh, D.N., (1979), "Credit Planning and Banking System – Some Issues" in S.L. Shetty (ed) p.117*). Intelligent utilization of credit by the commercial banks holds the key to promoting development and that private investment is an indispensable catalyst in this connection (*Shigao Horie (1967), "Economic Development- The Banking Aspects," The Per Jacobson Foundation, Sep. 22, p.5*). A rising rate of saving rate is essential for the growing requirement of capital formation in a growing economy. I the interest of social welfare and stable growth, the savings required for the planned rate of capital formation be, as far as possible, voluntary (*Naresh Jha, (1982), "Role of Banking in Rural Development," Southern Economist, April 15, p.30*).

The purposes of banking development in rural areas are:

(i) To mobilize deposits to meet the demand for rural development expenditure;

(ii) To remove regional variation in income generation by deployment of credit in the priority sectors and

(iii) To set the pace of economic growth in the rural sector so that the economy may achieve the objective of balanced growth (*Bhatia, B.S. & A.S. Chawla, (1984), " Banking and New Economic Programme," Published in S.D. Tripathi and K.K. Uppal (ed), Banking and New Economic Programme, Publication Bureau, P.K. Chandigarh*).

The importance of banking institutions is felt rather deeply in the under-developed economies in the sense that these are usually short of capital and the task of mobilization of resources and their deployment to the priority sectors belong to such institutions. In McKinnon's words, deposits may serve as a 'conduit' for capital formation, making deposits complementary assets (*Quoted by Lazarus E. Molho, (1986), "Interest, Rates, Savings and Investment in Developing Countries- A Re-Examination of the McKinnon Shaw Hypothesis, IMF Staff Papers, Vol. 33, No.1, March, p.91*). The availability of deposits with positive real rates of return may encourage both saving and capital formation. Shaw stressed the importance of positive real deposits as an inducement to save financially repressed economies.

According to the 'complementary' hypothesis McKinnon (*McKinnon, R.I. (1973), "Money and Capital in Economic Development," Brookings Institution, Washington D.C. p.67.*), in a self-financed economy, where indivisibilities in investment are important and the Government does not directly participate in capital formation, real cash balances serve as a 'conduit' for capital formation.

The basic idea is that in such an economy, accumulation of real cash balances must precede that of physical capital. But, since the demand for real cash balance is postulated to be positively and significantly related to the real rate of return on such balances, it follows that capital formation is a positive function of this rate of return, which is what the 'complementarily' hypothesis is all about. McKinnon asserts that private investment is quite sensitive to the real return on holding money and its stability.

In his test of the repressionist hypothesis for South Korea, McKinnon showed that the ratio of $M_2/GDP$ went up from 0.09 in 1964 to 0.33 in 1970, while the real return on one year time deposits changed from -12.6 per cent in 1964 to +12.6 per cent in 1970, with inflation falling from 35 per cent to 9 per cent over the same period.

According to Gurley and Shaw (*Gurley, J.G. and E.S, Shaw, (1967),*

*"Financial structure and Economic Development," in economic Development and Cultural Change, pp.258-260)*, financial development depends on real growth. In other words, it is essentially demand –following. Patrick (*Gupta, K.L. (1984), "Finance and Economic Growth in Developing Countries," Croom Helen, p.12)* distinguishes between supply-leading and demand-following financial development. According to him, demand-following development is the phenomenon in which the creation of modern institutions, their financial assets and liabilities, and related financial services is in response to the demand for these services by investors and savers in the real economy. In this sense, the evolutionary development of the financial system is a continuing consequence of the pervasive, sweeping process of economic development.

In supply-leading development, the creation of financial institutions and supply of their financial assets, liabilities and related financial services is in advance of its demand for them, especially the demand of entrepreneurs in the modern growth-inducing sectors. According to Patrick, both phenomena exist at different stages of development. The supply-leading role of banks, therefore, represents a situation in which banking development causes economic growth and its reverse is the demand –following role. The rate of physical capital formation has, thus, always been accorded a major role in the service of economic growth.

The structuralists' school maintains that for investment purposes, it is the saving in financial assets which are important. *Ceteris paribus,* an increase in the size of the financial sector leads to an increase in the amount of financial savings available as investible funds. It, therefore, follows that the size of the financial sector contributes directly to the rate of capital formation (*Fisher, B. (1981), "Interest Rate Ceilings, Inflation and Economic Growth in Developing Countries," Economics, p.23).* Financial structuralists knew that a widespread network of financial institutions and a diversified array of financial instruments have a beneficial effect on the saving – investment processes and hence, on growth.

Raymond Goldsmith (*Raymond W. Goldsmith, (1969), "Financial Structure and development," Yale University Press, New Haven, p.48),* by using a single equation model argued that the size of a country's financial structure, as proxied by the financial inter-relations ratio (M2/and the denominator of GNP) was determined by its per capita income, its growth and the actual rate of inflation. He used the financial inter-relations ratio as an indicator of financial deepening. This ratio is defined as the ratio of a set of financial assets to total wealth. Goldsmith suggested that financial development helped economic growth, implying thereby a supply-leading role (*Raymond W. Goldsmith, (1969), op. cit. p.100).*

Bhatia and Khatkhate (*Bhatia, R.J. and D.R. Khatkhate, (1975), "Financial Intermediation, Savings Mobilization and Entrepreneurial Development: The African Experience," IMF Staff Papers)* examined the relationship of financial deepening to growth in eleven African countries. As indicators of financial deepening, they used, alternatively, currency, demand deposits, time and saving deposits and also their total as proportions of GDP. They tried to test the relationship between these alternate measures of financial development and per capita income and the rate of growth of GDP by plotting the dependent and one of the independent variables at a time. The results could not show a relationship between financial deepening and financial repression.

Vogel and Buser (*Vogel, R.C. and S.A. Buser, in R.I. McKinnon (ed), (1978), "Money and Finance in Economic Growth and Development," Marcel Dekker Inc. New York)* tested the repressionist hypothesis for sixteen Latin American countries using pooled time-series data for the period 1971. As proxies for financial deepening they used three indicators i.e. Currency, demand deposits and time deposits, each expressed as a ratio of the GDP.

Alan Roe (*Alan R. Roe, "financial Intermediation and Economic Development: An Empirical Investigation" Mimeo, Undated*) developed a four equation model and one of the equations was the financial intermediation ratio, measured by M2/GDP.

The common practice in the empirical literature has been to use $M_1$ or $M_2$ as a measure of financial development. Gupta expanded this definition. He used the ratio of the currency outside banks and money with banks, quasi-money with banks, post-office saving deposits, bonds of other financial institutions, capital accounts of other financial institutions and change in life insurance liabilities (=assets) to GNP as the main indicator of financial development and is called the financial intermediation ratio (FIR). According to Gupta, in India, the FIR increased from 27.9 percent in 1961 to 38.2 per cent in 1977. The commercial banks having access to the central bank of the country tend to inject loanable funds on a large scale and at relatively lower rates; this would tend to reduce the profitability of lending business in the unorganized market (*Brahmananda, P.R. in G.L. Karkal (ed), (1967), "Unorganised Money Markets in India, pp.233-250*).

With reduced profitability of their lending activity and the shrinkage of their area of business, the indigenous agencies would get merged with the agencies in the organized sector. It was pointed out by Harrod and Domar (*Nickolas Kaldor, (1989, "Essays on Economic Stability and Growth"*, *Duckworth, pp. 233-250*) that, if say, the ratio of capital to annual output was 5: 1, a society would require to save 15 per cent of its annual income, if it was to expand its capacity to produce by 3 per cent per annum or 20 per cent of its income, if its rate of growth of output was to be 4 per cent, and so on. Hence, given the technical relation between capital and output, the potential rate of economic growth depends upon the proportion saved.

The relationship between Government and banking extend far beyond matters of regulation and control.

First, banks perform many services for the Government, including the extension of short-term and long-term credit, the holding of deposits and the performance of agency or brokerage functions as in the sale of treasury bonds to the public. Second, there is a wide range of relationships where the Government stands over the banks in the role of administrator, supervisor, umpire, policeman or guardian. And third, they may engage in supplementary or even competitive lending activities (*Charles R. Whittlesey, Arthur M. Freedman and Edward S. Herman (1963), "Money and Banking: Analysis and Policy," The Macmillan Co. New York, p.517*).

The economic viability of a scheme depends on the extent to which the linkages – both forward and backward – are being maintained. To ensure maintenance of backward linkages, there should be an assurance of the adequate and timely provision of all those inputs which go into production of the optimum output.

Similarly, to ensure the maintenance of forward linkages, there should be a guarantee that the output produced results in the generation of income sufficient enough to raise the people above the level of poverty and at the same time enable them to repay their loan.

In a few countries, banks were created by the Governments to exploit mineral resources and to build power plants on behalf of the Government to draw up and carry out a general plan, to promote production in all sectors of the economy, to obtain credit from abroad, to provide long-term finance to private enterprise in order to give fillip to the process of development. The importance of banks in stimulating the economic growth is evident from the fact that in some of the countries, the Governments had to establish these institutions to provide credit facilities for the developmental projects. The banking system, if not regulated to act differently, tends to become an instrument for siphoning off savings from the poorer regions to the richer and more progressive ones where returns on capital are high and secure (*Gunnar Myrdal, (1969), "Economic Theory and Under-developed Regions," University Paper back (Reprint), p.28*).

The most spectacular aspect of development in India has been in relation to bank coverage (*Rangarajan, C, (1982), "Innovations in Banking), Oxford and IBH Publishing Co. pp.2-4*). Another important dimension of growth of banking offices has been in relation to the spread of banking into rural areas.

The arguments generally presented in opposition to geographic expansion in banking (*Douglas D. Evanoff and Diana Fortier, (1986), "The Impact of Geographic Expansion in Banking: Some Axioms to Grind" FRB Chicago Economic Perspectives, May/June, p.24*) are:

(i) Geographic expansion will lead to significant increases in market concentration. Over time, a relatively small number of institutions will gain control of the local market place.

(ii) Anti-trust legislation is not effective in curtailing concentration.

(iii) Banking organization which compete with each other in a number of markets will, in effect, collude with one another by avoiding aggressive competition in one market, expecting similar behavior by rival firms in other markets (the mutual forbearance hypothesis)

(iv) Small banks are not able to compete with large banking organizations. Therefore, if increased geographic expansion is allowed, a significant number of bank failures will occur, and the number of small independent banks will significantly decline.

(v) Removing restrictions on geographic expansion will lead to excessive market power resulting in an inferior level of banking services.

(vi) Allowing expansion will lead to higher bank service prices.

(vii) Service accessibility will decline if geographic expansion is allowed.
Also, the number of bank alternatives from which financial services can be obtained will decline.

(viii) Geographic expansion will not significantly aid, and may actually hinder, rural areas because expansion will take place only in more attractive urban markets.

In the institutional model of development designed by Joseph Alois Schumpeter (1883-1950), economic development is the function of credit availability (*Schumpeter, J.A. (1984), "Theory of Economic Development (1911), quoted in O.S. Shrivastava, "Advanced Economics of Development and Planning")*. The role of the banking system is important because bankers risk the liquidity of their system. Development without credit is not possible and credit creation without development is equally impossible. Credit gives access to the social stream of goods before the entrepreneur has acquired the normal claim to it. Credit is, therefore, an indispensable ingredient in the process of economic development. Banks contribute through more diversified activities to the socio-economic uplift of a developing country. Credit policy is, therefore, a part of the monetary policy of central banks.

The central bank acts as a watchdog over various economic and social developments as an equitable distributor of bank finance. The concept of the independence of a central bank implies that the Government gives direction to the central bank only after consultations. The essence of central banking, according to Sayers, is discretionary control over the monetary system. The world economic conferences held in 1920 and 1922 at Geneva and Brussels, respectively, passed resolutions for setting up central banks in all countries to enable them, *inter alia*, to assist in the evolution of a sound banking system with an adequate number of branches for mobilizing the saving of the community.

The monetary policy of the central bank aims at providing adequate credit for essential productive purposes in a developing country. The central bank provides the state with the funds that it requires for purposes of development. It also ensures the flow of credit towards productive purposes to bring overall economic development. The wise performance of central banking functions helps in the speedy development of a strong nation (*Raman, A. (1968), Central Banking in India," pp. 1-20*). Careful planning leads to establishment of forward and backward linkages which, in turn, induce multiplier effects which indicate growth in the sectors, increasing output and generating employment, establishing innovations and strengthening the local service sector at the generation of external economies and thus make the entire local regional economy more conducive to growth (*Ashok Mitra, Problems of Regional Disparities-Commerce Pamphlet, 1967-68*).

The financing of the creation of basic infrastructure *viz.* roads, railroads, schools and power plants, is essential to the development process and often, it is an immediate pre-requisite of a major private investment project (*David Rockfeller, (1969), " Economic Development - the Banking Aspects," in Per Jacobson Foundation Lecture, Sep. 22, pp. 9-12*). In some cases, in fact, the banks actually do preliminary studies on their own and the look around for an entrepreneur to take over. In so doing, they give impetus to small and medium-sized industries, as well as in many cases, to large industrial complexes. Directly or indirectly, they foster in developing countries awareness in the early stages of development. They help in growth of secondary industry as well as development of the underlying infrastructure as the construction of steel mills or hydro-electric plants to stimulate sound economic growth.

In a developing economy, banks are expected to offer more and more credit, to increase the resources of industries to cause faster economic development ( *Radhaswami, M and S. V. Vasudevan, (1980), "A Text Book of Banking Law and Practice & Theory of Banking" pp. 521-522*). By fostering and institutionalizing savings and channeling funds in desired directions in consonance with the aims and priorities laid down in the plans it can influence the pace as well as the pattern of growth. It can redirect real resources into more productive channels with a high rate of social return in harmony with policy objectives.

It is in this context that the First Plan emphasized that the banking system had to be fitted into the scheme of development to make the process of savings and their utilization socially purposive (*Government of India, (1951), Planning Commission, First Five-Year Plan, p.38*).

The role the banks play distinguishes them from other classes of financial intermediaries. The fundamental shift in the pattern of financial flows gives a major role to the banking system different from other financial intermediaries. It determines the flow of finance due to credit creation. The power to create credit enables the banking system responsible not only for the right amount of bank credit consistent with monetary stability but also for the direction of credit flows. By choosing to create credit or by refusing to do it, the system can give or deny users or potential users of credit command over real resources (*Ghosh, D.N. (1979), Banking Policy in India-An Evolution*).

In centrally planned economies there are few of these with the catalytic changes in Soviet Union and Eastern Europe. The banking system has been assigned the specific function and responsibility to help economic enterprises in the fulfillment of their targets. Each economic enterprise was attached to a particular unit of the banking system and the enterprises were eligible for credit within a planned limit. Banks could not refuse credit so long as the actual needs were consistent with the statement of plan targets. While the banking system functioned as the agent on behalf of the Government for the planned distribution of credit, it was also responsible, at the same time, for efficient use of public resources. The distribution and control functions entrusted to the banking system were an integral part of the methods and policies of national economic management of the centrally planned economies (*Podoloski, T.M. (1973), "Socialist Banking And Monetary Control," p.76*). The Federal Reserve System in the United States of America (U.S.A) contributes to attainment of the nation's economic and financial goals through its ability to influence the availability and the cost of money and credit in the economy. As the nation's central bank, it attempts to ensure that money and credit growth over the longer run is sufficient to provide a rising standard of living for all the people (*Board of Governors of the Federal Reserve System, (1974), "The Federal Reserve System: Purposes and Functions" 6th ed. Washington D.C. p.2*).

In India, many studies have been made to analyze the implications of branch expansion programme on economic growth. Using log-linear model, Brahmananda (*Brahmananda, P.R. (1978), "The Falling Economy and How to Revive it," The Indian Economic Journal, Vol. 25, No.3, pp. 1-106*) stated that the growth - rate of money supply was well above the growth rate of real output. He employed a few indicators in the regression exercise to explain diminishing returns. In his empirical profile of production, Brahmananda applied the regression technique on a cross-section basis to say that there existed a high capital-output ratio (*Brahmananda, P.R. (1982), "Productivity in the Indian Economy – Rising Inputs for Falling Outputs," Himalaya Publishing Co. Bombay. pp.126-136*).

Padwal and Banyopadhyay (*Padwal, S. and R. Bandyopadhyay, (1973), " Bank Branch Location in Rural Areas – An OR Approach," Prajnan, Vol. II, No.2, (April-June)pp. 163-186*) examined the problem of bank branch location in rural areas. Their study pointed out that it was profitable for the bank to open the maximum number of branches in the earlier years of a Plan.

Varde (*Varde, S.D. (1973), "Efficacy of Rural Branches – An Empirical Pilot Study," Prajnab, Vol. Ii. No.2 (April-June) pp. 187-202*), in the empirical study on the efficacy of rural branches, maintained that the success of rural branches has to be judged in return to the objective of rural banking. The two-fold objective was to act as an active catalyst in the integrated socio-economic development of the area served by the branch and to become a commercially profitable unit of banking.

Varde, Palav and Sita (*Varde, S.D. , S.M. Palav and M. Sita, (1975), " Branch Expansion Planning for the Banking Industry', Prajnan, Vol.IV, No.2, (May-June), pp. 145-182*) carried out a study of on branch expansion planning for the banking industry and formulated a district-wise branch expansion plan for the Five-Year Plan period 1974-79. The objective of the study was to develop a branch allocation scheme for branches to be opened, so as to bring about the maximum reduction in the existing disparities in respect of coverage of bank offices. The study suggested that if banks felt that they had additional capacity to permit them to open new branches, it would not be incompatible to permit them to open them wherever they wished.

Basu (*Basu, S.K. "Determinants of Regional Imbalances in Banking Development" Indian Journal of Regional Science, Vol. XII, No.2, pp. 121-129*) scrutinized the inter-district variation in per-capita deposit and credit of commercial banks. The study pointed out that a rise in the degree of urbanization pushes per capita credit up from its average value, possibly more than it pushes per capita deposit. An increase in the number of bank offices relative to population raises per capita deposit more than it does per capita credit. There have, thus, been numerous studies on the role of banks in the economy. However, these studies have failed to formulate a clear-cut region-specific branch banking policy to be pursued by a country's central bank.

Mass hunger is hardly conducive to social stability. Social stability is a pre-requisite of any kind of national progress. A developing nation can achieve substantial economic progress after achieving four other important things;

(i) A considerable degree of literacy,

(ii) A large measure of social justice;

(iii) A reliable apparatus of Government and

(iv) A clear understanding of what development involves.

Therefore, an intelligent utilization of credit by commercial banks holds the key to promoting development after establishing the necessary socio-economic infrastructure in a developing country like India

As the leader of the consortium of credit institutions in the districts, the lead banks in India are expected to play a significant role. The primary task of the lead bank to ensure sufficient branch network by reaching into areas hitherto unexposed to commercial banking. Banks are expected to help in the uniform development of all regions in the country. Money from the surplus area has to be diverted to the backward area for the purpose of investment and development. The mechanism of credit creation is expected to be used to expand the potential business activities. Expansion of bank credit is to be followed, *inter alia*, also by an increased production and employment.

This present study reveals a positive and significant influence of bank branches and bank credit on economic development. The study surveys all the districts of the country to measure the spread effects made through the intermediation by lead banks. It identifies the leakages in the banking system and indicates innovative areas to improve the quality of life of the common citizen. It is also a guide for rationalizing the existing bank branches in India.

The following chapter traces the evolution of branch banking from its origin. Branch licensing policies pursued by the RBI are also presented.

# BANKING DEVELOPMENT
# IN INDIA – A HISTORIC PERSPECTIVE

In India, stress on banking development was laid in 1954 when the All-India Rural Credit survey Committee (*see Reserve Bank of India, (1978), "Functioning of Public Sector Banks – Report of the Committee," Bombay, pp. 7 & 8)* recommended an integrated system of rural credit, the main features of which were: (i) development of State-sponsored, State-partnered credit institutions; (ii) full co-ordination between credit and marketing and processing; (iii) administration through adequately trained and efficient personnel, and (iv) assignment of a crucial role to the Reserve Bank of India as a planner, mentor, supervisor and provider of finance in a significant way.

## Genesis

The first bank was started by M/s. Alexander & Co. in the year 1770 under the name of The Bank of Hindustan (*C.N. Cooper, (1963), "The Rise, Progress and Present Condition of Banking in India," pp. 50-65).* The first presidency bank *viz.* The Bank of Bengal was opened for business on May 01, 1806 under the name of Bank of Calcutta. The presidency banks were central banks of issue, bankers to the Government and the bankers' banks.

The Government made them private institutions in 1876 (*K. Chandrasekar, (1982), "Indian Banking in Historical Perspective," Southern economist, April, 15).* The three presidency banks of Bengal, Bombay and Madras were amalgamated to form the Imperial Bank of India in 1920.

War and post-war period gave an impetus to joint-stock banks (*I.P. Jain, (1953), "Indian Banking Analysed: Directory of Banking in India, Pakistan, Burma and Ceylon," Banking Experts, Madras, p.31).* Not only that a large number of banks came to the field but they also resorted to branch banking without limit.

On the eve of the nationalization of the Reserve Bank of India, the Imperial Bank, the Indian and the exchange banks together had 1260 offices including head offices, each office servicing on an average a population of about three lakh. The offices were located in about 475 towns. The remaining 2100 towns and almost all the villages were devoid of any banking facility. They depend entirely on indigenous bankers and co-operative institutions (*see Reserve Bank of India, (1982), History of Reserve Bank of India,*

*1935- 1951," Bombay).*In the economic history of India, indigenous banks have occupied a prominent place *(M.L.Tannan, (1947), Banking Law and Practice in India" p.1).*

Chanakya's Arthashastra (about 300 B.C) refers to merchant bankers who received deposits, advanced loans and carried out other functions very much akin to modern banking *(L.C. Jain, (1929), "Indigenous Banking in India," p.3).*Despite series of invasions from 6th century onwards and consequent political instability, individual bankers continued to flourish.

The Reserve Bank of India was established in 1936. The needs of the economy during the Second World War warranted a rapid expansion of banks. As a result, the number of scheduled banks rose from 55 in June 1937 to 1996 in June 1946. Their branches numbering 1278 in June 1938 rose to 3063 in June 1946. A large number of banks opened during this period had their offices either in Bengal pr in Punjab.

The Reserve Bank of India submitted its proposals for an Indian Bank Act in 1939 to the Government of India. The proposals were based on the general banking principles to safeguard the interests of the depositors and to facilitate economic development of the country by promoting the saving habit *(Jathar and Beri, "Indian Economics" (vol. II), p.443).* In view of strong public opinion for a banking legislation, the Government introduced a bill to enact the Banking Companies Act, 1945 in the legislative assembly on November 16, 1944. At that time, the number of non-scheduled banks increased from 2846 to 3469.

## Concentration of Economic Power

Unevenness in the spread of banking facilities was evident in the fact that commercial bank branches were concentrated only in centres of large population. At the end of 1956, 1752 centres had 4030 bank branches. In 1951, deposits from rural and semi-urban centres had accounted for 15 per cent of the total resources mobilized.

It was emphatically argued prior to nationalization that operations of the Indian commercial banks resulted in concentration of wealth and economic power which was against the accepted principle of socialistic pattern of society. In support of this contention, various facts were quoted. For instance,

(i)   In 1963, 188 persons dominated 75 per cent of the resources of the private sector banking. About 90 per cent members the Boards of Directors in banks consisted of industrialists and big businessmen.

(ii)  650 accounts in the country constituted two thirds of total advances of the banking system.

(iii) Almost every industrial house in this country controlled one or the other bank. Let us take the case of largest commercial banks.

| Name of the Bank | | Controlled by |
|---|---|---|
| Central Bank of India | : | Tata Group |
| Bank of India | : | Khatau – Mafatlal Group |
| Punjab National bank | : | Dalmia, Jain Group |
| Bank of Baroda | : | Walchand – Hirachand Group |
| United Commercial Bank | : | Birla Group |
| Hindustan Commercial Bank | : | J.K. Group |
| Hindustan Mercantile Bank | : | Tata Group |

The aforesaid industrial groups controlled a number of industries. They were thereby enjoying a position of monopoly in their business.

(iv) A single director of bank was a common director of many other industrial concerns and with his command over the bank; he was able to turn the bank in to the power house for his industrial empire.

(v) The following statement indicates the interlocking of some of the directors of large Indian banks to other industrial concerns:

| Name of the Bank/Director | No. of Companies with which he was connected |
|---|---|
| **BANK OF INDIA** | |
| 1. A D. Shroff | 23 |
| 2. K.M.D. Thackersey | 28 |
| 3. Jagmohan P. Goenka | 11 |
| 4. Jai Singh Vithal Das | 16 |
| 5. Giridhari Lal Mehta | 11 |
| 6. Ambala Sarabhai | 16 |
| 7. Madan Mohan Mangal Das | 17 |
| 8. Bhajan Das C. Mehta | 10 |
| 9. N.K. Petigara | 12 |
| 10. Ram Niwas Ruia | 38 |
| **CENTRAL BANK OF INDIA** | |
| 11. C.H. Bhabha | 9 |
| 12. C.P. Wadia | 6 |
| 13. S.S. Khambata | 6 |
| 14.Jamshetji Jeejibhoy | 9 |
| 15. C.B. Parikh | 16 |
| 16. Dharamsey Khatau | 29 |
| 17. J. Harivallabhdas | 21 |
| 18. H.H.M. Sir J.M. Scindia | 8 |
| **PUNJAB NATIONAL BANK** | |
| 19. Kamalanayan Bajaj | 21 |
| 20. C.L. Bajoria | 11 |
| 21. A.K. Jain | 8 |
| 22. S.P. Jain | 13 |
| **UNION BANK OF INDIA** | |
| 23. K.R.P. Shroff | 4 |
| 24. Bal Krishna Harivallabdas | 7 |
| 25. Jai H. Mehta | 24 |

26. Patilal H.Shah                     22

27. Pallanji S. Mistry                 24

**BANK OF BARODA**

28. Naval Tata                         10

29. Tulsidas Kilachand                 11

30. R.B. Birla                         9

31. K.P. Goenka                        15

32. Arvind Mafatlal                    15

**UCO BANK**

33. E.P. Goenka                        12

34. Yogendra M. Mafatlal               8

These directors not only borrowed loans from their own banks, but also borrowed from other banks by way of mutual accommodation of one another's companies.

## Money Creation

Under the fractional reserve system, banks create deposits. Deposit creation by any bank depends on obtaining excess reserves. Normally, the reserves will accrue to a bank as the bank's customers deposit cheques drawn on other banks. However, if the depositors fail to deposit the entire sum received and take out some cash instead, the receiving bank will obtain fewer rupees in deposits and hence, fewer excess reserves. The chain of deposit creation will contract as a result. The critical valuable turns out to be the relationship between currency held by the public and their demand deposits. The higher the ratio of currency to demand deposits, the smaller the deposit multiplier. Leakages refer to elements that held to a reduction in the value of the demand deposit multiplier. Time deposit leakage differs from the cash leakage. Cash flows out of the banking system, whereas time deposit accounts remain in the system.

## Money Multiplier and the Banks

The Government and the RBI create currency between them. The Government provides the RBI with rupee securities and with their backing the RBI issues currency. So long as the Government of India is willing to borrow from the RBI and so long as the RBI cannot refuse, there is no limit to the amount of currency that the Government of India and the RBI between them may create. Part of the total currency in circulation becomes reserve with which the banking system creates deposit money. The bankers know that all deposit holders do not withdraw all their deposits on a single day. Therefore, they keep only a small amount of cash in relation to their deposit liabilities. The Reserve Bank of India Act, 1934 requires all scheduled commercial banks to maintain cash reserve ratio between 3 and 15 per cent of total deposit liabilities.

If and when the banking system finds itself with more currency than is adequate to meet the cash reserve and the cash on hand requirement, it is willing and usually able to make loans and advances and credit the corresponding amounts to the deposit accounts of the debtors. It is, thus, that deposit money is created on the basis of a fractional reserve.

There are two principal sources from which additional cash accrues to the banking system on the basis of which it may create additional deposit money. *(V.G. Pendharkar, (1967), "Bank Deposits in the Indian Economy – A Note on Creation and Leakages" in 'Economic and Political Weekly', Spl. No. August).*

(i) RBI credit to the Government: When the Government of India requires money, the RBI does not refuse and the Government is given credit from the RBI. The Government of India issues securities. The RBI accepts them and credits the deposit account of the Government to that extent. The Government begins to draw on this account. It issues cheques in payment for goods and services it purchases from the public; the public deposits these cheques with the banks from where they move to the RBI and are credited to the deposit accounts of the banks with the RBI. All these do not happen on a single day. But, in principle, the bankers' deposits with the RBI increase by the amount of credit extended by the Reserve Bank of India to the Government of India. This accrual of additional cash in the banking system provides the base for expansion of the deposit money.

Additional deposits created and additional cash flows out of the banking system simultaneously. A part of it is, however, retained as additional cash reserves in the bankers' deposits with the RBI in order to maintain the cash reserve ratio. A part flows into the hands of the public to meet the additional currency needs in accordance of the Currency – Deposit Ratio. The balance remains as additional cash on hand with the banks.

Let us suppose, the RBI extends additional credit to the Government of India amounting to ₹ 100 crore. In consequence and in due course the bankers' deposits with the RBI increase by the same amount.

For illustration, let us suppose that the cash reserve ratio is 10 per cent that is 0.10; that the currency – deposit ratio is 0.30; and that the cash on hand with the banks is 1.5 per cent of the deposit liabilities. Then, if we denote the additional deposits by 'D', we have ₹ 100 crore = D x (0.1+0.3 + 0.015) = 0.415 D OR D = ₹ (100/0.415) crore = ₹ 240.964 crore.

This is additional money deposit money created. To this we should add the additional currency amounting to ₹ (240.964 x 0.3) crore = ₹ 72.29 crore with the public. Thus, the total money supply additionally created consequent to an initial accretion of cash worth ₹ 100 crore in the banking system is ₹ (240.96 + 72.29) crore = ₹ 313.25 crore. This is the money multiplier.

On completion of the process of additional deposit creation, as currency worth ₹ 72.29 crore flows into the hands of the public and cash worth ₹ 3.61 crore into the banking system as additional cash on hand (₹ 72.29 + 3.61 Crore), ₹ 75.90 crore worth of securities move from the banking department of the RBI to the issue department of the RBI to support the issue of additional currency.

The other source from which additional cash may accrue to the banking system is as under:

(ii) RBI's credit to banks: If there is demand for additional money supply from the public and the banks have no resources to meet the demand, the banks approach the RBI for accommodation. Such demand can be speculative. If the RBI considers that the additional money supply is necessary and desirable, it provides the required accommodation.

RBI grants loans and advances to the banks and credits them to the bankers' deposits with the RBI. The subsequent process of expansion of money supply is as follows.

The RBI, let us suppose, extends credit worth ₹ 100 crore to the banks. It will lead to the same additional money supply of ₹ 240.96 crore of deposit money and ₹ 72.29 crore of currency.

However, there is a difference when monetary expansion takes place through the RBI's credit to banks; if the RBI has no securities in its banking department to transfer to the issue department to support the issue of additional currency worth ₹ 75.90 crore (₹ 72.29 crore + ₹ 3.61 crore), the RBI must extend additional credit to the Government of India worth ₹ 75.90 crore.

The process does not end there. The RBI's credit to the Government of India worth ₹ 75.90 crore leads to additional deposits of ₹ 182.89 crore (i.e. ₹ 75.90 crore × ₹ 2.40964 crore).

This, in turn, requires RBI's additional credit to the Government of India to support the issue of additional currency worth ₹ 57.61 crore (i.e. ₹ 182.89 crore × ₹ 0.315 crore) (currency – deposit ratio is 0.3 and cash on hand with banks 0.015), and so on.

At the end of the process, it will appear that concomitant to the RBI's credit to the banks worth ₹ 100 crore, the RBI would have extended to the Government of India credit worth ₹ 75.90 crore/(1-0.759) crore (75.90/0.241) i.e. ₹ 315 crore. Consequently, the RBI's credit to the banks worth ₹ 415 crore (₹ 100 crore + ₹ 315 crore) (i.e. the RBI's concomitant credit to the Government of India of ₹ 315 crore) forms the base for creation of deposit money by the banking system.

Hence, the additional deposits created would amount to ₹ 415 x ₹ 2,40,964 crore i.e. ₹ 1,000 crore. To this we should add ₹ 1000 × ₹ 0.3 crore i.e. ₹ 300 crore being the additional currency with the public so that, the resulting increase in the money supply turns out to be ₹ 1300 crore. We may note that the currency issued by the RBI but resting with the banks as additional cash on hand amounting to ₹ 15.00 crore is not regarded part of the money supply.

Thus, a part of the RBI's credit to Government arises out of currency needs of the public and cash on hand needs of the banks and is concomitant to the RBI's credit to banks. The latter cannot, therefore, be considered in isolation (ibid).

During the last week of March banks customarily resort to window dressing. The methods, *inter alia*, include discounting of cheques received from various financial and non-financial institutions and issuing short-term deposit receipts against them. When the cheques are realized in April, the proceeds of the cheques are credited to various institutions. Thus, they adjust their funds position. A few others resort to granting of credit to a borrower who does not require any bank loan and create a deposit out of it. These instances indicate that meeting the business (loans and deposits) target becomes a ritual.

## Leakages

At certain centres bank funds were not utilized for creation of assets or for increased productive use in the economy despite regulating mechanism. As a result, secondary reserves were not created. A few instances are narrated below.

## Bad and Doubtful Debts

Details of these sub-standard assets are generally not published. However, the provisions made against such items are indicated in the balance sheet of banks.

They arise due to varied reasons which include wrong identification of beneficiaries under various Government – sponsored welfare schemes. Revelations in the media from time to time indicate that small borrowers generally do not default and are generally honest to repay bank loans as per schedule.

Leakages in the form of defaulters came to light in the nineteen eighties along with 'loan melas' or credit camps. The Central Vigilance Commission categorically declared that the mass lending programmes have led to squandering of public funds. The absence of accountability has affected the performance of banks. There is no accountability fixed when the banks' Boards sanction various loans. Corrupt and unproductive banking practices such as loan melas and write –off of bank funds indicated the increasing role of a middle men.

The RBI never published figures relating to the amount involved in loan melas. The Banking regulation Act, 1949 did not require a bank to disclose the figures of bad and doubtful debts to the public.

According to a press release published on February 23, 2016, ten public sector banks with non-performing assets (NPAs) over 8 per cent each, together accounted for over half the total bad loans (NPAs) in the banking industry. Details of the banks and NPAs in Rupees crore in brackets are as follows: (i) Bank of Baroda (₹ 38,934 cr.) (ii)Bank of India (₹ 36,519cr.) (iii) Bank of Maharashtra (₹ 8,302 cr.) (iv) Central Bank of India (₹ 17,564 cr.) (v) Dena Bank (₹ 7,916 cr.) (vi) IDBI Bank (₹ 19,615 cr.) (vii) Indian Overseas Bank (₹ 22,672 cr.) (viii) Punjab National Bank (₹ 34,338 cr.) (ix) UCO Bank (₹ 14,932 cr.) and (x) United Bank of India (₹ 6,722 cr.), totaling a little more than ₹ 2 lakh crore and accounted for more than half of the total (gross) NPAs of the banking sector.

The stress on the balance sheets of the public sector banks is an outcome of gross NPAs or bad loans crossing ₹ 4 lakh crore as on December 31, 2015 plus, banks requiring an additional ₹ 40,000 – ₹ 60,000 crore towards meeting regulatory prescriptions on capital requirement in the next fiscal year. According to India Ratings (Ind – Ra), public sector banks require ₹ 3.7 lakh crore over fiscal years 2017-2019 to meet capital adequacy norms.

According to the published data on non-performing assets (NPAs) by the Reserve Bank of India relating to March 2015 (Source: Statistical Tables Relating to Banks in India dated 23rd December, 2015) out of a total of ₹ 63548 billion advances (gross) outstanding (based on off-site returns submitted by domestic scheduled commercial banks), a total of ₹ 2987 billion were non-performing assets (Annexure-XIV).

The break-up of NPAs among the domestic scheduled commercial banks indicate that 34.5 per cent of the total priority sector advances and 65.5 per cent of the non-priority advances were NPAs.

It is observed from the data on public domain relating to accounts with credit limit of more than ₹ 2 lakh that 23 per cent of the total borrowal accounts belonged to large borrowers who enjoyed 92 per cent of the bank credit of all scheduled commercial banks, indicating clearly that small borrowers have been neglected or ignored by them. A common citizen is one of the small borrowers. Inclusive growth is, therefore, a myth.

## Write-offs - a Scam

The Banking Regulation Act, 1949 does not require a bank to disclose the amount of bad and doubtful debts to the public. Banks write-off loans periodically to window-dress their balance sheets in the course of their normal business. As per information obtained by a non-governmental organization (NGO), under the Right to Information (RTI) Act, 2005, 29 public sector banks had written off ₹ 1, 14 lakh crore of bad debts (NPAs) between 2013 and 2015 as they were unable to recover their dues.

In accordance with the Supreme Court directions, the RBI submitted on 29th March, 2016, a list of big defaulters who have failed to repay bank loans of over ₹ 500 crore each with a plea not to disclose their names public as it would affect the livelihood of the employees of these defaulter corporate adversely.

According to Dr. K.Chakrabarty, former Deputy Governor of the Reserve Bank of India who had handled the Supervision department of the RBI from 2009 to 2014, technical write-offs by Indian banks are inequitable and is a big 'scam' and therefore, it should be stopped (*The Indian Express dated 8th February, 2016*).

There is a reason on the part of banks to write off loans though a loan is technically their assets. According to Shri M. Narendra, former Chairman and Managing Director of Indian Overseas Bank, it benefits banks in terms of tax liability. Moreover, the bad loan no longer stays in the bank's books. Write-offs happen when a loan becomes non-recoverable or dead asset. It is done after making 100 per cent provisioning.

The write – off instruction comes from the Head Office of the Bank. According to the Master Circular on Income recognition and Asset Classification issued by the RBI, technical or prudential write-off is the amount of non-performing asset (loan) which are outstanding in the books of the branches of banks, but have been written off (fully or partially) at the Head Office level. Amount of technical write – off should be certified by statutory auditors.

Non-performing assets (NPAs) reflect poorly on the bank and are eager to write it off or remove it from the balance sheet and reduce tax liability. Some banks write-off accounts to sell them to asset reconstruction companies (ARCs) at lower prices and make easy money out of it. Banks generally do not want to take on the tedious recovery process. Selling the assets to ARCs is a quick-fix solution for banks. According to the published news item, in some cases, bank officials cut sweet deals with the promoter of defaulting companies to write-off loans.

If it is the Head Office of a bank that approves write-offs, loans are sanctioned by a credit approval committee comprising the Chairman, executive directors and general managers of a bank. This mechanism was put in place in 2012 by the Union Finance Ministry. These committees can approve credit proposals up to ₹ 400 crore in case of major public sector banks and ₹ 250 crore in the case of others. If the loan proposal is above this limit, it has to be vetted by the bank's board committee. Some banks blindly follow the decisions without going in for any due diligence on their own.

According to Shri K.K.Srinivasan, former Member of the (Life) Insurance Regulatory Development Authority of India, boards of public sector banks have senior officials from the Government as well as the RBI on their boards. The irony of NPAs of public sector banks is that they have happened right under the nose of RBI officers who are on boards of these banks. Thus, in a way the RBI becomes directly responsible for the banks' decisions on credits that became NPAs. A regulator should not be a part of the apex business decision-making body (board of directors) of regulated entities.

It was reported in 1994 that the principal cause of bank failures in the United States of America (U.S.A) was frauds. In India, incidence of frauds has not allowed to assume unmanageable heights. 'Fraud' is defined as an intentional misrepresentation of material facts by one or more individuals to management (employees or third parties) in order to secure an unfair or unlawful or unjust gain.

It is said that dishonesty is contrary to the very concept of banking and without conscience; fidelity and integrity there cannot be any bank operating in any country. Although fraud is universal and can occur in any profession, banks which deal with money are more susceptible and the degree of temptation is higher.

As the custodians of the public money, banks are meant to display the highest degree of integrity instead of searching for scapegoats. Fraud prone areas include cash balances kept with them at vault/safe/counters/automated telling machines (ATMs)/in transit, unauthorized operations in dormant accounts and they are being frequently reported by the press.

Entries in suspense accounts, for instance, if not reversed on location of differences, and are not balanced at regular intervals give room for fraudulent activities.

In view of the greater autonomy enjoyed by the banks and the accountability entrusted with them following the financial sector reforms, the role played by banks in checking frauds through proper housekeeping and internal checks becomes more crucial to arrest leakages. Banks have always been directed to ensure that bank credit is used for the desired productive and economic activities connected not at all connected with speculations/or in real estate.

Capital markets, real estate market and commodities market have been classified as sensitive sectors as fluctuations in prices of underlying assets in these sectors could adversely affect the asset quality of banks. In 2014-15, sensitive sectors accounted for 18.5 per cent of the total loans and advances of banks, as per the report on trend and Progress of Banking in India, 2014-15.

The Hon'ble Supreme Court intervened, as per the news published in the public domain, to examine if the Reserve bank of India and the Union Government could take shelter behind the confidentiality clause in the Reserve bank of India Act, 1934 for holding back the names of defaulters of big loans amounting to ₹ 500 crore and above individually (Press Trust of India – Dated 13th April, 2016). The Supreme Court Bench questioned why borrowers borrow from banks to set up companies and then declare them sick to enjoy with the public money on the one hand and harassing the poor farmers who fail to repay due natural calamities on the other. However, the Watchdog (Regulator) of the banking industry has expressed the view that disclosure of the individual names would lead to an adverse impact on the Indian economy. The matter had been referred to the Hon'ble Court by a public interest litigation and the case assumed importance in view of huge sum of money worth lakh of crore of rupees involved.

## Menace of Banking Frauds

India has emerged as a popular one among cybercriminals – mostly hackers and other malicious users who use the internet to commit such crimes identified as identity theft, spamming, phishing and other types of fraud. As per a Study conducted by the Assocham - Mahindra, total number of cyber crimes registered during 2011, 2012, 2013 and 2014 stood at 13,301, 22,060, 71,780 and 1, 49,254 respectively. With increasing use of information technology (IT) enabled services such as e-governance, online business and electronic transactions, protection of personal and sensitive data have assumed paramount importance. It is further stated that mobile frauds are an area of concern as around 50 per cent of financial transactions are done via mobile devices and are likely to grow. The increasing use of smart phones and tablets for online banking and other financial transactions have increased the risks of frauds.

Andhra Pradesh, Karnataka and Maharashtra have witnessed the highest number of *cyber crimes registered under the IT Act* in India. Importantly, these three states together contribute more than 70 per cent to India's revenue from IT and IT related industries. Documents obtained under the Right to Information (RTI) Act, 2005 from the RBI relating to only those cases where the amount involved in each case is ₹ One lakh and above as on 20th February, 2011 *and published as an Abstract in the Australian Journal of Business and Management Research, New South Wales Research Centre Australia (NSWRCA) in April 2015 (Vol.4 No.12) (See Menace of Frauds in the Indian Banking Industry: An Empirical Study – by Dr. Madan Lal Bhasin)*, *inter alia*, reveal the following:

Mumbai tops the list of cities with the highest number of frauds reported by banks. Top – ranking States with more cases of bank frauds as on 20th February, 2011 include

Andhra Pradesh, Bihar, Delhi, Gujarat, Haryana, Karnataka, Madhya Pradesh, Maharashtra, Punjab, Rajasthan, Tamil Nadu, Uttar Pradesh and west Bengal.

According to the analysis of big cases looked into by the Central Bureau of Investigation (CBI), bankers sometimes exceed their discretionary powers and grant loans to unscrupulous borrowers on fake/forged documents. In April 2015, In April 2015, the Governor of the RBI has written to the Prime Minister's Office (PMO) seeking " concerted action in the country's 10 biggest bank frauds allegedly involving prominent real-estate, media and diamond firms that are being probed by the CBI" (page 10, *ibid*).

Frauds in banks and political loans are added to 'costs' and are Corruption costs recovered from customers.

The Report of the Committee set up to enquire into various aspects of frauds and malpractices in banks (*A. Ghosh Committee*) in 1992 observed that frauds were not committed due to any lacuna in the systems and procedures of the banks but due to non-observance of guidelines by the banks. Subsidies and grants meant to the under-privileged and economically poorer sections of the community have been diverted to richer sections by unscrupulous bank officials unethically.

Most of the rural bank credit programmes had the policy pronouncements from the political representatives and therefore, there was obvious political interference and inept corruption in the politically motivated mass lending programmes and loan waiver schemes at many levels. Once politicians started presiding over a function organized by a bank, for instance, borrowers of bank credit were led to believe that the credit lent to them were grants made by the government to them and therefore, there was no need to repay. Thus, established norms and practices were ignored and the extraneous pressures weakened the health of the system.

Most of the beneficiaries under the poverty alleviation programmes came into the fold of banks accidentally because plan targets were required to be achieved. As a result, the beneficiaries were given assets which could not perhaps be managed by them. Borrowers, therefore, in general, were more likely to repay when they perceived the opportunity of getting a new loan under another Scheme by which they could get a fresh loan from the bank to repay the existing bank loan.

Certain types of transactions did not require the sanction of the RBI. For instance, the Famine Relief Fund, Chief Ministers' relief funds, the Prime Minister's relief fund and other such funds recognized or sponsored by State/central Governments were exempted from any prior approval of the RBI i.e. 1 per cent of the previous year's published profit of the bank or ₹ 1 lakh whichever was higher was allowed to be utilised by the Indian banks for these purposes. However, loss-making banks also have donated for these schemes.

Illiterate landless labourers often became victims of a few corrupt bank officials and village workers. Subsidies and grants meant to be given to the poor people have been diverted and indirectly enjoyed by them, thus, making mockery of development, as per the published news items. .

A credit transaction is complete only when the borrower repays the amount borrowed from the bank to enable the banker to lend further.

## Consolidation in Asian Countries

The Asian financial crisis of 1997-98 underlined the risks to economic stability and growth that a weak or vulnerable financial sector could pose. This led to restructuring and consolidation in many of the financial sectors in a few countries.

In Hong Kong, the monetary authority provides 100 per cent foreign direct investment (FDI) in the banking sector with its prior approval. This has led to tie-ups with mainland banks.

In Indonesia, Indonesia Bank Restructuring Agency has divested many of its holdings in the banking sector as part of the Government's privatization programme. Government has approved FDI in listed banks up to 99 per cent.

In Malaysia, Bank Negara has implemented a financial master plan to strengthen its domestic banks and to create a level playing field for foreign banks since 2007. FDI has been capped at 30 per cent. In Singapore, FDI has been capped at 40 per cent.

The Bank of Thailand announced its master plan in January 2004, aiming to remove obstructions in mergers and amalgamations and restructure the financial organizations in to full service institutions or retailers.

In the developed U.S. market consolidation has taken place. Citigroup has been dethroned as the sole $ 1 trillion banking organization in the U.S. with the mergers of Bank of America and Fleet Boston and J.P. Morgan Chase and Bank One.

The consolidation of banks is being viewed as a win-win situation for all the constituents as under:

For banks, sound financial position, large assets, benefits of core banking solution, net working and the state of the art technology, large profits, improved investor confidence, etc.

For customers, it results in better and competitive pricing of all products including improved services with upgraded technology.

The Government and the RBI will be benefitted with better monitoring, less number of chief executive officers with whom to interact, and for better surveillance.

Rating agencies would offer improved rating of Indian banks. Ultimate safety of funds, better investment opportunities, negotiable environment, international level standards for Indian banks would attract foreign institutions, investors, depositors and non-resident Indians.

All other entities dealing with these Indian banks would be satisfied with sound and safer investments, contracts and other obligations.

## Financial Inclusion

Financial inclusion has been accorded top priority by the Reserve Bank of India with the broad objective of taking banking products and services to all sections of the society in general, and vulnerable groups such as weaker sections and low income groups in particular, at an affordable cost in a fair and transparent manner in all villages by regulated mainstream institutional players. Accordingly, banks have been advised by the RBI to pursue Board approved three-year Financial Inclusion Plan (FIP) since 2010. With the inception of the Pradhan Mantri Jan Dhan Yojana (PMJDY) in August 2014, the Government of India has accorded top priority to the pursuit of financial inclusion. 'Financial inclusion' is being viewed as 'money at the bottom of the pyramid'.

'Inclusive growth' means broad based growth, shared growth and pro poor growth, meant to decrease the rapid growth rate of poverty through structural transformation of the society. Indicators of human development *viz*. literacy/education level, skill development, maternal and infant mortality rates, gender equity, employment creation, market expansion, levels of consumption and production are visible signs of inclusive growth. Inclusive growth, thus, is indicative of the benefits and fruits of overall growth attained at the grass root level. Planning Commission, therefore, made inclusive growth their explicit goal in the 11th Five – Year Plan (2007-2012).

An increase in investment leads to provision of adequate linkages and social overheads *viz.* public hospitals, public educational and technical institutions, public transport and other public utilities for the benefit of the common citizens. This includes all-weather roads, posts and telecommunication, uninterrupted availability of power supply at a stable voltage and frequency, water for irrigation, sanitation, clean drinking water, pollution-free environment, fuel, railways for freight, ports and airports. Integrated value chain finance for creation of such basic infrastructure *viz.* connectivity, communication, schools, hospitals and power plants is therefore, a pre-requisite for development. An investment in education, health, basic amenities and environment through better governance, thus, serves the best interests of the common citizens. However, Annexure VIII and IX indicate the latest status of inadequacy, requiring more attention to progress..

Financial inclusion pursued by banks includes Business Correspondent/Business Facilitator (BC/BF) model, credit delivery procedures for the Micro and Small Enterprises (MSE) and adoption of Information and Communication Technology (ICT) solutions. There exists a positive and significant intermediation of bank branches/bank credit to improve the quality of life. This may be felt from the movement of key indicators of human development, quality of life of the citizens, gradual reduction and eventual removal of poverty, malnutrition, diseases, illiteracy, squalor and inequalities among the various regions of the country.

India's growth has been the focus of studies by various illustrious institutions such as the United Nations, World Bank, Foundations, Non-Governmental Organizations and Civil Society Organizations.

The RBI is a member of the Alliance for Financial Inclusion (AFI) which serves as one of the partners for the G20 Global Partnership for Financial Inclusion. An integrated chain of innate machinery to facilitate spread effects already exists. Centrally Sponsored Schemes (CSS) are funded through Gross Budgetary Support (GBS) for Central plans. Central assistance is provided to states. Lead banks have been assigned the task of developing the districts by playing a major role. Welfare schemes are required, therefore, to reach the ultimate target for effective inclusive growth. For instance, for the benefit of farmers, the Rashtriya Krishi Vikas Yojana was launched to enable the states to prepare district level agricultural plans that take account of local conditions. Under the Environment (Protection) Act, 1986, the Central Government may intervene where the water table falls.

The objective of the Rajiv Gandhi Grameen Vidyutikaran Yojana (RGGVY) is providing power to all villages and this would facilitate rapid expansion of irrigation in eastern India. RBI also notified on April 24, 2008 that banks could engage individuals as Business Facilitators and a range of service providers to act as Business Correspondents.

Micro finance/micro credit has generally taken one of the following three forms: i) Self-Help Group (SHG) programme that has linkages with banks ii) cooperatives or iii) Grameen bank branches. Organized SHGs consist of 10 to 12 people with similar socio-economic demographic characteristics (e.g., low-income women in rural or urban slums). The purpose of the SHGs is to help the members save small amounts of money on a regular basis, to create an internal insurance fund for members to draw on in times of emergencies, to empower the members through collective decision-making, and to extend uncollateralized loans to group members. They are all linked to various designated bank branches.

Micro credit extended to the small borrowers by various commercial banks is reckoned as part of priority sector advances by the RBI and the Government of India. Micro credit is defined as the provision of thrift, credit and other financial services and products of very small amount to the poor in the rural, semi-urban and urban areas for enabling them to raise their income level and thus improve their living standards. In sum, micro credit is a linkage between the underprivileged citizens who do not have any security to offer to procure even a small loan, and banks themselves.

According to the RBI, banks have covered 99.7 per cent villages. SLBCs have been mandated to prepare a roadmap for the purpose of providing banking services to cover villages with population less than 2000 to allot them to banks in a time bound manner.

## Origin of Branch Licensing Policies

It was widely recognized that without close surveillance by the central banking authority, soundness of the banking system could not be ensured. Regulatory measures by the Government included (i) the Banking Companies (Inspection) Ordinance, 1946 and (ii) the Banking Companies (Restriction of Branches) Act, 1946. The former empowered the Reserve Bank of India to conduct inspection of banks and accounts of any banking company, while under the latter Act, every bank was required to obtain the prior sanction of the Reserve Bank of India before opening a new branch or changing the location of an existing one.

Immediately after the Independence and partition, banks shifted their head offices and their liabilities from Pakistan to India. They could not transfer their assets to India.

Extensive powers of regulation and control over the activities of banks were assumed by the Reserve Bank of India under the Banking Companies (Control) Ordinance promulgated in September, 1948. The Ordinance of 1948 also vested in the Reserve Bank of India the authority to determine the lending policy to be followed by all banking companies in general. Yet, a large number of banks had come into existence and this was because there was no restriction on the floatation of a new bank (*T.A. Vaswani, (1968),*

*"Indian Banking System," pp.207-236)*. The unhealthy state of Indian banking in 1949 brought the Banking Regulation Act, 1949 into force. The Act required all banks – the existing and new ones – to obtain a license from the Reserve Bank of India for the purpose of carrying on banking business in India. The Reserve Bank's power regarding licensing of banks is defined in Section 22 of the Banking Regulation Act, 1949.

Section 22 provides that no company can carry on banking business in India unless it holds a license issued in that behalf by the Reserve Bank of India (RBI). Further, such a license may be issued subject to such conditions as the Reserve Bank may think fit to impose. Thus, in terms of this Section, no new or existing banking company, whether Indian or foreign, can start or carry on banking business unless it obtains in the first instance a license for that purpose from the Reserve Bank of India.

## Objectives of Branch Licensing Policy

The restriction to start a bank office is a potent weapon in the hands of the Reserve Bank of India not only to control indiscriminate expansion by banks but also to assist and promote economic growth through a vigorous and positive branch licensing policy designed to promote the twin objectives of mobilization of resources and development of the banking habit particularly in the rural areas.

The Reserve Bank's powers to regulate and control the branch expansion of banks are contained in Section 23 of the Banking Regulation Act, 1949. The Section stipulates that no bank can open a new place of business without obtaining the prior permission of the Reserve Bank. In the case Indian banks, this restriction is also applicable to opening of new offices outside the country. Another important provision of the Section refers to the criteria which the Reserve Bank may follow in dealing with applications of banks for grant of permission to open new branches. The Section provides that before granting such permission, the Reserve Bank may require to be satisfied by an inspection under Section 35 of the Act or otherwise, in regard to the following matters: (i) the financial condition and history of the company; (ii) the general character of its management; (iii) the adequacy of its capital structure; (iv) earning prospects, (v) whether the opening of new office will serve public interest.

## Nationalsation of RBI

The Reserve Bank of India (RBI) was nationalized in January 1949. The policy of consolidation of banks was taken up and as a consequence, the total number of bank branches declined from 2,852 in December 1949 to 2,779 in December 1950, by weeding out uneconomic units (branches/offices). A few banking institutions declared themselves as non-banking companies. In pursuance of the recommendations of the Rural Banking Enquiry Committee, the Imperial Bank was acquired by the State Bank of India and was established on July 01, 1955.

Nationalisation of the Imperial Bank heralded the entry of the public sector banks into the commercial banking business. This was one of the steps initiated by the Government in the process of public ownership and control of the commanding heights of the economy in accordance with Parliament's mandate of December 1954 for the adoption of a socialistic pattern of society.

It also reflected the recognition of the fact that the banks are among the most important institutions at the command of any community for achieving its social and economic objectives.

Following the reorganization of the princely states, state-associated banks were brought under the control of the State Bank of India, as suggested by the All-India Rural Credit Survey Committee in 1954.

As a result of the closure of a few banks and merger of small banks with bigger ones, the number of banks operating in the country declined to 359. The closure of Laxmi Bank and Palai Central Bank in 1960 necessitated an insertion of a new section in the Banking Regulation Act, 1949 in September 1960, vesting Reserve Bank of India with wider powers to enforce compulsory liquidation and merger of weak banking companies. The move marked a major step in the direction of preventing unsound working of banks and eventual liquidation. As a result, 59 banks went into compulsory/voluntary liquidation between 1959 and 1967 while 204 weaker/non-viable banks were amalgamated or merged with sound banking companies. Consequently, the number of bank branches increased from 4,847 to 6,984 between 1959 and 1967 and further to 7,650 in December 1968.

The branch licensing policy of the RBI came up for discussion at the meeting of the National Credit Council for a revision in April 1968. It was resolved that at least 50 per cent of the total number of branches to be opened should be in rural and semi-urban areas. Further, at least half of them should also be in unbanked centres.

## Social Control of Banks

In spite of expansion of banking activities, commercial banking was, in general, deficient in terms of geographical and functional coverage. Less than 200 account holders dominated three-fourths of the total resources of private banking and about 90 per cent of the directors of banks were industrialists and businessmen. Each leading industrialist family had been closely associated with the promotion and directions of one or more banking concerns. Easy credit availability to industrial houses was one of the powerful factors responsible for the growth of monopolies and concentration of economic power. Just 19 per cent of borrowal accounts with outstanding credit of over ₹ 10,000/- each claimed as much as 96 per cent of total credit and 435 accounts out of over a million accounts accounted for more than 28 per cent i.e. ₹ 635 crore of total bank credit as at end March 1967.

Being predominantly urban-oriented and controlled by a few large business groups, the private sector banks were not properly equipped to assist in the attainment of the socio-economic objectives. The credit requirements of agriculture, small-scale industries, transport operators, small traders, artisans and other weaker sections of the community continued to remain neglected.

Although agriculture provided the means of living to nearly seventy five per cent of the country's population and contributed almost half the gross national product, its share in total bank credit was barely 1.0 per cent as at end-June 1967.

Similarly, the share of small-sector which accounted for 40 per cent of aggregate industrial output was just 6.5 per cent. The share of retail traders in the total credit too was less than 2.0 per cent. The bulk of deposits collected from the public was being lent to organized sectors of industry and trade.

As the multitudes of weaker sections of the society were at the mercy of private money lenders who were exploiting them by charging exorbitant rates of interest, the Government introduced the scheme of social control in 1968 over banks with the main objectives of achieving a wider spread of bank credit, preventing its misuse, directing a large volume of bank credit flow to priority/neglected sectors and making credit a more efficient instrument of economic development.

## Lead Bank Scheme

The National Credit Council constituted five study groups to enable the banking system to adjust itself to the demand conditions emerging from the structural changes in the economy in 1968. One of the study groups was headed by Prof. D.R. Gadgil which was asked to suggest an organizational framework for the implementation of social objectives. The findings of this group revealed uneven distribution of credit not only among different states but also among different sectors and non-availability of finance for small entrepreneurs and other weaker sections of the community. The group, therefore, recommended adoption of an 'Area Approach' to evolve schemes for the proper growth of banking and credit structure in rural areas.

## Service Area Approach

The Service Area Approach (SAA) was introduced in April 1989 for planned and orderly development of rural (centres with not more than 10,000 population) and semi-urban (centres with population between 10,001 and 1,00,000) areas by all scheduled commercial banks including regional rural banks. Under this Approach, each bank branch was assigned to serve a designated area of 15 to 25 villages and the branch was responsible for meeting the credit needs of its service area. The primary objective of this Approach was to increase productive lending and forge effective linkages between bank credit, production, productivity and increase in income levels. The scheme was reviewed from time to time to make appropriate changes to make it more effective. The SAA was reviewed in December 2004. Since then the scheme is applicable only for Government-Sponsored programmes.

The Reserve Bank of India had earlier endorsed the idea of area approach under the Chairmanship of Shri F.K.F. Nariman who headed the Committee of Bankers on Branch Expansion Programme of public sector banks and introduced the Lead Bank Scheme in December 1969 under which all districts were allotted to public sector commercial banks for opening branches, conducting surveys and assisting the overall development of the district concerned to discharge their social responsibilities.

The Nariman committee felt that priority should be given to unbanked centres. Based on the above considerations, 1350 centres consisting of (i) all unbanked places classified as towns as per 1961 census, (ii) all unbanked treasury centres and (iii) certain other centres identified by the banks themselves as offering the potential for development, were allotted to various scheduled commercial banks. Offices at these centres were expected to open before the end of 1970.

The Lead Bank Scheme administered by the Reserve Bank of India since 1969 aims at coordinating the activities of banks and other developmental agencies through various fora in order to achieve the objective of enhancing the flow of bank credit to priority sector and other sectors and to promote banks' role in overall development of the rural sector. For coordinating the activities in the district, a particular bank is assigned the lead bank responsibility of the district. The lead bank is expected to assume leadership role for coordinating the efforts of the credit institutions and Government.(*See Master Circular – Lead Bank Scheme, RBI/2014 – 15/94 – RPCD.CO.LBS.BC.No.9/02.01.001/2014-15 dated July 1, 2014*).Annexure –I illustrates the present status.

The Lead Bank Scheme initially covered the then existing 335 districts in the country. One of the main functions of the lead banks was to identify centres in their respective lead districts offering scope for branch development and to ensure that such centres were covered by bank branches as quickly as possible.

The lead bank scheme has last been reviewed by the High Level Committee of the Reserve Bank of India in 2009. The Committee held wide ranging discussions with various stakeholders *viz.* State Governments, banks, development institutions, academicians, non-governmental organizations (NGOs) and other agents of development.

As on June 30, 2014 25 public sector banks and one private sector bank (The Jammu & Kashmir Bank Ltd.) have been assigned lead bank responsibilities in 671 districts of the country.

For this purpose, banks surveyed the districts allotted to them and they approached the Reserve Bank for permission to open branches as and when such centres were identified by them. They were required to circulate the centres identified by them in their lead districts to other banks and also to other small regional banks operating in the area and invoked their co-operation for expansion of branch banking in the districts. The success of the scheme in terms of branch expansion was judged by the quickness with which banks were able to have offices at all identified centres.

Where the business potential or any other special circumstances that were brought to the notice of the Reserve Bank warranted intensive banking facilities, more bank branches could be allowed.

Their satisfactory working and ability to meet the demands of the depositors were matters of vital importance. While dealing with applications of banks for opening branches outside the country, in addition to the criteria laid down under section 23, factors such as impact on the foreign exchange position, capacity of the bank to face competition of banks already established and adequacy of its resources to meet unforeseen contingencies were also taken into account.

Under the Potential Linked Credit Plans (PLPs), planning starts with identifying block-wise/activity-wise potential estimated for various sectors. They take in to account the long term physical potential, availability of infrastructure support, marketing facilities, and policies/programmes of the Government.

Controlling offices of commercial banks and Head Office of the Regional Rural Bank (RRB) and the Lead Bank circulate the accepted block-wise/activity-wise potential to all their branches for preparing the Branch Credit Plans (BCPs) by their respective branch managers. Details of the lead banks as on March 31, 2016 are given below:

# LEAD BANKS AND THEIR DATE OF REGISTRATION AS BANKS

| LEAD BANK/ADDRESS | DATE OF REGISTRATION |
|---|---|
| 1. Allahabad Bank,<br>No.2, N.S. Road,<br>Kolkata – 700 001. | 17-04-1865 |
| 2. Andhra Bank,<br>Dr. Pattabhi Bhavan,<br>5-9-11, Saifabad,<br>Hyderabad – 500 004. | 20-12-1923 |
| 3. Bank of Baroda,<br>Baroda House,<br>Baroda (Vadodara) -396 006. | 20-7-1908 |
| 4. Bank of India,<br>Nariman Point,<br>Mumbai – 400 021. | 07-9-1906 |
| 5. Bank of Maharashtra,<br>Shivaji Nagar,<br>Pune – 411 005. | 16-9-1935 |
| 6. Canara Bank,<br>No. 112, J.C. Road,<br>Bengaluru – 560 002. | 01-7-1906 |
| 7. Central Bank of India,<br>Nariman Point,<br>Mumbai – 400 021. | 21-12-1911 |
| 8. Corporation Bank,<br>Corporate Centre,<br>Mangaladevi temple road,<br>Pandeshwar,<br>Mangaluru – 575001. | 28-5-1906 |
| 9. Dena Bank,<br>Dena Corporate Centre,<br>Bandra-Kurla complex,<br>C-10, 'G' block, Bandra (East),<br>Mumbai – 400 051. | 26-5-1938 |
| 10. Indian Bank,<br>Corporate Office, 254 -260,<br>Avvai Shanmugam Salai,<br>Royapettah, Chennai – 600 014. | 05-3-1907 |

11. Indian Overseas Bank,                          20-11-1936
    Central Office, No 763,
    Anna Salai.
    Chennai – 600 002.

12. Oriental bank of Commerce,                      19-2-1943
    Plot No.5, Sector 32,
    Industrial Area, Gurgaon – 122 001.

13. Punjab National Bank,                           19-5-1894
    No.7, A.V.B. House,
    Bhikaji Cama Place,
    New Delhi- 110066.

14. Punjab & Sind Bank,                             24-6-1908
    No.21, Rajendra place,
    New Delhi – 110 008.

15. State Bank of India,                            1-7-1955
    Nariman Point,
    Mumbai -400 021.

16. State bank of Hyderabad,                        25-4-1941
    4th Floor, Gunfoundry – Abids,
    Hyderabad – 500 001.

17. State Bank of Mysore,                           19-5-1913
    No. 646, Kempa Gowda Road,
    Bengaluru – 560 009.

18. State Bank of Patiala,                          14-11-1917
    The Mall,
    Patiala – 147 001.

19. State Bank of Travancore,                       12-9-1945
    Thiruvananthapuram – 695 012.

20. Syndicate Bank,                                 20-10-1925
    Door No. 16/355 & 16/365 A,
    Udupi, Manipal – 579 104.

21. Union Bank of India,                            11-11-1919
    Nariman Point,
    Mumbai – 400 021.

22. United Bank of India,                           12-10-1950
    No.11, Hemant Basu Sarani,
    Kolkata – 700 001.

23. UCO Bank,                                                  06-1-1943

    No.10, B.T.M. Sarani,

    Kolkata -700 001.

24. Vijaya Bank,                                               02-5-1931

    No. 41/2, M.G. Road,

    Near Trinity Circle,

    Bengaluru – 560 001.

25. The Jammu & Kashmir Bank Ltd,                             01-10-1938

    M.A. Road,

    Sri Nagar.

    Jammu & Kashmir.

The Districts allotted to these 25 banks for overall development are annexed to this Chapter. How the lead bank scheme is jointly operated is explained in the following paragraphs. In brief, banks have been given predominant role to play the developmental role economically and socially.

A special Block Level Bankers' Committee (BLBC) meeting is convened for each block to finalize the plan ensuring that the Block Credit Plan (BCP) is in tune with the potentials identified activity-wise in accordance with the Government sponsored programmes. All the BCPs of the district are aggregated by the Lead District Manager (LDM) to form the District Credit Plan.

## Merger of Public Sector Banks - Consolidation

It has been proposed in compliance to the prudential norms to merge the public sector banks into six major banks known as Anchor Banks. The particulars of the Six Anchor Banks are as under:

1. State Bank of India (Anchor Bank)

   Merging (i) State Bank of Bikaner & Jaipur (ii) State Bank of Hyderabad (iii) State

   Bank of Mysore (iv) State Bank of Patiala (v) State Bank of Travancore and (vi) Bharatiya Mahila Bank;

2. Punjab National Bank (Anchor Bank)

   Merging (i) Allahabad Bank (ii) Corporation Bank (iii) Indian Bank and (iv) Oriental

   Bank of Commerce;

3. Canara Bank (Anchor Bank)

   Merging (i) Indian Overseas bank (ii) Syndicate Bank and (iii) UCO Bank;

4. Union Bank of India (Anchor Bank)

   Merging (i) Central bank of India (ii) Dena Bank and (iii) IDBI Bank Ltd;

5. Bank of India (Anchor Bank)

   Merging (i) Andhra Bank (ii) Bank of Maharashtra and (iii) Vijaya Bank;

6. Bank of Baroda (Anchor Bank)

   Merging (i) Punjab & Sind Bank and (ii) United Bank of India.

In view of this latest development in May 2016, the lead banks in each district of India would assume responsibility as per the directions of respective Anchor Banks. This study, assumes more relevance due to this historic fact and responsibilities assigned to them.

## Role of Banks Board Bureau

The Banks Board Bureau (BBB) headed by former Comptroller and Auditor General dealt with the issue of consolidation of public sector banks to ensure mergers. The BBB was expected to be replaced by a holding company for all the public sector banks. Until the legislation is in place, the BBB would perform the job of the holding company deciding on policy matters and appointments, as per the minutes of the meeting held on 8th April, 2016 in the presence of the RBI Governor Dr. Raghuram Rajan published by the Times of India.

## Monitoring the Performance at Districts

The performance of the credit plans is reviewed in the various for a created under the LBS as under:

At Block Level, by the Block Level Bankers' Committee (BLBC);

At District Level, by the District Consultative Committee DCC) and District Level Review Committee (DLRC);

At State Level, by the State Level Bankers' Committee (SLBC).

BCP also resolves operational problems in implementation of the credit programmes of banks. LDM is the Chairman of the BLBC. The representatives of Panchayati Samities are also invited to attend the meetings every six months.

DCCs are constituted as a common forum at district level for the constituent bankers and Government agencies/development departments to coordinate the activities in implementing various schemes sponsored under the LBS at each quarter

## Role of Lead District Managers

The effectiveness of the LBS depends on the dynamism of the district Collectors and the LDMs with the supportive role of the Regional/Zonal Office of the banks.aart from convening the meetings of DCC/DLRC and other routine meetings to resolve outstanding issues, other duties of LDMs include the following:

- ➤ Drawing up and monitoring the road map for banking penetration;
- ➤ Monitoring implementation of DCP;
- ➤ Associating with the setting up of Financial Literacy Centres (FLCs) and financial literacy camps;
- ➤ Associating with rural branches of banks;
- ➤ Convening quarterly public meetings at various locations in the district;
- ➤ Coordinating with the Lead District Officer of the RBI to generate awareness of the banking policies and regulations relating to common citizens;
- ➤ Obtaining feedback from the public and providing grievance Redressal to the extent possible at the meetings;
- ➤ Facilitating appropriate machinery for the purpose of grievance Redressal, if necessary.

DLRC meetings are presided over by the District Collector and attended by members of the DCC. Local Members of Parliament (MPs)/Members of legislative Assembly (MLAs) 'Zilla Parishad' Chiefs also are invited to these DLRC meetings. The agenda items in these meetings include opening of new bank branches, distribution of Kisan Credit Cards, Self-Help Group – credit linkage programmes, etc. However, responses to queries from public representatives are accorded highest priority and are attended promptly. The follow-up of DLRC's decisions is required to be discussed at the DCC meetings.

The State-Level Bankers' Committee (SLBC) is an apex inter-institutional forum to create adequate coordination machinery in all states, on a uniform basis for development of the State. The SLBC is chaired by the Chairman & managing director (CMD0 of the convenor bank/Executive Director of the convenor bank each quarter. The Chief Minister/Finance Minister and Senior level officers of the State/RBI (Deputy Governor/Executive Director) are invited to attend the SLBC meetings. Further, the State Chief Ministers are encouraged to attend at least one SLBC meeting in a year.

It has been provided to include institutions and academicians engaged in research and studies, etc. that have implications for sustainable development in agriculture and MSME sector as special invitees. These activities of Non- governmental Organizations (NGOs) in facilitating and channeling credit flow to the low income households are expected to increase in future to ensure inclusive growth, as there have been success stories presented as models at the SLBC meetings.

As per the recommendations of the Expert Group constituted by the Government of India to go in to the nature and magnitude of the problem of low credit-deposit (C-D) ratio across the country and to suggest steps to overcome the problem, the C-D ratio of banks is required to be monitored at different levels on the basis of the following parameters:

| Institution/Level | Indicator |
| --- | --- |
| Individual banks at Head Office | Credit as per place of Utilization + Total resource support provided by the States |
| State Level (SLBC) | Credit as per place of Utilization + Total resource Support provided by the States. |
| District Level | Credit as per place of Sanction |

Banks have been advised that in the districts having C-D Ratio is less than 40, Special Sub-Committees (SSCs) of District Consultative Committee (DCC) may be set up to monitor the C-D Ratio; the district with C-D Ratio of less than 20 is required to be treated on a special footing; districts having C-D Ratio between 40 and 60 are monitored by the DCC.

The SSCs draw up Monitorable Action Plans (MAPs) for improving the C-D Ratio in their districts on a self-set graduated basis.

The RBI monitors the performance in this regard through Monitoring Information System (MIS). Annual Action Plans are prepared with the sub-sectors *viz.* agriculture and allied activities, micro and small enterprises, education, housing and others under priority sector and medium industries. SLBC convenor banks compile/consolidate State-wise, bank group-wise Financial Inclusion Plans for the 3 years in the prescribed format.

Branches of Foreign Banks

So far as foreign banks were concerned, foreign exchange considerations remained paramount, and no new branches of these banks were allowed except on very special considerations. In any case, no foreign bank was permitted to open an office at any inland station. These banks were permitted to open branches in a limited scale and that too only in port towns. In this Study, performance of branches of foreign banks is not included.

## Rural and Semi-Urban Centres

The Reserve Bank, in its policy announced in February 1970 established a linkage between rural and semi-urban branches. It laid down a ratio of one urban branch for every two branches opened in rural and semi-urban areas as at the end of 1969 (1:2). For banks having 60 per cent or fewer number of branches in rural and semi-urban areas as at end December 1969, the ratio was to be one urban branch for every three branches opened in rural and semi-urban areas (1:3).

A study by the Reserve Bank in 1971 revealed a substantial deposit potential at the metropolitan centres and therefore, in November 1971, the above ratio for branch expansion was changed into one urban branch and one metropolitan or port town branch for every two branches opened after October 1971 in rural and semi-urban areas in the case of banks having more than 60 per cent of their branches in rural and semi-urban areas (1:1:2), for other banks the ratio was to be one urban branch and one metropolitan or port town branch for every 3 branches opened in rural or semi-urban areas (1:1: 3).

The branch licensing policy was revamped to give a boost to rural branch expansion in 1977; the Government also directed banks to open branches at all unbanked community development blocks before the end of June 1978.

As this could not materialize, a new policy based on the recommendations of the James Raj Committee on public sector banks, the Dantwala Committee on regional rural banks and the Kamath working group on multi-agency approach to agricultural financing, was announced for 1978-1981. A redeeming feature of the policy was to have a district to district approach and gave priority to deficit districts for opening bank branches. A deficit district was defined only in terms of population criterion i.e. those districts in which the average population per bank branch was higher than the national average.

The currency of the policy was extended up to March 1982 to enable banks to utilize the licenses pending with them. A revised policy to co-terminate with the Sixth Five-Year Plan was formulated. The aim was to achieve, by the end of 1985, a banking coverage of one bank branch for an average population of 17,000 in the rural and semi-urban areas on the basis of 1981 census. The identification of centres for establishment of new branches was done in consultation with State Governments. The district consultative committees organized under the lead bank scheme, where both the Government and institutional agencies were represented and were also involved in the process.

At the end of 1985 it was found there were wide spatial gaps not covered by bank branches. Therefore, it was decided to provide banking facilities on a selective basis to bridge the gap. The branch expansion programme was to terminate with the Seventh Five-Year Plan. The block- level coverage was required to cover an area of about 200 square kilometers (kms) to enable to provide banking facilities within 10 kms.

For identifying the centres the Group consisting of representatives of the lead bank, two other banks having good network of branches in the district, a representative of a regional rural bank in the district and a nominee of the district administration, was required, *inter alia*, to study the concerned block map.

After identifying the centres, the list was sent to the district consultative committees to expedite consideration of the lists by convening special meetings and forwarded to the State Government Secretary/ Director/institutional Finance to prepare a consolidated list of centres in order of priority and to forward the same along with block maps to the Task Forces set up at the Regional Offices of the Reserve Bank of India to monitor and implement the branch expansion programme.

The main objectives of nationalisation of commercial banks are summed up in the preamble to the Banking Companies (Acquisition and Transfer of Undertaking) Act, 1969 as follows:

"To control the commanding heights of the economy and to meet progressively and serve better the needs of development of the economy in conformity with national policy objectives and for matters connected therewith or incidental thereto" (*See Preamble to the Banking Companies Act, 1969*).

Social justice demands equal opportunity for all citizens. Growth and social justice, *inter alia*, constitute the guiding principles of India's Five-Year Plans. These were sought to be promoted through increased emphasis on rural development and extending credit assistance to the economically and socially weaker sections of the society. Banks deployed bank credit to agricultural and rural development directly and through schemes such as the poverty-alleviation programmes.

In the growth strategy, emphasis has been laid on the simultaneous attainment of the objectives of economic growth and social justice. In brief, the objectives of the branch expansion policy of commercial banks have been to promote monetization and monetary integration of the economy; filling in the gaps in the financial infrastructure, meeting the credit needs of all productive deployment of investible funds so as to maximize economic growth with stability and social justice (*Text of the Statement made by the Prime Minister in Parliament, (1969), 'The Banker', July, P. 366 and also the Government of India – Nationalisation of Banks – A Symposium* )

## Role of the Central Bank

Sections 17 and 18 of the Reserve Bank of India (RBI) Act, 1934 relate to advances by the RBI in general and advances to banks against such security as it may consider sufficient. Institutions such as the Industrial Development Bank of India (IDBI), National Bank for Agriculture and Rural Development (NABARD), National Housing Bank (NHB), Export –Import Bank of India (EXIM Bank), Deposit Insurance & Credit Guarantee Corporation, Unit Trust of India, Small Industries Development Bank of India (SIDBI),etc and research institutions, training institutes were also set-up by the RBI.

Even where the RBI does not have absolute authority as a watch dog, it can still influence decisions by virtue of its shareholdings. As adviser, consultant and monitor, RBI has been advising the banks and financial institutions on matters of national importance, taking part in consultations and conducting inspections and monitoring through various periodical statements and reports. Also, it trains the personnel engaged in these institutions by imparting regular and short-term courses in various training colleges.

## Regional Rural Banks (RRBs)

The Government appointed in 1975 a Working Group under the Chairmanship of Shri M. Narasimham, to review the flow of institutional credit especially to the weaker sections of the community. The Working Group recommended the formation of state-sponsored, regionally based and rural oriented regional rural banks, combining the local feel and familiarity with rural problems which the cooperatives possess and the degree of business organization, ability to mobilize deposits, access to central money markets and a modernized outlook which the commercial banks have. It was clearly emphasized that the role of banks would be to supplement and not supplant other institutional agencies in the field. The first five RRBs were established on October 02, 1975. The RRBs were sponsored primarily by public sector banks.

Although the RRBs were permitted to undertake all banking business activities as defined in the Banking Regulation Act and might engage in one or more forms of business as specified in the Act, they were advised to confine themselves to the financing of small scale industries, small business activities, small and marginal farmers, landless agricultural labourers, artisans and other weaker sections of the rural community either directly or indirectly or through the medium of co-operative outlets like farmers' service societies (FSSs) and primary agricultural credit societies (PACSs). They could provide loans for both production and consumption purposes within specified limits. The operational area of each RRB was generally confined to an area of one to three revenue districts with homogeneity in agro climatic conditions and rural clientele. The RRBs were required to open their branches in the unbanked and under - banked centres where the commercial banks were weak and unable to cater to the needs of the weaker sections. Each branch could cover one to three blocks and be in a position to finance five to ten farmers' service societies. The number of RRB branches increased from 17 in June 1976 to 14,051 in 1989 of which many of them were opened in unbanked centres. By June 1978, lead banks had carried out surveys in 380 districts to provide comprehensive credit for growth.

The number of RRBs increased to 196 in June 1989 to cover 370 districts of India. The RRBs had – as their major objectives – development of the rural economy through provision of credit and other facilities for agriculture, trade, industry and other productive activities in rural areas. As the small man's bank, they were expected to cater primarily to the credit needs of weaker sections of the community such as small and marginal farmers, agricultural labourers, rural artisans and village/cottage industries. They provided short-term and medium-term loans to various beneficiaries.

Though banks formulated development plans for their respective lead districts, there was no uniform methodology adopted in the preparation of the credit plans. Long gaps existed between the dates of launching of the plans and acceptance of commitments by the participating financial agencies.

There was an obvious failure to align the plans with the development programme of the Government and inadequacy of thrust and focus on agricultural and allied activities. Instead of fixation of scheme-wise targets, only the financial allocation for all schemes in a sector was made, but, ironically without the plans reflecting the position of financial resources available for deployment in the districts.

## District Credit Plan

The new credit plan launched in 1980 was comprehensive one indicating credit targets for the institutional credit agencies in districts on a block-wise, scheme-wise and bank-wise basis. The plan was based on detailed guidelines issued by the RBI in 1979 to the lead banks indicating, *inter alia*, the objectives, contents, approach to estimation of credit outlays for different purposes and the uniform methodology to be followed to enable them to implement from 1980. The lead banks were advised in April 1989 to invite local Members of Parliament (MPs)/Members of Legislative Assembly (MLAs) to the District Level Review Committee (DLRC) meetings convened.

## Annual Action Plan

Annual Action Plans were required to be prepared by the lead banks in December each year indicating sectoral, scheme and institution group-wise break-up of total credit outlays. One of the features of the new plan was the introduction of participatory planning by the constitution of a district level task force comprising representatives of the central co-operative bank, commercial banks having a large number of branches in the district and the district plan official, besides the district convenor of the lead bank. The lead banks were also advised to develop their own systems of carrying out evaluation studies of the implementation of credit plans of their lead districts periodically. The banks were reminded in January 1981 to take corrective steps to remove regional imbalances in credit deployment. The credit plans to be prepared were intended to enable the credit plan to switch over to the financial year (April-March) to bring about greater co-ordination between the Government and the banks in the formulation and implementation of various programmes.

While preparing schemes for inclusion in the district credit plans, the lad banks were required to keep in view the directives issued by the Government and the RBI regarding deployment of their resources for specified sectors/sub-sectors especially in respect to agriculture, the weaker sections and other developmental programmes. The new plans were intended to improve the capability of the lead banks for formulation of area-specific bankable schemes and thereby improve the credit absorption capacity of the rural sector, especially of capital-deficit areas/weaker sections.

Besides carrying out economic surveys of the district and preparing credit plans, the lead banks identified growth centres or under-banked centres and allotted them to other co-ordinator banks for opening branches.

## Non-Banking Working Day

Based on the recommendations of the Indian Banks' Association, the RBI issued instructions to banks to implement the non-banking working day scheme by which rural branches utilised one day in the week for field visits and for updating the house-keeping. On such a day, no public transactions were handled and the banking personnel were devoting the entire day for services connected with deposit mobilization and recovery of advances.

The ultimate goal of all these schemes under the country's economic policy was to improve national welfare through the monetary policy.

## Consultative Meetings

Recognizing the importance of high level forum for the review of the functioning of public sector banks in various states, the nationalized banks (Management and Miscellaneous Provisions Scheme, 1970), framed under section 9 of the Nationalsation Act, provided for setting up of regional consultative committees, six in all for the six geographical regions in the country. Each regional consultative committee was presided over by the Union Finance Minister and consisted of the representatives of the state governments generally at the Ministers' level and the chief executives of various public sector banks functioning in that region. The Governor and Deputy Governors of the Reserve Bank of India attended these meetings.

These committees were important fora at which the public sector banks in respective region were reviewed. More importantly, these meetings provided an opportunity to discuss the development programmes of the state governments and their expectations from the banks and on the other to the representatives of the state governments to understand and appreciate the practical difficulties faced by banks in their developmental tasks.

In order to ensure corrective action in matters of policy involving public interest, the Finance Minister held periodical meetings with the chief executives of public sector banks and the Governor of the RBI. Besides meeting the chief executives, the Finance Minister used to hold meetings with the representatives of all the public sector banks in order to have a feel of the interest of the employees in the functioning of these banks. These meetings were attended by the chief executives of these banks also and were held in two separate sessions –one with the representatives of workers and the other with the representatives of officers.

The Finance Minister also reviewed periodically the performance of each public sector bank with its chief executives and senior officers. At these meetings, various aspects of each bank's performance in its different areas of activities were discussed for taking specific action to improve the functioning of the banks ( *Bhagwati P. Agrawal, (1982), "Commercial Banking in India – After Nationalisation –A study of their Policies and Progress." Classified Publishing Co., New Delhi, pp. 254 -255).*

In the consultative committee meetings of the Ministry of Finance, various facets of the working of public sector banks came up for detailed discussion. The discussions he held in Parliament as also in consultative committees enabled the Government to take appropriate measures in the light of the suggestions made.

## Priority Sectors

An attempt was made to broaden the industrial base by stipulating flow of funds to certain sectors. The concept of priority sectors was, therefore, intended to ensure that credit assistance from the banking system flowed in an increasing measure to those sectors of the economy, which, though contributing significantly to national income, did not receive adequate support of institutional finance in the past.

At a meeting of the National Credit Council held in July 1968, it was emphasized that banks should increase their involvement in the financing of priority sectors viz. agriculture and small-scale industries.

Providing adequate bank credit to priority sectors was one of the objectives of nationalisation of banks in 1969. Banks were advised by the RBI to make credit available for productive purposes to deserving borrowers of small means on the basis of integrity and credit worthiness of borrowers concerned. The description of priority sectors was also formalized in 1972 on the basis of the report submitted by the Informal Study Group constituted by the RBI.

The Small Loans Guarantee Scheme, 1971 covered credit facilities granted by commercial banks including RRBs to farmers and agriculturists, transport operators, retail traders, small business enterprises and professional and self-employed persons. Effective from March 1972, the guarantee cover was extended to credit facilities granted under the differential rate of interest scheme.

At a meeting of the Union Finance Minister with the Chief executives of public sector banks held in March 1980, it was agreed that banks should aim at raising the proportion of their advances to priority sectors to 40 per cent by March 1985.

The revised guidelines made operational with effect from July 20, 2012. The following categories are the specific eligible activities under priority sector:

(i) Direct agriculture i.e. loans to individual farmers including Self-Help groups (SHGs) or Joint Liability Groups (JLGs*), i.e.* groups of individual farmers directly engaged in agriculture and allied activities *viz.* dairy, fishery, animal husbandry, poultry, bee-keeping and sericulture 9up to cocoon stage);

(ii) Indirect agriculture i.e. loans to corporate including farmers' producer companies of individual farmers, partnership firms and cooperatives of farmers directly engaged in agriculture and allied activities;

(iii) Micro and Small Enterprises i.e. micro enterprises engaged in manufacturing units where investment in plant and machinery does not exceed ₹ 25 lakh and in micro enterprises in service sector where the investment does not exceed ₹ 10 lakh. Small enterprises are those in manufacturing sector where the investment is more than ₹ 25 lakh but does not exceed ₹ 5 crore, and in service sector the investment is more than ₹ 10 lakh but does not exceed ₹ 2 crore;

(iv) Khadi and village industries;

(v) Education;

(vi) Housing;

(vii) Export credit;

(viii) Certain others (micro) – specified by the RBI/Government.

(ix) Priority sector includes certain Weaker Sections including persons with disabilities who belong to the following category:

(a) Small farmers are those who hold more than I hectare, but less than 2 hectares of land; marginal farmers are those who hold up to I hectare of land. For purpose of priority sector loans, 'small and marginal farmers' include landless agricultural labourers, tenant farmers, oral lessees, and share croppers, whose share of land holding is within above prescribed limits;

(b) Artisans, village and cottage industries where individual credit limits do not exceed ₹ 50,000/-;

(c) Beneficiaries of Swarnajayanti Gram Swarozgar Yojana (SGSY), now National Rural Livelihood Mission (NRLM);

(d) Scheduled Castes and Scheduled Tribes;

(e) Beneficiaries of Differential Rate of Interest (DRI) scheme;

(f) Beneficiaries of Swarna Jayanti Shahari Rozgar Yojana (SJSRY);

(g) Beneficiaries under the Scheme for Rehabilitation of Manual Scavengers (SRMS);

(h) Loans to Self-Help Groups (SHGs);

(i) Loans to distressed farmers indebted to non-institutional lenders;

(j) Loans to distressed persons other than farmers not exceeding ₹ 50,000/- per borrower to prepay their debt to non-institutional lenders;

(k) Loans to individual women beneficiaries up to ₹ 50,000/-

(l) Loans sanctioned under (a) to (k) above to persons from minority communities as may be notified by Government of India from time to time;

In States, where one of the minority communities notified is, in fact, in majority, item (l) will cover only the other notified minorities. These States/Union Territories are Jammu & Kashmir, Punjab, Meghalaya, Mizoram, Nagaland and Lakshadweep.

## Social Banking

Social banking according to the Estimates Committee of the Eighth Lok Sabha constituted bankers' participation in schemes and programmes that had content dominantly social in relevance which is future-oriented in context and welfare –oriented in content.

Social banking activities proposed to impart stability to the socio-economic life of the target population. The Committee wanted, therefore, the entire banking system to serve as an effective instrument in the process of accelerated economic growth of the society with emphasis on the uplift of the poorer sections. Guidelines on 'Payment Banks' and 'Small Finance Banks' had been issued on 27ᵗʰ November, 2014. These differentiated banks are required to further the cause of financial inclusion.

## "Garibi Hatao"

"Garibi Hatao" (Remove Poverty) was the guiding slogan of anti-poverty programmes formulated mostly during the Sixth Five-Year Plan.In general, they aimed at distributing a few assets in favour of the poor, with a view to brining about social justice.

Twenty-Point Programme was launched in 1975; it was restructured during the Seventh Five-Year Plan (1985-90); it contained 15 points for financing by the banking sector which included, *inter alia*, (i) eradication of poverty, (ii) rising productivity, (iii) reducing income inequalities, (iv) removing social and economic disparities and (v) improving the quality of life. The 15 points are as under:

1. Attack on rural poverty;
2. Strategy for rain-fed agriculture;
3. Better use of irrigation water;
4. Bigger harvests;
5. Enforcement of land reforms (bank credit to allottees of surplus land for undertaking productive activities);
6. Special programme for rural poor;
7. Health for all;
8. Justice to scheduled castes and scheduled tribes;
9. Equality for women;
10. Housing for all;
11. Improvement of slums;
12. New strategy for foresting;
13. Concern for the consumer;
14. Energy for the villages and
15. A responsive administration.

Other programmes included or substituted envelop the National Scheme of Training of Rural Youth for Self-Employment (TRYSEM), Integrated Rural Development Programme (IRDP), Self-Employment Scheme for Educated Unemployed Youth (SEEUY) and Self-Employment Programme for the Urban Poor (SEPUP). 'Swachh Bharat' (Clean India) has been advocated since 2014.

There were many voluntary schemes such as community development programme, Drought Prone area Programme, Hill Area Development Programme, etc. for the uplift of weaker sections of the community. The focus was on providing employment opportunities to reduce inequality and poverty through these measures.

It was reported by the media on 20th April, 2016 that the State Government of Gujarat has detected Government employees holding 4 to 5 acres of land holdings were in possession of BPL card holders and enjoyed subsidies , thus forcing for a review.

## Minimum Needs Programme

The minimum needs programme attempted to provide essential infrastructure and special services to the weaker sections of the population. The Draft Five- Year Plan (1978-83) indicated nine items of minimum needs which included elementary education, adult education, rural health, rural water supply, rural roads, rural electrification, housing for rural landless labour households, environmental improvement and improvement of urban slums.

The twenty first century has witnessed certain schemes which are operated through banks to promote social justice *viz*. Sampoorna Grameen Rozgar Yojana (September 2001); National Pension Scheme (January 2004); Mahatma Gandhi National Rural Employment Guarantee (February 2006); Aam Aadmi Bima Yojana (2007); Rashtriya Krishi Vikas Yojana (August 2007); Gramin Bhandaran Yojana (March 2007); Bachat Lamp Yojana (2009); National Rural Livelihood Mission (June 2011); Sabla (for girls) (2011); Rajiv Awas Yojana (2013); Sakshan (for boys) (2014); Pradhan Mantri Jan Dhan Yojana (August 2014); Atal Pension Yojana (May 2015); Deen Dayal Upadhyaya Gram Jyoti Yojana (2015); Digital India

Programme ( July 2015); Pradhan Mantri Suraksha Bima Yojana (May 2015); Sukanya Samriddhi Yojana (January 2015); Smart Cities Mission (June 2015); Pradhan Mantri Awas Yojana (June 2015).

The objectives of all these plans are also similar as advocated and practised earlier under different names aiming to promote social justice.

Swachhta Status Report

The Swachhta Status Report based on survey conducted by National Sample Survey Organization (NSSO) between July 2014 and June 2015, covering 3788 villages and 2907 urban blocks, shows that nearly 96 per cent in villages and 99 per cent in urban areas use sanitary toilets that have access to them. The report also reflects a gradual shift in people's attitude towards household toilets in rural areas – an achievement in the face of resistance to having toilets in residential premises. The report further states that 46 per cent of urban population who do not have household sanitary toilets are using community toilet complexes. However, there is a long way to meet the target of complete sanitation by October 2019 as 52 per cent of the rural population and about 7.5 per cent in urban areas still defecate in the open, according to the Survey. It was found that about 55 per cent of toilets were being cleaned by people employed by the Panchayati or the municipal body and in 17 per cent cases, residents were cleaning them on their own or by their welfare association. Nearly 23 per cent of such toilets were not being cleaned at all. Likewise, community/public toilets in 8.6 per cent wards were not being cleaned by anybody (*TOI, Mumbai dated 14th April, 2016*).

The Union ministry of Urban Development has written to all state governments to amend their municipal ward laws to incorporate provisions for on the spot fine, penalty or cleaning charge from people caught defecating or littering in the open and to enforce by October 2018 (*TOI, Mumbai dated 16th April, 2016*).

## Business Correspondents/Business Facilitators

A significant number of banking outlets operate in branchless mode through

Business Correspondents (BCs) and Business Facilitators (BFs). Dominance of BCs in rural areas can be gauged from the fact that almost 91 per cent of the banking outlets were operating in branchless mode on March 31, 2015.

It was thought that careful planning would lead to establishment of forward and backward linkages in backward regions which, in turn, induce multiplier effects which

reflect in growth in the sectors, increasing output and generating employment, establishing innovations and strengthening the local service sector at the generation of external economies and thus, make the entire local regional economy more conducive to growth. RBI Governor, Deputy Governors, Executive Directors and top management visited villages across the country under the outreach programmes to boost financial inclusion through financial literacy. Involvement of public sector bank personnel will accelerate the process.

The RBI advised all scheduled commercial banks and urban co-operative banks on November 11, 2005 on financial inclusion to make available a single basic savings bank deposit 'no-frills' account known as a 'small account' - either with 'nil' or very low minimum balance as well as charges that would make such accounts accessible to vast sections of population.

The charge -free services available in the account include unlimited deposit and limited withdrawal of cash at a bank branch on four occasions in a month, as well as automated teller machines, receipt/credit of money through electronic payment channels or by means of deposit/collection of cheques drawn by Central/State Government agencies and departments.

## Panchayati Raj Institutions

There are various preliminary tasks assigned to the bank branches under the Service Area Approach, including survey of village profiles, development agencies at the block-level, their developmental programmes, formulation of village/branch credit plans, SHGs. The controlling offices of banks are required to monitor the implementation of the Service Area Approach which merged the erstwhile Village Adoption Scheme since April 1, 1989.

Panchayati Raj Institutions (PRIs) are the primary means of delivery of the essential services that are critical to inclusive growth. The 73rd and 74th Amendments to the Constitution of India have led to the establishment of about 2,50,000 elected institutions of local self-government of them 2,38,000 are located in rural areas. There are about 540 duly elected Members of Parliament, 4500 elected members of State Assemblies, 3.2 million Panchayati Raj members out of which 1.2 million are women. 27 targets at national level fall in 6 major categories *viz.* (i) income and poverty (ii) education (iii) health (iv) women and children (v) information and (vi) environment.

There are 13 State specific targets in addition to the national ones on GDP growth, agriculture, employment, poverty rate, literacy ratio, gender equality, infant mortality/maternal mortality rate, total fertility rate, child malnutrition, anemia among women and girls and sex-ratio.

India is a union of 29 states and 7 union territories. As of 2011, with an estimated population of 1 billion, India is the World's second most populous country. India occupies 2.4 per cent of the Word's land surface area and is a home to 17.5 per cent of the World's population. The Thar Desert in western Rajasthan is one of the most densely populated deserts in the World.

The bank branches have been functioning in every district of the country to transform the lives of the Indians through their service. The next chapter points out the level of structural transformation achieved through intermediation at the State-level in terms of certain socio-economic indicators. An attempt has also been made to measure the development at the district-level.

# DEVELOPMENT INDICATORS
# AND THE PROGRESSION

According to Prof.Muhammad Yunus – the Nobel laureate for Peace in 2006 - who spearheaded micro credit in Bangladesh, micro finance originated in India. In Bangladesh, it reached 115 million people in 30 years through Self-Help Groups (SHGs). At that rate, India should have been fully covered by SHGs by then.

Financial inclusion pursued by banks envelopes positive changes by improving the quality of life of the underprivileged sections of the community. It is assumed, thus, that bank branches serve as a model at local, district, state and national level to meet the aspirations of the common citizens. Public utilities such as public transport, public hospitals, public schools, public parks, public entertainment halls, any infrastructure for public use are likely to enhance the quality of life of the common citizen. The 12 digit 'Aadhaar' card by the Unique Identification Authority of India has been made a legal document for identifying and reaching out to the common citizens in India to enable them to realize *spread effects*. The following paragraphs attempt to measure the progressive economic growth and development achieved in India, assuming that the development has been aided mainly by the banks and their branches at grass roots level.

## Branch Banking Service

The data published by the Reserve Bank of India excluding bank credit extended for food procurement, relating to March 2015 indicate that rural and semi-urban branches together accounted for 63.4 per cent in the total number of branches of scheduled commercial banks and account for more than 62 per cent of total number of bank accounts across the country. However, they could mobilize 25 per cent of total deposits accounted by them.

However, the share of extended credit in rural and semi-urban areas across the country stood at less than 20 per cent in the total, thus indicating that there exists a vast scope for lending in these deserving parts of the country.

The ultimate purpose of providing banking facilities as stimulant in remote areas is development, to initiate sectoral growth in terms of output, employment opportunities and income to all people for a better social life promoted through real economic growth. How far the widening and deepening of banking facilities has stimulated development at the State and district levels is a common query of the common citizen who has a right to know.

For the purpose of this Study, certain universally accepted socio-economic indicators using secondary data are employed. The latest secondary data are given in the Annexure to enable the reader to ascertain the present position. This chapter has 3 sections.

## Section-I

In the present section, an endeavour is made to analyse the impact of expansion of bank branches in terms of

(i) Population covered by a bank branch
(ii) Per capita income;
(iii) Per capita daily calorie intake;
(iv) Rural poverty ratio;
(v) Literacy rate and
(vi) Urbanization.

In tables (4.1 to 4.7) data for two representative years corresponding to the beginning of post-nationalisation era or end of pre-nationalisation era (as per availability of earlier data) and the latest year for which the same data were available in 1990 (when the empirical model was tested) are reproduced. The latest data are, however, presented in the annexure for further research.

The mean, standard deviation and coefficient of variation on the one hand and rank correlation coefficients between branch expansion and each of the said socio-economic indicators on the other have been worked out as part of the analysis. The data and results are presented in these tables.

The analyses are made with particular reference to 13 major Indian States where 89.5 percent of the total new branches were opened between July 1969 and June 1990. The states are: (i) Andhra Pradesh (ii) Bihar, (iii) Gujarat, (iv) Karnataka, (v) Kerala, (vi) Madhya Pradesh, (vii) Maharashtra (viii) Odisha, (ix) Punjab, (x) Rajasthan, (xi) Tamil Nadu (xii) Uttar Pradesh and (xiii) West Bengal

Table 4.1 indicates that the population coverage in these states has narrowed down disparities considerably since 1977. The coefficient of variation also has decreased from 68.77 to 11.07 during the same period. The Table indicates that population covered by a bank branch, and its mean value have decreased substantially from 89.15 in 1965 to 16.48 in 1987. These point out that a notable degree of reduction in the inequalities pertaining to branch coverage in these major states. However, the coefficient of variation increased from 30.11 in 1978 to 31.94 in 1981 due to backlog in opening branches in 1981.

A review of the progress in implementation of the branch licensing policy also confirmed this view. The review made in 1981 revealed a large number of authorizations were pending with banks. The backlog was mainly on account of lack of infrastructural facilities at the centres identified for opening offices and manpower resources. The Reserve Bank of India had to extend, as a result, the currency of the policy up to 1982 to enable the banks to utilize the licenses already issued to them.

As regards Table 4.2, mean value of per capita income increased between 1971 and 1987 from ₹ 659.92 to ₹ 2670.00. On the other hand the coefficient of variation did not change significantly and, thus existing tendency of wide disparities in terms of per capita income persisted.

Table 4.3 reveals that mean value increased during the period 1971 and 1978. The coefficient of variation declined from 18.63 in 1971 to 9.11 in 1978, indicating that existing disparities in terms of calorie intake had narrowed down.

Table 4.4 indicates that mean value of rural poverty ratio has decreased from 49.63 in 1965 to 38.72 in 1984. On the contrary, coefficient of variation has increased from 22.77 in 1965 to 26.29 in 1984, indicating that the existing disparities have widened in these states in terms of rural poverty ratio. Table 4.5 indicates the progressive literacy level that narrows down disparities.

From Table 4.6, it may be observed that the mean value increased from 20.32 in 1971 to 28.44 in 1981. The coefficient of variation tended to decline during the same period from 34.96 in 1971 to 30.20 in India suggesting a narrowing down of disparities in terms of urbanization.

Table 4.1
Population Covered per Bank Branch
(in thousands)

| States | 1965 | Rank | 1971 | Rank | 1978 | Rank | 1981 | Rank | 1984 | Rank | 1987 | Rank |
|---|---|---|---|---|---|---|---|---|---|---|---|---|
| Andhra Pradesh | 80 | 8 | 75 | 8 | 20 | 7 | 19 | 7 | 16 | 3 | 14 | 1 |
| Bihar | 215 | 12 | 205 | 12 | 31 | 13 | 29 | 13 | 20 | 10 | 19 | 11.5 |
| Gujrat | 37 | 15 | 34 | 1 | 16 | 4 | 14 | 4 | 17 | 7 | 16 | 7.5 |
| Karnataka | 40 | 4 | 37 | 35 | 15 | 3 | 13 | 3 | 17 | 7 | 16 | 7.5 |
| Kerala | 37 | 1.5 | 35 | 2 | 12 | 1.5 | 11 | 2 | 16 | 3 | 15 | 4 |
| Madhya Pradesh | 118 | 10 | 114 | 10 | 26 | 9.5 | 24 | 9.5 | 21 | 12 | 19 | 11.5 |
| Maharashtra | 46 | 6 | 4 | 6 | 19 | 6 | 17 | 6 | 17 | 7 | 15 | 4 |
| Odisha | 218 | 13 | 210 | 13 | 29 | 11 | 27 | 11.5 | 21 | 12 | 19 | 11.5 |
| Punjab | 45 | 5 | 41 | 5 | 12 | 1.5 | 10 | 1 | 16 | 3 | 15 | 4 |
| Rajasthan | 73 | 7 | 70 | 7 | 24 | 8 | 21 | 8 | 18 | 9 | 17 | 9 |
| Tamil Nadu | 39 | 3 | 37 | 3.5 | 18 | 5 | 16 | 5 | 16 | 3 | 15 | 4 |
| Uttar Pradesh | 122 | 11 | 117 | 11 | 30 | 12 | 27 | 11.5 | 21 | 12 | 19 | 11.5 |
| West Bengal | 89 | 9 | 86 | 9 | 26 | 9.5 | 24 | 9.5 | 16 | 3 | 15 | 4 |
| M | 89.15 | | 85.00 | | 21.38 | | 19.38 | | 17.85 | | 16.46 | |
| SD | 61.31 | | 59.18 | | 6.43 | | 6.19 | | 2.03 | | 1.82 | |
| CV | 68.77 | | 69.02 | | 30.11 | | 31.94 | | 11.38 | | 11.07 | |

Note :    M - Mean          SD - Standard Deviation          CV - Coefficient of variation
Source :  Reserve Bank of India,      Report on Currency and Finance,    Various issues.

Table 4.2
Per Capita Income (Rs.)

| States | 1971 | Rank | 1987 | Rank |
|---|---|---|---|---|
| Andhra Pradesh | 627 | 7 | 2333 | 8 |
| Bihar | 415 | 13 | 1802 | 13 |
| Gujrat | 827 | 2 | 3223 | 3 |
| Karnataka | 698 | 5 | 2486 | 6 |
| Kerala | 592 | 8 | 2371 | 7 |
| Madhya Pradesh | 534 | 10 | 2020 | 11 |
| Maharashtra | 808 | 3 | 3493 | 2 |
| Odisha | 473 | 12 | 1957 | 12 |
| Punjab | 1121 | 1 | 4719 | 1 |
| Rajasthan | 560 | 9 | 2150 | 9 |
| Tamil Nadu | 648 | 6 | 2732 | 5 |
| Uttar Pradesh | 497 | 11 | 2146 | 10 |
| West Bengal | 779 | 4 | 2988 | 4 |
| M | 659.92 | | 2648.70 | |
| SD | 182.12 | | 800.78 | |
| CV | 27.59 | | 29.98 | |

Source : Government of India, Economic Survey, 1971-72 and 1988-89.

Table 4.3
Per Capita Daily Calorie Intake

| State | 1971 | Rank | 1978 | Rank |
|---|---|---|---|---|
| Andhra Pradesh | 2111 | 8 | 2369 | 5 |
| Bihar | 2219 | 5 | 2354 | 6 |
| Gujrat | 2151 | 6 | 2225 | 9 |
| Karnataka | 2132 | 7 | 2462 | 4 |
| Kerala | 1586 | 13 | 2135 | 11 |
| Madhya Pradesh | 2390 | 4 | 2304 | 8 |
| Maharashtra | 1919 | 12 | 2129 | 12 |
| Odisha | 2020 | 9 | 2161 | 10 |
| Punjab | 3319 | 1 | 2787 | 1 |
| Rajasthan | 2662 | 2 | 2715 | 2 |
| Tamil Nadu | 1920 | 11 | 2071 | 13 |
| Uttar Pradesh | 2514 | 3 | 2534 | 3 |
| West Bengal | 1961 | 10 | 2337 | 7 |
| M | 2223 | | 2353 | |
| SD | 414.39 | | 214.37 | |
| CV | 18.63 | | 9.11 | |

Source : Government of India, Planning Commission.

Table 4.4
Rural Poverty Ratio (Per cent)

| States | 1965 | Rank | 1984 | Rank |
|---|---|---|---|---|
| Andhra Pradesh | 41.2 | 10 | 38.7 | 8 |
| Bihar | 53.0 | 7 | 51.4 | 1 |
| Gujrat | 51.0 | 8 | 27.6 | 11 |
| Karnataka | 54.4 | 6 | 37.5 | 9 |
| Kerala | 61.6 | 1 | 26.8 | 12 |
| Madhya Pradesh | 40.7 | 11 | 50.3 | 2 |
| Maharashtra | 60.5 | 3 | 41.5 | 7 |
| Odisha | 60.9 | 2 | 44.8 | 4 |
| Punjab | 26.0 | 13 | 13.8 | 13 |
| Rajasthan | 30.0 | 12 | 36.6 | 10 |
| Tamil Nadu | 57.8 | 5 | 44.1 | 5 |
| Uttar Pradesh | 49.8 | 9 | 46.5 | 3 |
| West Bengal | 58.3 | 4 | 43.8 | 6 |
| M | 49.63 | | 38.72 | |
| SD | 11.30 | | 10.18 | |
| CV | 22.77 | | 26.29 | |

Source :(i) Government of India, Planning Commission. (ii) Reply to Unstarred Question No. 1989 in the Rajya Sabha on March 12, 1989

Table 4.5
Literacy Rate (Per cent)

| State | 1971 | Rank | 1981 | Rank |
|---|---|---|---|---|
| Andhra Pradesh | 24.6 | 9 | 29.9 | 9 |
| Bihar | 19.9 | 12 | 26.2 | 12 |
| Gujrat | 35.8 | 4 | 43.7 | 4 |
| Karnataka | 31.5 | 7 | 38.5 | 7 |
| Kerala | 60.4 | 1 | 70.4 | 1 |
| Madhya Pradesh | 22.1 | 10 | 27.9 | 10 |
| Maharashtra | 39.2 | 3 | 47.2 | 2 |
| Odisha | 26.2 | 8 | 34.2 | 8 |
| Punjab | 33.7 | 5 | 40.9 | 5.5 |
| Rajasthan | 19.1 | 13 | 24.4 | 13 |
| Tamil Nadu | 39.5 | 2 | 46.8 | 3 |
| Uttar Pradesh | 21.7 | 11 | 27.2 | 11 |
| West Bengal | 3.2 | 6 | 40.9 | 5.5 |
| M | 28.99 | | 460.44 | |
| SD | 10.87 | | 12.03 | |
| CV | 34.68 | | 31.40 | |

Source : National Census Report, 1971 and 1981.

Table 4.6

Urbanisation (Per cent)

| States | 1971 | Rank | 1981 | Rank |
|---|---|---|---|---|
| Andhra Pradesh | 19.3 | 7 | 23.3 | 7 |
| Bihar | 10.0 | 12 | 12.5 | 12 |
| Gujrat | 28.0 | 3 | 31.1 | 3 |
| Karnataka | 24.3 | 5 | 28.9 | 4 |
| Kerala | 16.2 | 10 | 18.7 | 10 |
| Madhya Pradesh | 16.3 | 9 | 20.3 | 9 |
| Maharashtra | 31.2 | 1 | 35.0 | 1 |
| Odisha | 8.4 | 13 | 11.8 | 13 |
| Punjab | 23.7 | 6 | 27.7 | 5 |
| Rajasthan | 17.6 | 8 | 21.0 | 8 |
| Tamil Nadu | 30.3 | 2 | 33.0 | 2 |
| Uttar Pradesh | 14.0 | 11 | 17.9 | 11 |
| West Bengal | 24.8 | 4 | 26.5 | 6 |
| M | 20.32 | | 23.44 | |
| SD | 7.10 | | 7.14 | |
| CV | 34.96 | | 30.20 | |

Source : National Census Report, 1971 and 1981.

## Association Between Indicators of Development and Branch Banking

In order to examine the association between development indicators and branch banking, two rank correlation coefficients have been worked out as appropriate to the relevant years based on the data for 13 major states as cross sections. The northern region is represented by Bihar, Madhya Pradesh, Punjab, Rajasthan and Uttar Pradesh, the eastern region by Odisha and West Bengal, the Western region by Gujarat and Maharashtra and the Southern region by Andhra Pradesh, Karnataka, Kerala and Tamil Nadu.

It may be observed that branches in these major states formed more than 89 percent of the new branches opened by all banks during the post-nationalisation period. The results are presented in Table 4.7.

The value of the rank correlation coefficients between per capita income and population per branch indicates a high degree of association between the two. However, during the two years of analysis there is not any difference in the coefficient values.

The rank correlation coefficients indicate only a marginal increase from 0.72 in 1971 to 0.73 in 1987.

Table 4.7

Rank Correlation Coefficients between Population Per Branch and
Socio-economic Indicators

| | Indicators | 1965 | 1971 | 1978 | 1981 | 1984 | 1987 |
|---|---|---|---|---|---|---|---|
| (i) | Per Capita Income | – | 0.72 | – | – | – | 0.73 |
| (ii) | Calorie Intake | – | 0.26 | 0.12 | – | – | – |
| (iii) | Rural Poverty Ratio | 0.10 | – | – | – | 0.45 | – |
| (iv) | Literacy Rate | – | 0.71 | – | 0.68 | – | – |
| (v) | Urbanisation | – | 0.65 | – | 0.64 | – | – |

The manifold expansion in the number of bank branches has, thus, not at all influenced the relative positions of the states in respect of their per capita income. These branches could not generate adequate economic activities and create assets to raise the per capita real income of the common citizen. The results also indicate there had been leakages in the process of intermediation.

The latest position of these indicators is presented State-wise in Annexure – VII, VIII, IX, and X. The trend requires further scrutiny and analysis. Diversion of bank credit by the borrowers and rising non-performing assets (Annexure – XIV) in the system confirm that all bank branches could not deploy funds to economic units to generate output, employment and income in the country.

As regards calorie intake, it may be observed from Table 4. 3 it may be observed that it has not been significantly associated with branch banking facilities for both years -0.26 in 1971 and -0.12 in 1981. This signifies the absence of any noticeable impact created by expansion of bank branches upon the living standards of the under-privileged and common citizens measured in terms of calorie intake.

The banks did not devote much attention to increase in the supply of nourishing food items like pulses, eggs, fish and milk. Table 4.4 points to lack of any association between poverty and branch banking. However, the value of correlation coefficients has changed from 0.10 in 1965 to – 0.45 in 1984, indicating the positive role played by rural bank branches. States that have registered an increase in number of poor people during the period included Andhra Pradesh, Bihar, Madhya Pradesh, Rajasthan, Uttar Pradesh and West Bengal. One reason could be misuse of funds earmarked for anti-poverty programmes. Annexure X reveals the latest published status.

Mid-day Meal Scheme was being pursued by many states. National Rural Health Mission was launched in 2005 with over five lakh Accredited Social Health Activists (ASHAs) one for every 1000 population in18 Special Focus States and in tribal pockets. 30,000 Primary Health Centres were launched during the Eleventh Five-Year Plan with 3 staff nurses to provide round the clock services. 6,500 Community Health Centres with 7 specialists and 9 staff nurses; 1,800 Taluka or sub- divisional hospitals and 600 district hospitals in 2,012. Mobile Medical Units in each district have been provided on completion of District Health Action Plans in 2008. United grants and annual maintenance grants to every sub-centre were released regularly.

In terms of literacy rate, it is observed from Table 4.5 that association between education and a bank has not undergone any significant change during the period 1971- 1981. The values of correlation coefficients are 0.71 and 0.68, respectively. As a result, it can be mentioned that though education was one of the priority sectors for the bank lending; only a negligible portion of bank credit has been allocated for the spread of education.

As regards urbanization, the value of correlation coefficients are 0.65 and 0.64 in 1971 and 1981, respectively (Table 4.6) indicating that there has not been much change in the degree of association between branch banking facilities and urbanization.

Urbanization is an indicator of development. Although urbanization had taken place, improvement in area such as sanitation, clean water supply, environmental protection; public transport, communication and other basic needs for the human welfare have not been paid required attention. Degree of urbanization has, however, been measured only through the density factor of population. Cosmetic structures in the cities failed to meet the basic needs such as clean air to inhale, uninterrupted power supply, clean drinking water supply to the needy urban population and pollution-free environment in many parts across India. Annexure – VII reveals that no significant qualitative reformation has happened in urban centres.Urbanization has, thus, been a population shift from rural to urban areas; the gradual increase in the proportion of people living in urban areas and the reason for which each society adapts to the change. Therefore, the urbanization achieved in India has been due to a higher birth rate and migration from rural areas and a centre was defined urban based on the population criterion and not due to any qualitative development in terms of clean environment, clean drinking water supply, sanitation, uninterrupted electric power supply and other facilities to sustain the quality of life.

The planning commission's data on reduction of people below poverty line from 37.2 per cent in 2004-05 to 29.8 per cent in 2009-10 was also attributed due to the Government's 'inclusive growth' policy like National Rural Employment Guarantee Programme (NREGP), Pradhan Mantri Gram Sadak Yojana, Sarva Shiksha Abhiyan, Bharat Nirman and several others. In other words, about 47 million people have been lifted from poverty by increasing their purchasing power.

According to the Planning Commission, incidence of poverty has increased in the north east region since 2004-05 and specifically in Assam, Meghalaya, Manipur, Mizoram and Nagaland. Other States with high incidence of poverty are Bihar (53.5 per cent), Chhattisgarh (48.7 per cent), Jharkhand (39.1 per cent) and Uttar Pradesh (37.7 per cent). However, in States like Himachal Pradesh, Karnataka, Madhya Pradesh, Maharashtra, Odisha, Sikkim, Tamil Nadu and Uttarakhand the decline was about 10.0 per cent during the same period.

According to the Human Development Report, India ranks 130 among the 177 countries. The International Food Policy Research Institute's Global Hunger Index ranks India 94th among 118 countries surveyed. The World Food Program estimates half of our children suffer from severe or moderate malnourishment due to persisting poverty. Around 365 million people or one-third of our population remained BPL. These estimates for 2011-12 were based on an expenditure of ₹ 32 and ₹ 26 by an individual in the urban and rural areas respectively at 2010-11 prices. This provisional figure represents one-third of the world's poor population, indicating persisting poverty measured in terms of minimum required level of calories is 2100 for rural and 1800 for urban individuals.

The criterion of global standard of calculating poverty at the U.S. $1.25 a day at 2005 purchasing power parity remains only a dream to more than 300 million Indians. 67 out of 1000 children born in India die before the age of five. Despite a national policy for compulsory primary education, only 50.0 per cent our children have access to proper formal education.

According to the multi-dimensional poverty indicators developed by the Oxford Poverty and Human Development Initiative and applied by the Human Development Index (HDI) 2010, the proportion of BPL families in India is 55.4 per cent of the population. Bihar fares poorest with 61.4 per cent of the BPL, while Kerala has the lowest fraction of 40.9 per cent of BPL people. West Bengal rates 13th in HDI despite being the 6th largest contributor to Gross Domestic Product (GDP).

The Micro and Small Enterprises (MSE) sector, for instance, accounts for the manufacturing segments and remains a source of strength for real economic growth. As per the Reserve Bank's extant guidelines to banks, 60 per cent of MSE advances should be directed towards micro enterprises. Banks have been advised that the allocation of 60 per cent of MSE advances to micro enterprises is to be achieved by 2012-13.

Distribution of bank credit to small and marginal farmers continues to be low. The persisting non-performing assets are also leakages. High percentage of over dues have accrued in the past as there were no proper linkages – forward and backward – to increase the return from land like irrigation, electricity, marketing facility, etc. which adversely affect recycling of bank funds. A credit transaction is complete only when the borrower repays the amount in full with interest.

Some of the causes stated by the Indian Banks' Association (IBA) Bulletin include unrealistic assessment of credit requirement of borrowers, delay in sanctioning and disbursing credit, target-oriented approach, ignorance of the viability of the credit proposals, lack of integrated approach and stipulation of unrealistic repayment schedules.

There are Lead Banks in each district. The number of districts assigned to lead banks stood at 586 in March 2015. Any positive impact on progressive economic development of the concerned district depends on collaborative efforts by all participants including the district collector to facilitate enhancement of entrepreneurial skills of people to increase the absorption capacity of credit.

The Lead Bank Scheme has, *inter alia*, revealed that there existed noticeable inter-regional disparities, as a result of the impact of branch banking facilities. Identification of requisite details for subsequent rectification by the concerned authority may ultimately lead to probable adequate coverage in terms of credit or investment or infrastructure, thus attaining financial inclusion.

The lead banks were advised in April 1989 to invite local Members of Parliament and Members of Legislative Assembly to the District Level Review Committee meetings as and when convened. The development funds allocated to the elected representatives also find a place in bank branches. How and where the funds were utilized by them were beyond the scope of the branch managers of banks as they were expected to perform to meet the business targets.

The Micro and Small Enterprises (MSE) sector, for instance, accounts for the manufacturing segments and remains a source of strength for real economic growth.

As per the Reserve Bank's extant guidelines to banks, 60 per cent of MSE advances should be directed towards micro enterprises. Banks have been advised that the allocation of 60 per cent of MSE advances to micro enterprises is to be achieved by 2012-13.

Annual Action Plans are also required to be prepared by the lead banks each year indicating sectoral, scheme-wise and institution group-wise break-up of the total credit outlays as part and parcel of the participative planning by the district level task force comprising banks – both commercial and co-operative banks having dominance over the district and the district plan officer besides the district convener of the lead bank of area –specific bankable schemes and thereby improving the credit absorption capacity of the rural segments. The task force is also required to prepare evaluation studies of the implementation of the credit plans through greater co-ordination between the government and banks in the development and welfare programmes introduced by the Government from time to time. Plan for the scheduled castes and scheduled tribes also are included in the report.

The lead banks, as consortium leaders, constituted consultative committees at district level to serve as a forum for discussion among the banks and other financial institutions exchanging information about lending to the priority sectors in the districts, identifying bankable schemes and evolving methods of financing them in a coordinated manner allotting unbanked centres identified during the survey.

The district survey report and district census reports are also available with the Committee of which the District Collector is the Chairman. Representatives of all the commercial banks, cooperative banks, regional rural banks, term lending financial institutions and developmental agencies in the field of agriculture, small-scale industries, etc operating in the district participate with the lead bank representative who is the convener besides the concerned government departments. They maintain liaison with the related departments of the respective state government.

Regional Consultative Committees (RCCs) were set-up in six geographical regions in the country, presided over by the Union Finance Minister and having representatives of the state governments at the ministers' level and chief executives of various public sector banks functioning in the region. Governor and Deputy Governors of the RBI attended these meetings to review and discuss various developmental programmes and to take appropriate measures in the light of performance and suggestions made during these discussions. ( Data provided in the Annexure are as per these six geographical regions).

Banks have thus formulated comprehensive economic surveys and credit plans for their implementation in their respective lead districts. The district credit plan is a blue print for action by banks and other financial institutions. These plans are in tune with the plans formulated by the Planning Commission. There are District Consultative Committees functioning to effectively monitor overall progress of the lead bank scheme.

Credit plans are comprehensive indicating credit targets for the institutions in each district on a block-wise, scheme – wise and bank-wise basis, as suggested by the RBI in March 1979.

Under Rajiv Gandhi Jeevandayi Arogya Yojana, health insurance scheme for the poor was practiced in 25 districts of the State of Maharashtra; the poor people are being treated for various ailments and also undergo life saving surgeries. Maharashtra has adopted the Pre-Conception and Pre-Natal Diagnostic Techniques (PCPNDT) Act, 1994 to protect the girl children. The Maharashtra Medical Council-the watchdog of professional ethics among doctors takes action against violators of this Act As a result, the sex ratio in Maharashtra remained at a higher level.

Micro level planning thus aims at tackling the local problems at grass root level with optimum utilization of readily available regional human and natural resources to satisfy specific regional ends like provision of basic infrastructure subsequent to the financial intermediation or monetization or credit utilization. The Planning Commission, in an affidavit to the Supreme Court, has stated in September 2011 that of the 40.74 crore BPL population in the country, 35.98 crore of them have been touched by the Public Distribution System (PDS). The latest official secondary data on poverty indicators are presented in Annexure – X.

# Section -II

An attempt was made to measure the development that has taken place due to the spread effects of intermediation at the grass root level. Data used are available on the public domain. They are presented in **Annexure - I.** District- wise data (as on March 31, 2016) indicate the progress achieved through intermediation with their lead banks. Districts are presented Region and State/Union Territory-wise. Their source is the Annexure - I to Master Circular of the Reserve Bank of India on Lead Bank Scheme i.e. (*RBI/2014 – 15/94 – RPCD.CO.LBS.BC.No.9/02.01.001/2014-15 dated July 1, 2014*).

Data on Number of 'Bank Branches' refer to the number of branches of scheduled commercial banks as on 31ˢᵗ March, 2015 published in 2016. Sex-Ratio, Density of population and Literacy rates are as per the Government of India National Census 2011 Report.

## District-wise Analysis

In brief, some districts of certain states and Union Territories have performed better in terms of these select indicators. For instance, in recent years, Bihar and Madhya Pradesh have been beneficiaries of bank branches and as a result, agricultural production has increased in these States.

In Kandhamal district of Odisha, bank branches have catered to the educational and healthcare activities.

In Punjab, in general, lower sex-ratio persists due to gender bias and bank branches have no impact on this indicator of development.

In Uttar Pradesh, there is scope for bank credit to educational needs through the bank branches.

In the Union Territory of Andaman & Nicobar Islands, sex-ratio and literacy rate were lower in Nicobar, as compared with the territory average, despite the presence of 37 bank branches.

In undivided Andhra Pradesh, literacy rate was lower than the State average of 67 per cent in districts of Kurnool, Mehabub Nagar and Nizamabad where density of population was lower than the state average.

In the North-Eastern region, all districts of Arunachal Pradesh, Assam, Manipur, Meghalaya, Mizoram, Nagaland and Tripura require more intermediation through bank branches for overall development.

In Bihar, although districts of Arwal and Sheohar had a higher density of population, they are not served with adequate number of bank branches. On the contrary, districts of Rohtas and Sheikhpure with lower density of population had more number of bank branches.

While Dadra & Nagar Haveli with a density of population of 698 per square k.m, had 24 bank branches, Daman & Diu with a much higher density of population had only 18 bank branches. In these Union territories, the sex-ratio was much less than the all-India average.

The experience of a few countries has suggested that commercial bank branch network exerted a profound influence on the pace and quality of development in their respective economies at a particular point of time. The quality and the crucial role the banks play in economic development of a country may, therefore, be felt from key indicators like improvement in the quality of life of the citizens, gradual reduction and eventual removal of (i) poverty, (ii) malnutrition, (iii) diseases, (iv) illiteracy, (v) squalor, (vi) unemployment and (vii) inequalities among the various regions of the country. This study has annexed certain secondary data/Statements/Tables at the end to enable a common citizen to understand the present stage.

In Kachchh district of Gujarat, the density of population remained the lowest at 46 and there were 208 bank branches.

In Haryana, the gender bias persisted and as a result, the presence of a number of bank branches failed to impact the quality of life of the common citizens.

In Leh district of Jammu & Kashmir, there were more bank branches for a meager local population.

In Karnataka, the literacy rate remained low despite the presence of a number of bank branches and 'education' was a priority sector for deployment of bank credit in most of its districts.

In Kerala, the presence of bank branches has been felt across the State, improving the quality of life of the common citizen in terms of better sex-ratio, literacy rate and healthcare.

Banks create credit through banking transactions/operations. Deployment of funds (credit) to the productive sectors of the economy promotes/generates economic growth and development, thereby promoting equality and social harmony. Increases in the total money supply also come about primarily as a result of lending and investing activities of the banking system in the form of derivative deposits.

If the deployment of credit is well planned to assist productive investment, it would generate surplus income and, thus, enhance the repayment capacity of the borrower. The surplus income generated would also create additional deposits to cause an increase in money supply which is known as 'multiple credit creation'.

Branch banking, thus, speeds up the mobility of supply of credit and helps achieving a balanced growth of a country's economy. Thus, bank branches serve as arteries in a human body, supplying funds to various needy sectors and sections of the community.

They induce economic activities and to produce goods and services required by the citizens. Transfer of these resources and promotion of exchange activities, thus increase productivity which is, the basis for real growth and development.

## All-India Variables

In India, with rapid and massive branch expansion since the nationalisation of major banks in 1969, banks have, thus, grown into large institutions with their branch network spread far and wide. Annexure - XII presents the All –India position of bank branches, aggregate deposits, aggregate credit and investment since 1950-51 along with population data.

As revealed in the earlier chapter, the number of bank branches increased from 2,765 in 1950-51 to 1, 30,482 in 2014-15. As a result, the average population covered by a bank branch has declined from 65,000 in 1969 to 10,000 in 2015. This sort of geographical expansion of bank branches epitomizes the interaction of a changing economic scene. During the period, banks made efforts to remove poverty as well. Over the time path of development, the Indian economy has faced additional problems of integrating a vast, pluralistic and diverse nation across strong regional and communal lines and of protecting itself against major external threats.

The discussion in the earlier paragraphs reveals that, as a result of the supply-leading and demand-following roles played by the bank branches it is possible to establish an important linkage between the real and banking sector. The inter - dependence of banks among (i) increased number of bank branches, (ii) the newly tapped sources of savings. (iii) banks' intermediation with different sectors and (iv) the eventual structural changes in the economy assumes much significance.

## Production and Growth

Growth implies increased output at a rate faster than the rate of growth of population. National is the aggregate of the net value added, *inter alia* in different sectors of the entire economy consisting of States and Union territories. It is the establishment of a link between growth and productivity that makes for an increase in the rate of economic growth.

In India, agriculture is the major sector which contributes to the national exchequer. Increased production and distribution also satisfy the basic human need. Agricultural sector provides employment directly by raising agricultural production and indirectly by stimulating the income and saving of the cultivators.

Accelerated growth in agriculture has been the objective of Indian Planning over the decades. The banking system in India has been assigned a significant role to narrow down chronic disparities while widening and deepening its activities. Poverty alleviation programmes including integrated rural development programme were also assigned to the banks as part of social banking.

The nationalisation of the Reserve Bank of India (RBI) in 1949 has paved the way for the linkage between central banking functions and the socio-economic objectives of the Government. Besides, Indian banks have been given the responsibility of acting as the prime movers in the process of planned development.

The Reserve Bank of India (RBI), through its branch licensing policies sought to bring about rapid economic development of different sectors of the economy by letting commercial banks in to areas where even orthodox banks in developed countries have feared to tread. The Indian banks have, thus, not only attempted to bring about a more equitable distribution of wealth and facilities to promote welfare of all citizens, but, engaged themselves also in social reformation.

The objective of the RBI's monetary policy has been attainment of growth with justice, in accordance with the macro-economic policies pursued by the Government. Extension of the monetized sector and of the banking habit, narrowing down seasonal and regional gaps between the supply of and demand for funds, availability of adequate funds to priority sectors and preferred sections and development of social overheads for meeting the requirements of industry and agriculture are important aspects of the Reserve Bank's evolving promotional role.

## Capital - Output

Banks in India which work within the framework of national guidelines have an obligation to promote the ideal of social welfare in the process of intermediation. By rendering a greater part of capital judiciously and productively, the banking system is expected to facilitate speedy and balanced growth of the national economy.

Economic growth is a function of the rate of incremental capital formation. The central bank of the country exists for promoting and maintaining a high level of production and real income in the country and fostering growth and development of a country's resources in the best national interest.

The relationship between capital formation and output also assumes special importance in the context of a developing country like India. It is also a practice to use the level and nature of change in the capital-output ratios to draw inferences about the efficient utilization of credit. As deposits create credit, there exists a relationship between the number of bank branches and national output or income.

## Savings and Investment

Bank branches are established to mobilize the financial savings and transform them in to investment assets or capital formation. The emergence of savings depends largely on the branch network and these branches are, therefore, partners in productive enterprises. Bank deposits and credit are important segments of financial assets/liabilities of the household sector. Indian banks widened their areas after the nationalisation of major banks in 1969 with a view to ensuring credit to economically backward regions, neglected sectors and poorer sections of the community.

There exists an establishment of a link between economic growth/development and the banking system through deployment of credit. In India, there are major sectors which envelope other tiny but vital sectors.

## Agriculture and Development

It was optimistically reckoned that from increased agricultural output would emerge a lasting solution to the problem of rural poverty and hunger. During the post-nationalisation period, agriculture and allied activities such as fishing, poultry, forestry, etc were treated as priority sector for extending concessional credit to enable the banks to make the sector more productive with stipulated targets and to deploy credit.

The strategy entrusted with banks was, thus, to transform the traditional subsistence farming sector in to a modernized sector mainly to increase output, using technology.

It is observed that total food grains (cereals and pulses) production has increased from 50.01 million tonnes in 1952-53 to 252.68 million tonnes in 2014-15 while the total area under cultivation increased from 109.48 million hectares in 1957-58 to 122.00 million hectares in 2014-15. Yield of food grains per hectare has increased from 630 kilogramme (kg) per hectare to 2379 kg per hectare during the same period.

Production of oilseeds (groundnut, castorseed, sesamum, nigerseed, rapeseed and mustard, linseed, safflower, sunflower, and soyabean) has increased from 6.40 million tonnes in 1954-55 to 26.68 million tonnes in 2014-15 just the area under cultivation of oil seeds increased from 13.00 million hectares in 1958-59 to 25.73 million hectares in 2014-15. Yield per hectare increased from 481kg per hectare in 1950-51to 1037 kg per hectare in 2014-15, as per the data published by the Ministry of Agriculture, Government of India.(**Annexure- V**)

According to the Government of India, Ministry of Agriculture & Farmers Welfare released in September, 2015, gross irrigated area for agricultural production has increased from 25.64 million hectares in 1955-56 to 92.58 million hectares in 2012-13, while the net sown area increased from 129.16 million hectares to 139.93 million hectares during the same period, indicating a large gap between the gross irrigated area and net sown area.

The National Bank for Agriculture and Rural Development (NABARD), *inter alia*, provides refinance facilities to all scheduled commercial banks that lend to this major productive sector. In Madhya Pradesh and Bihar, credit to agriculture and allied activities has shown positive impact. This may be observed from the data published at district-level.

According to the Union Agriculture Secretary, the credit mechanism did not work the way it was expected to perform by ensuring agriculture credit reaching small and marginal farmers According to him mass suicide by farmers in Maharashtra was attributed to this fact and debt burden due to high interest loan from local money lenders. The Times of India published in its Mumbai edition on April

12, 2016. Thus, instead of playing the role of facilitator, a few bankers have focused on petty politics. For instance, populist sops have been the norms for decades and there was no investment in irrigation, setting up of food processing industry, crop insurance scheme, marketing facilities, etc. as linkages to foster agricultural output in most of the States.

## Small – Scale Industries

The small-scale industrial sector is a dynamic and subsidiary sector. The Government recognizes the need to spread the rural and cottage industries with a view to be more productive.

These industries account for more than 35 per cent of the gross value of output in the manufacturing sector and over 40 per cent of the total exports from India. It also provides employment to millions of citizens. The small-scale industries have been given more importance over successive Plans to give impetus to the industrial sector in terms of growth in output, employment and income. Small – scale industry is a priority sector for the banks as well.

Small-scale industries have been merged with the agro and rural industries to form the micro, small and medium enterprises (MSMEs) with effect from October 02, 2006, consequent to enactment of Micro, Small and Medium Enterprises Development Act, 2006.

The Small- Scale industries (SSI) sector covers a wide spectrum of industries categorized under (a) small-scale industrial undertakings, (b) ancillary industrial undertakings, (c) export oriented units, (d) tiny enterprises, (e) small-scale service enterprises, small scale service business enterprises, (g) artisans, village and cottage industries, and (h) women entrepreneurs' enterprises in which women entrepreneurs have not less than 51 per cent financial holding. These enterprises assist mining, chemicals and petrochemicals, defence products, fertilizer, food processing, heavy industries, manufacturing industries, retail trade, textiles, tourism, etc. Bank credit to this sector has considerably increased over the years.

India occupies 2.4 per cent of world's land area with more than 6,30,000 villages. In rural India, 400 million citizens are without electricity. Although they are connected with electricity, there is no uniformity in electricity distribution. It is observed that there has been a sharp growth in electricity generation between 2004 and 2012. The faster pace of electrification with indirect bank credit has not drastically changed the lives of average citizens.

India has mineral resources in all states and is characterized by highly uneven geographical distribution. Adequate access to credit to exploit these mineral resources especially in the north-eastern states would have increased their share in the national income, indicating that regional dimension was missing in credit deepening by bank branches.

## Justice Delivery

Prompt justice to the citizens is one of the requisites of development, It is said that justice delayed is justice denied. A recent study conducted by a Bengaluru – based NGO *viz.* Daksh on 18 lakh cases reviewed from 21 High Courts in the country in collaboration with the Union Law Ministry to analyse data from its own database as well as other published data on the Indian judiciary, (published by Times of India, Mumbai in March 2016 (Source : *Daksh)*) has found that the average pendency of a case - the time it takes for a case to be disposed of – in the Allahabad High Court (HC) is over three and half years or 1337 days. The Allahabad HC tops the chart among the 21 HCs covered by the study, followed by Bombay HC (Mumbai) which takes 1245 days of average pendency of a case. The Gujarat HC is third with 1186 days for disposal of a case. The Sikkim HC has the lowest average pendency of 281 days. The oldest case yet to be disposed of is of January 1, 1958.The Study has also reviewed 17 lakh cases in 417 district courts, the oldest case being of November 22, 1931.

## Migration of Bank Funds

The credit dispensation policy of the scheduled commercial banks in India, which accounted for about ninety – nine per cent of total banking business in the country, has been designed to restrict the flow of funds from rural and semi-urban areas to the developed urban and metropolitan areas in accordance with the objectives of Five-Year Plans for a balanced development with a view to reducing the existing inter-regional disparities. Bank branches opened by the scheduled commercial banks since July 1969 in unbanked centres were expected to *inter alia*, remove the persisting economic disparities and social barriers.

Though in 1969, the share of rural deposits was only 3 per cent in the total, it formed 10 per cent in the total in 2015. With a view to ensuring even distribution of utilization of funds in the entire country, the Reserve Bank of India stipulated in February 1977 that 60 per cent of deposits mobilized in the rural and semi-urban areas by the bank branches should be deployed in the respective areas by March 1979. However, the bank funds seemed to have flowed from the under-developed rural sector to the comparatively developed urban centres aiding widening disparities.

This is evident from the data published in 2016. The total amount of bank credit deployed in urban areas was higher than the total deposits mobilized there, whereas the reverse was true for the rural areas.

For instance, bank credit sanctioned in the State of Maharashtra but utilised in other states amounted to ₹ 2084 billion in March 2015; bank credit utilised in the State of Maharashtra but sanctioned in other states amounted to ₹ 88 billion; however, total credit utilised in the State of Maharashtra amounted to ₹ 17776 billion while total bank deposits mobilized amounted to ₹ 21500 billion in March 2015

The data published by the RBI for the same period relating to accounts with credit limit of more than ₹ 2 lakh suggest that there were only 2 per cent small borrowers utilizing 2 per cent of total bank credit at an interest rate at 6 per cent or less across the country. The rest 98 per cent of bank credit were lent out at more than 6 per cent. The status report published, thus, indicates that the predominant poor segment of population who were provided with concessional rate of bank credit were not adequately served by the large number of existing bank branches.

For instance, the credit flow to tiny/micro/small borrowers who were deployed credit up to Rupees 2 lakh individually constituted 77 per cent across the country in terms of number of accounts. They had, however, been actually provided with only 8.2 per cent of total bank credit. Thus, the data on the public domain indicates that 11000 account holders enjoyed 31.5 per cent of bank credit of ₹ 1 billion and above across the country in March 2015.

## Credit – Deposit Ratio

The Credit – Deposit (CD) ratio is a major indicator of deployment of funds mobilized by the bank branches at a particular centre. The level of economic activity, credit absorption capacity, market conditions and credit policy determine the CD ratio at that centre.

Population group-wise outstanding credit (excluding credit extended to food procurement) of scheduled commercial banks according to place of sanction and as per place of utilization data relating to March 2015 indicates that funds mobilized from rural and semi-urban areas have mostly been utilised in comparatively more developed urban and metropolitan areas indicating migration of bank funds.

Although borrowal accounts were more than 60 per cent in rural and semi-urban areas together, the two sectors together utilised only 20 per cent of the total deployed bank credit across the country. All these indicate that inequalities continue and disparities widen further.

More over Annexure – XI reveals that although 13 bank branches located in Lakshadweep mobilized deposits amounting to ₹ 7618 million in March 2015, only ₹ 694 million has been utilized as credit in the Union Territory indicating a CD ratio of 9.1 per cent.

The State of Maharashtra requires a special mention. A total of ₹ 21500 billion of deposits have been mobilized while a total credit of ₹ 177763 billion have been deployed in the industrious State, thus indicating that migration of funds from Maharashtra to elsewhere. In the Western Region, the CD ratio was only 28.2 per cent. Similarly, the Union territories of Dadra & Nagar Haveli and Daman & Diu had a lower CD ratio of 36.2 per cent and 33.6 per cent, respectively, posing themselves as blockage of fund flow. The demand for bank's resources for utilization by the local population has, perhaps been ignored to supply to other comparatively developed regions.

In the Eastern Region comprising States of Bihar, Jharkhand, Odisha, Sikkim and the Union territory of Andaman& Nicobar Islands, the CD ratio has been low. Only West Bengal has achieved a CD ratio of 60 per cent, stipulated for rural and sub-urban centres across our country, as a State.

CD ratio of each of the States located in the North-Eastern Region ranged between 27 per cent and 40 per cent.

On the contrary, Chandigarh, Delhi, Andhra Pradesh, Tamil Nadu and Telangana have utilized more than 100 per cent of resources mobilized from their own area of jurisdiction, indicating that bank credit have been deployed excessively in these developed parts of our country.

## Section - III

Inter and Intra-Regional Inequalities in Select Banking Indicators

In the following pages, analysis of the inter and intra-regional variations in widening and deepening aspects of development of banking sector is provided only for the years 1972 and 1988. Analysis of the latest data presented in the annexed statements may be undertaken by successive researchers.

The aspects covered in this analysis are:

 I. Number of bank branches per thousand population;
 ii. Total bank credit per thousand population;
 iii. Bank credit to agricultural sector per thousand population;
 iv. Bank credit to small-scale industries per thousand population;
 v. Number of bank branches per hundred square kilometers of area;
 vi. Total bank credit per hundred square kilometers of area;
 vii. Bank credit to agricultural sector per hundred square kilometers of area; and
 viii. Bank credit to small-scale industries per hundred square kilometers of area.

Initially, the eight ratios cited above were computed. While using data on population of 1981 adjustments have been incorporated to arrive at 1972 and 1988 population figures _viz._ It has been assumed that population grew at 2.3 percent and 2.0 percent, respectively, during the period 1972-1981 and 1981-1988. Mean and coefficient of variation (C.V.) for each of these ratios are worked out for all-India, five regions (for north-eastern region, in the analysis, only Assam is included, separate measure are not provided) and 17 States. The relevant results for 1972 and 1988 are presented in tables 4.8 and 4.9.

(It may be noted that States like Andhra Pradesh, Bihar and Uttar Pradesh were undivided in 1988. However, at the time of publication of this book, they are found reorganized and therefore, due care needs to be taken while doing further research. The officially published data annexed are as at 31ˢᵗ March, 2016.

## Population Coverage

Inter and intra-regional inequalities in per capital banking facilities are examined below:

### Table 4.8

### MEAN VALUE OF THE AND COEFFICIENT OF VARIATION IN NUMBER OF BANK BRANCHES PER THOUSANDS OF POPULATION (Based on district data for the years 1972 & 1988)

| Sn. | States | 1972 | | 1988 | |
|---|---|---|---|---|---|
| | | MEAN | CV | MEAN | CV |
| 01 | Haryana | 0.03 | 66.7 | 0.08 | 12.5 |
| 02 | Himachal Pradesh | 0.03 | 33.3 | 0.13 | 23.1 |
| 03 | Jammu & Kashmir | 0.02 | 50.0 | 0.11 | 27.3 |
| 04 | Punjab | 0.05 | 40.0 | 0.11 | 18.2 |
| 05 | Rajasthan | 0.02 | 50.0 | 0.07 | 28.6 |
| 06 | Assam | 0.01 | 100.0 | 0.08 | 137.5 |
| 07 | Bihar | 0.01 | 100.0 | 0.05 | 20.0 |
| 08 | Odisha | 0.01 | 1.0 | 0.06 | 16.6 |
| 09 | West Bengal | 0.02 | 150.0 | 0.06 | 83.3 |
| 09 | West Bengal* | 0.01 | 100.0 | 0.05 | 20.0 |
| 10 | Madhya Pradesh | 0.01 | 100.0 | 0.07 | 28.0 |
| 11 | Uttar Pradesh | 0.01 | 100.0 | 0.07 | 28.6 |
| 12 | Gujarat | 0.04 | 25.0 | 0.08 | 25.0 |
| 13 | Maharashtra | 0.03 | 100.0 | 0.07 | 57.0 |
| 14 | Andhra Pradesh | 0.02 | 50.0 | 0.07 | 28.6 |
| 15 | Karnataka | 0.05 | 60.0 | 0.10 | 40.0 |
| 16 | Kerala | 0.04 | 50.0 | 0.09 | 33.3 |
| 17 | Tamil Nadu | 0.04 | 50.0 | 0.07 | 33.3 |
| | Northern Region | 0.03 | 66.7 | 0.10 | 30.0 |
| | North .Eastern Region** | 0.01 | 100.0 | 0.08 | 137.5 |
| | Eastern Region | 0.01 | 200.0 | 0.06 | 50.0 |
| | Eastern Region* | 0.01 | 100.0 | 0.05 | 20.0 |
| | Central Region | 0.01 | 100.0 | 0.07 | 28.6 |
| | Western Region | 0.03 | 66.7 | 0.07 | 42.8 |
| | Southern Region | 0.04 | 50.0 | 0.08 | 50.0 |
| | ALL- INDIA | 0.02 | 100.0 | 0.08 | 50.0 |
| | ALL- INDIA | 0.02 | 100.0 | 0.07 | 57.1 |

*Excluding Kolkata    ** Same as that of Assam

Table 4.9

## MEAN VALUE OF AND COEFFICIENT OF VARIATION IN BANK CREDIT PER THOUSANDS OF POPULATION

(Based on district data for the years1972 & 1988)

| Sn. | States | 1972 | | 1988 | |
|---|---|---|---|---|---|
| | | MEAN | CV | MEAN | CV |
| 01 | Haryana | 0.53 | 86.8 | 8.47 | 29.9 |
| 02 | Himachal Pradesh | 0.09 | 144.2 | 6.63 | 80.9 |
| 03 | Jammu & Kashmir | 0.25 | 208.0 | 5.54 | 130.6 |
| 04 | Punjab | 0.70 | 81.4 | 13.35 | 55.8 |
| 05 | Rajasthan | 0.21 | 87.5 | 4.00 | 61.0 |
| 06 | Assam | 0.31 | 122.6 | 4.78 | 137.7 |
| 07 | Bihar | 0.22 | 109.0 | 2.39 | 67.3 |
| 08 | Odisha | 0.10 | 110.0 | 4.65 | 74.8 |
| 09 | West Bengal | 1.95 | 375.0 | 9.77 | 300.0 |
| 09 | West Bengal* | 0.12 | 100.0 | 2.44 | 48.4 |
| 10 | Madhya Pradesh | 0.24 | 191.6 | 4.69 | 119.8 |
| 11 | Uttar Pradesh | 0.25 | 180.0 | 3.65 | 101.4 |
| 12 | Gujarat | 0.85 | 136.0 | 8.81 | 90.5 |
| 13 | Maharashtra | 1.90 | 413.0 | 13.78 | 329.0 |
| 14 | Andhra Pradesh | 0.58 | 178.0 | 8.42 | 148.0 |
| 15 | Karnataka | 0.94 | 174.0 | 11.40 | 132.6 |
| 16 | Kerala | 0.70 | 94.2 | 10.45 | 53.3 |
| 17 | Tamil Nadu | 1.55 | 192.0 | 13.80 | 170.0 |
| | Northern Region | 0.36 | 125.0 | 7.15 | 83.9 |
| | North Eastern Region** | 0.31 | 122.6 | 4.78 | 137.7 |
| | Eastern Region | 0.80 | 545.0 | 4.94 | 316.0 |
| | Eastern Region* | 0.15 | 120.0 | 2.89 | 77.0 |
| | Central Region | 0.25 | 184.0 | 4.11 | 113.0 |
| | Western Region | 1.46 | 409.0 | 11.68 | 296.0 |
| | Southern Region | 0.91 | 191.0 | 10.67 | 139.0 |
| | ALL- INDIA | 0.65 | 448.0 | 7.10 | 227.0 |
| | ALL -INDIA | 0.56 | 434.0 | 6.77 | 221.0 |

*Excluding Kolkata    ** Same as that of Assam

Table 4.10

## MEAN VALUE OF AND COEFFICIENT OF VARIATION IN BANK CREDIT TO AGRICULTURE PER THOUSNADS OF POPULATION
(Based on district data for the years 1972 & 1988)

| Sn. | States | 1972 MEAN | CV | 1988 MEAN | CV |
|---|---|---|---|---|---|
| 01 | Haryana | 0.04 | 75.0 | 3.44 | 24.7 |
| 02 | Himachal Pradesh | 0.01 | 200.0 | 1.29 | 75.2 |
| 03 | Jammu & Kashmir | 0.01 | 100.0 | 0.68 | 88.2 |
| 04 | Punjab | 0.06 | 83.3 | 4.29 | 36.4 |
| 05 | Rajasthan | 0.06 | 266.7 | 1.36 | 50.7 |
| 06 | Assam | 0.02 | 150.0 | 1.33 | 157.8 |
| 07 | Bihar | 0.01 | 100.0 | 0.59 | 47.5 |
| 08 | Odisha | 0.01 | 100.0 | 1.03 | 36.8 |
| 09 | West Bengal | 0.21 | 366.7 | 0.78 | 46.1 |
| 09 | West Bengal* | 0.02 | 150.0 | 0.72 | 34.7 |
| 10 | Madhya Pradesh | 0.02 | 200.0 | 1.28 | 73.4 |
| 11 | Uttar Pradesh | 0.02 | 200.0 | 0.87 | 55.1 |
| 12 | Gujarat | 0.09 | 55.9 | 1.96 | 121.0 |
| 13 | Maharashtra | 0.09 | 155.5 | 1.58 | 39.2 |
| 14 | Andhra Pradesh | 0.07 | 71.4 | 2.39 | 42.3 |
| 15 | Karnataka | 0.16 | 106.0 | 3.43 | 64.7 |
| 16 | Kerala | 0.09 | 133.0 | 2.44 | 69.0 |
| 17 | Tamil Nadu | 0.18 | 144.0 | 2.18 | 31.0 |
|  | Northern Region | 0.05 | 220.0 | 2.13 | 77.5 |
|  | North .Eastern Region** | 0.02 | 150.0 | 1.33 | 157.8 |
|  | Eastern Region | 0.09 | 544.0 | 0.74 | 48.6 |
|  | Eastern Region* | 0.01 | 200.0 | 0.72 | 46.2 |
|  | Central Region | 0.02 | 200.0 | 1.05 | 70.4 |
|  | Western Region | 0.09 | 122.2 | 1.74 | 91.4 |
|  | Southern Region | 0.12 | 133.0 | 2.65 | 59.0 |
|  | ALL INDIA | 0.07 | 300 | 1.61 | 89.0 |
|  | ALL INDIA | 0.06 | 183.0 | 1.61 | 89.4 |

*Excluding Kolkata    ** Same as that of Assam

### Table 4.11
## MEAN VALUE OF AND COEFFICIENT OF VARIATION IN BANK CREDIT TO SMALL INDUSTRIES SECTOR PER THOUSNADS OF POPULATION
### (Based on district data for the years 1972 & 1988)

| Sn. | States | 1972 MEAN | CV | 1988 MEAN | CV |
|---|---|---|---|---|---|
| 01 | Haryana | 0.19 | 142.1 | 1.72 | 65.1 |
| 02 | Himachal Pradesh | 0.01 | 100.0 | 1.27 | 144.0 |
| 03 | Jammu & Kashmir | 0.04 | 125.0 | 0.77 | 145.5 |
| 04 | Punjab | 0.18 | 177.8 | 2.53 | 100.0 |
| 05 | Rajasthan | 0.24 | 375.0 | 0.53 | 81.1 |
| 06 | Assam | 0.05 | 120.0 | 0.64 | 112.5 |
| 07 | Bihar | 0.03 | 166.6 | 0.32 | 87.5 |
| 08 | Odisha | 0.02 | 100.0 | 0.46 | 69.6 |
| 09 | West Bengal | 0.24 | 362.5 | 0.99 | 169.7 |
| 09 | West Bengal* | 0.02 | 250.0 | 0.59 | 93.2 |
| 10 | Madhya Pradesh | 0.05 | 220.0 | 0.62 | 137.0 |
| 11 | Uttar Pradesh | 0.05 | 220.0 | 0.52 | 123.0 |
| 12 | Gujarat | 0.15 | 127.0 | 1.69 | 91.7 |
| 13 | Maharashtra | 0.20 | 345.0 | 1.53 | 230.0 |
| 14 | Andhra Pradesh | 0.07 | 200.0 | 1.06 | 147.0 |
| 15 | Karnataka | 0.09 | 178.0 | 1.33 | 188.0 |
| 16 | Kerala | 0.13 | 146.0 | 2.44 | 69.0 |
| 17 | Tamil Nadu | 0.28 | 239.0 | 1.95 | 133.0 |
|  | Northern Region | 0.18 | 344.4 | 1.26 | 127.8 |
|  | North .Eastern Region** | 0.5 | 120.0 | 0.64 | 112.5 |
|  | Eastern Region | 0.10 | 520.0 | 0.54 | 176.0 |
|  | Eastern Region* | 0.02 | 200.0 | 0.42 | 93.0 |
|  | Central Region | 0.05 | 220.0 | 0.56 | 132.1 |
|  | Western Region | 0.18 | 300.0 | 1.60 | 177.0 |
|  | Southern Region | 0.13 | 262.0 | 1.32 | 151.0 |
|  | ALL- INDIA | 0.12 | 350.0 | 0.97 | 171.0 |
|  | ALL- INDIA | 0.11 | 336.0 | 0.69 | 169.0 |

*Excluding Kolkata    ** Same as that of Assam

## I. Number of Bank Branches Per Thousand Population

From Table 4.8, it may be seen that number of bank branches per thousand population in various districts of each state grew substantially over the period 1972-1988. At the All-India level, this measure grew from 0.02 to 0.08 over the period. For 1988, the set figure ranges between 0.05 in the case of Bihar and West Bengal (0.05) and 0.13 in the case of Himachal Pradesh. For many of the States, the corresponding values are in and around the All-India value, whereas, Bihar, Odisha and West Bengal have relatively small value as compared to All-India. Himachal Pradesh, Jammu & Kashmir, Punjab and Karnataka have values much above the All-India level. Number of bank branches to cover population per district, as seen from the table, is more in the case of northern region and less in the eastern region on the national level. Variation in the value of the measure under reference, among the districts of the corresponding states, has narrowed significantly over the period of analysis. In the case of All-India, the coefficient of variation value has declined from 100 to 50.

A similar pattern emerges in the case of all states except Assam and West Bengal. Thus, in tune with the popular belief and expression, banking facilities in terms of number, have expanded at the micro-level almost uniformly in most of the States of the country. There are also indications that the intra-regional disparities have tended to decline significantly.

## II. Bank Credit per Thousand Population

Results presented in Table 4.9 reveal the following: Mean bank credit per thousand population in a district grew from ₹ 0.65 lakh to ₹ 7.10 lakh in the case of All-India in the period 1972-1988. An almost similar growth pattern has been experienced in the states too. As compared to the All-India figure of 7.10 for 1988, Haryana, Punjab, West Bengal, Gujarat, Maharashtra, Andhra Pradesh, Karnataka, Kerala and Tamil Nadu have obtained higher values. In Punjab, West Bengal, Maharashtra, Karnataka, and Tamil Nadu, the said value is very high.

On the other hand, Jammu & Kashmir, Rajasthan, Assam, Bihar (in particular), Odisha, Madhya Pradesh and Uttar Pradesh have lower values. Only Himachal Pradesh has the same as the All-India value.

The micro-level difference in disbursal of bank credit has tended to come down. However, for West Bengal and Maharashtra, the value of coefficient of variation is very high (300 and 329, respectively).

Although per capita bank credit in the districts have grown, the difference among the States in this respect persist, indicating the disparities in banking potential among the regions of the country i.e many States significantly lag and some States have a notable advantage.

States belonging to the Western and Southern regions have an edge over the rest of the States. Perhaps, the urban-rural characteristics dictate this feature. The high variation among districts in Maharashtra and West Bengal substantiates this point, where the influence of metropolitan cities of Bombay and Calcutta can hardly be over-emphasized.

## III. Agricultural Credit per Thousand Population

Agricultural credit per thousand population on an average for the districts have also grown substantially over the period of analysis.(see Table 4.10). The normal average rose from ₹ 0.07 lakh to ₹ 1.71 lakh during the period 1972-1988. The inter-district variation also tended to disappear (the coefficient of variation for All-India is 89 in 1988 as compared to 300 in 1972). A similar  trend is noticed  for the States too. However, in1988, in particular, Haryana, Punjab, Andhra Pradesh, Karnataka, Kerala and Tamil Nadu (i.e. States located in the Northern and Southern regions) received more credit to agriculture through banks.

Thus, although the magnitude and variation in agricultural credit per thousand population in the districts of various States have changed as their flow has been in the desirable direction, it appears, that there are inter-regional disparities.

## IV. Bank Credit to Small-Scale Industries per Thousand Population

The results presented in Table 4.11, in this respect, indicate as under:

There is more than an eight-fold increase in the average availability of bank credit to small-scale industries per thousand population in a district at the national level. It increased from ₹ 0.12 lakh to ₹ 0.97 lakh. In 1988, the States of Haryana, Himachal Pradesh, Punjab, Gujarat, Maharashtra, Karnataka, Kerala and Tamil Nadu had a good record. But the States of Bihar and Odisha have fared badly. The inter-district variation in values has come down from 352 to 177 in the case of All-India and all States too.

However, there is still a high inter-district variation in respect of West Bengal, Karnataka and in particular, Maharashtra. The above observations reveal that while the use of bank credit to small-scale Industries under the priority sector criteria at the micro level of the country, has improved, it still needs close re-examination. The influence of urban and metropolitan centres and random process of industrialization (Kerala) probably tend to explain banks' ability and willingness to disburse credit.

The following computed measures reveal the mean and coefficient of variation in the ratios under reference based on States as cross sections for All-India for the years 1972 and 1988.

| | | 1972 | | 1988 |
|---|---|---|---|---|
| | Mean | Coefficient of Variation | Mean | Coefficient of Variation |
| **No. of Bank Branches Per Thousand Population.** | 0.02 | 50.0 | 0.08 | 25.0 |
| **Bank credit Per Thousand Population.** | 0.76 | 105.2 | 8.64 | 55.8 |
| **Bank credit to Agriculture per Thousand Population.** | 0.06 | 100.0 | 1.83 | 60.6 |
| **Bank credit to small-scale industries per Thousand Population** | 0.11 | 90.9 | 1.27 | 59.0 |

These figures also indicate that each measure of banking indicators, on an average for a State, increased and inter-state variations in them have tended to narrow down. However, in absolute terms variations in credit disbursal, agricultural credit and credit to small-scale industries per thousand population have been higher. It can also be observed that the share of agricultural credit, out of total bank credit, has increased from 7.8 to 21.1 percent during the period of study and that of credit to small-scale industries remained stationary at 14.5 percent. This indicates, yet once again, that by stipulations in bank credit, agricultural sector continued to get increasing attention, in general, among the States.

## (b) Area Coverage

In the analysis pertaining to earlier cited banking indicators per hundred kilometers, the influence of Kolkata, in a major way, and a certain extent Mumbai (Bombay), upon the all India value, is significantly and seriously felt. Considering the above, it was difficult to compare and comment on the State level features. However, subject to this limitation, and in a nut shell, the following points may be noted (See Tables 4.12 and 4.13)

## Table 4.12
## MEAN VALUE OF AND COEFFICIENT OF VARIATION IN NUMBER OF BANK BRANCHES PER HUNDRED SQUARE KILOMETERS AREA
### (Based on district data for the years 1972 & 1988)

| Sn. | States | 1972 MEAN | CV | 1988 MEAN | CV |
|---|---|---|---|---|---|
| 01 | Haryana | 0.69 | 97.1 | 2.90 | 31.0 |
| 02 | Himachal Pradesh | 0.29 | 105.2 | 1.77 | 88.8 |
| 03 | Jammu & Kashmir | 0.32 | 106.2 | 1.95 | 87.2 |
| 04 | Punjab | 1.31 | 58.0 | 4.54 | 46.0 |
| 05 | Rajasthan | 0.19 | 63.2 | 1.04 | 53.8 |
| 06 | Assam | 0.18 | 66.6 | 0.90 | 58.8 |
| 07 | Bihar | 0.38 | 107.8 | 3.40 | 55.0 |
| 08 | Odisha | 0.13 | 61.6 | 1.37 | 56.2 |
| 09 | West Bengal | 18.75 | 385.8 | 62.50 | 375.2 |
| 09 | West Bengal* | 0.67 | 122.0 | 3.86 | 78.0 |
| 10 | Madhya Pradesh | 0.19 | 126.3 | 1.30 | 113.8 |
| 11 | Uttar Pradesh | 0.44 | 102.2 | 3.00 | 59.3 |
| 12 | Gujarat | 0.75 | 76.0 | 2.08 | 73.6 |
| 13 | Maharashtra | 4.55 | 445.9 | 11.62 | 397.0 |
| 14 | Andhra Pradesh | 3.64 | 403.0 | 10.77 | 407.0 |
| 15 | Karnataka | 0.72 | 97.2 | 2.36 | 79.7 |
| 16 | Kerala | 2.80 | 61.4 | 7.86 | 62.1 |
| 17 | Tamil Nadu | 1.97 | 144.0 | 5.63 | 172.0 |
|  | Northern Region | 0.54 | 116.7 | 2.26 | 79.2 |
|  | North -.Eastern Region** | 0.18 | 66.6 | 0.90 | 58.8 |
|  | Eastern Region | 6.85 | 630.2 | 19.56 | 635.9 |
|  | Eastern Region* | 0.41 | 139.0 | 3.09 | 72.8 |
|  | Central Region | 0.33 | 118.0 | 2.24 | 82.6 |
|  | Western Region | 2.94 | 524.0 | 7.59 | 462.0 |
|  | Southern Region | 2.27 | 376.0 | 6.86 | 379.0 |
|  | ALL -INDIA | 2.04 | 863.0 | 6.69 | 799.0 |
|  | ALL -INDIA | 1.13 | 359.0 | 3.95 | 436.0 |

*Excluding Kolkata    ** Same as that of Assam

## Table 4.13
## MEAN VALUE OF AND COEFFICIENT OF VARIATION IN NUMBER OF BANK BRANCHES PER HUNDRED SQUARE KILOMETERS AREA
### (Based on district data for the years 1972 & 1988)

| Sn. | States | 1972 MEAN | CV | 1988 MEAN | CV |
|---|---|---|---|---|---|
| 01 | Haryana | 13.99 | 91.9 | 311.12 | 43.6 |
| 02 | Himachal Pradesh | 0.80 | 130.0 | 98.90 | 101.6 |
| 03 | Jammu & Kashmir | 5.92 | 225.2 | 151.50 | 190.4 |
| 04 | Punjab | 21.36 | 100.0 | 576.41 | 80.4 |
| 05 | Rajasthan | 2.60 | 155.4 | 63.56 | 98.3 |
| 06 | Assam | 4.67 | 113.7 | 78.99 | 94.9 |
| 07 | Bihar | 10.44 | 148.8 | 159.60 | 106.2 |
| 08 | Odisha | 1.74 | 128.1 | 119.04 | 115.2 |
| 09 | West Bengal | 4755.55 | 399.0 | 28581.80 | 397.0 |
| 09 | West Bengal* | 8.52 | 195.0 | 202.60 | 105.0 |
| 10 | Madhya Pradesh | 4.15 | 263.3 | 112.50 | 201.5 |
| 11 | Uttar Pradesh | 10.80 | 237.8 | 204.30 | 154.3 |
| 12 | Gujarat | 19.84 | 204.9 | 269.70 | 136.4 |
| 13 | Maharashtra | 1038.80 | 506.0 | 9028.30 | 498.0 |
| 14 | Andhra Pradesh | 218.20 | 433.0 | 3794.00 | 461.0 |
| 15 | Karnataka | 19.18 | 252.0 | 319.50 | 209.0 |
| 16 | Kerala | 50.54 | 114.0 | 991.00 | 85.46 |
| 17 | Tamil Nadu | 149.60 | 306.0 | 1839.00 | 294.0 |
|  | Northern Region | 8.69 | 163.9 | 220.12 | 138.5 |
|  | North-.Eastern Region** | 4.67 | 113.7 | 78.99 | 94.9 |
|  | Eastern Region | 1695.27 | 668.0 | 8129.00 | 740.0 |
|  | Eastern Region* | 7.41 | 188.0 | 162.40 | 108.0 |
|  | Central Region | 7.84 | 263.6 | 163.43 | 172.5 |
|  | Western Region | 608.60 | 656.0 | 5330.30 | 641.0 |
|  | Southern Region | 114.70 | 494.0 | 1927.00 | 543.0 |
|  | ALL- INDIA | 352.89 | 1280.1 | 2517.53 | 1104.0 |
|  | ALL -INDIA | 114.40 | 1331.0 | 1196.60 | 1106.0 |

*Excluding Kolkata    ** Same as that of Assam

Table 4.14
## MEAN VALUE OF AND COEFFICIENT OF VARIATION IN BANK CREDIT TO AGRICULTURE PER HUNDRED SQUARE KILOMETERS AREA
(Based on district data for the years 1972 & 1988)

| Sn. | States | 1972 MEAN | CV | 1988 MEAN | CV |
|-----|--------|-----------|-----|-----------|-----|
| 01 | Haryana | 1.12 | 83.9 | 123.52 | 30.4 |
| 02 | Himachal Pradesh | 0.09 | 155.5 | 60.73 | 73.4 |
| 03 | Jammu & Kashmir | 0.10 | 130.0 | 15.57 | 131.2 |
| 04 | Punjab | 1.63 | 90.8 | 162.34 | 26.8 |
| 05 | Rajasthan | 0.31 | 151.6 | 20.19 | 70.7 |
| 06 | Assam | 0.29 | 134.3 | 16.32 | 69.9 |
| 07 | Bihar | 0.52 | 128.8 | 40.88 | 86.1 |
| 08 | Odisha | 0.11 | 109.1 | 23.33 | 75.9 |
| 09 | West Bengal | 498.99 | 400.0 | 467.28 | 356.5 |
| 09 | West Bengal* | 0.86 | 112.0 | 51.03 | 53.5 |
| 10 | Madhya Pradesh | 0.28 | 207.1 | 24.21 | 137.8 |
| 11 | Uttar Pradesh | 0.64 | 126.6 | 42.79 | 66.3 |
| 12 | Gujarat | 1.59 | 98.1 | 49.66 | 113.9 |
| 13 | Maharashtra | 16.67 | 457.0 | 143.85 | 259.0 |
| 14 | Andhra Pradesh | 7.68 | 391.0 | 289.60 | 386.0 |
| 15 | Karnataka | 2.18 | 100.0 | 75.09 | 85.8 |
| 16 | Kerala | 6.34 | 159.0 | 189.20 | 69.06 |
| 17 | Tamil Nadu | 14.00 | 278.0 | 121.60 | 68.0 |
| | Northern Region | 0.69 | 147.8 | 62.38 | 107.8 |
| | North-.Eastern Region** | 0.29 | 134.3 | 16.32 | 69.9 |
| | Eastern Region | 204.93 | 625.0 | 156.88 | 566.0 |
| | Eastern Region* | 0.56 | 138.0 | 39.84 | 78.0 |
| | Central Region | 0.48 | 154.0 | 34.62 | 92.0 |
| | Western Region | 10.16 | 565.0 | 104.10 | 274.0 |
| | Southern Region | 7.12 | 350.0 | 178.00 | 367.0 |
| | ALL- INDIA | 30.92 | 1515.0 | 96.84 | 490.0 |
| | ALL -INDIA | 3.44 | 737.0 | 77.45 | 404.0 |

*Excluding Kolkata      ** Same as that of Assam

Table 4.15
### MEAN VALUE OF AND COEFFICIENT OF VARIATION IN BANK CREDIT TO SMALL INDUSTRIES SECTOR PER HUNDRED SQUARE KILOMETERS AREA (Based on district data for the years 1972 & 1988)

| Sn. | States | 1972 MEAN | CV | 1988 MEAN | CV |
|---|---|---|---|---|---|
| 01 | Haryana | 4.78 | 140.8 | 66.28 | 73.4 |
| 02 | Himachal Pradesh | 0.10 | 30.0 | 21.84 | 159.2 |
| 03 | Jammu &Kashmir | 0.88 | 157.9 | 23.74 | 180.2 |
| 04 | Punjab | 6.03 | 192.0 | 190.54 | 119.2 |
| 05 | Rajasthan | 0.41 | 156.1 | 8.27 | 118.5 |
| 06 | Assam | 0.68 | 133.8 | 10.54 | 90.8 |
| 07 | Bihar | 1.47 | 175.5 | 21.50 | 123.0 |
| 08 | Orissa | 0.30 | 156.6 | 11.36 | 100.5 |
| 09 | West Bengal | 583.80 | 386.0 | 1715.00 | 385.8 |
| 09 | West Bengal* | 2.36 | 339.0 | 61.07 | 198.0 |
| 10 | Madhya Pradesh | 0.90 | 353.3 | 15.94 | 218.7 |
| 11 | Uttar Pradesh | 2.10 | 266.7 | 30.49 | 167.8 |
| 12 | Gujarat | 3.45 | 176.0 | 54.69 | 136.0 |
| 13 | Maharashtra | 92.41 | 499.8 | 708.25 | 486.0 |
| 14 | Andhra Pradesh | 26.62 | 453.0 | 448.90 | 459.0 |
| 15 | Karnataka | 1.87 | 238.0 | 41.99 | 260.0 |
| 16 | Kerala | 7.98 | 126.0 | 109.90 | 87.3 |
| 17 | Tamil Nadu | 31.37 | 328.0 | 217.00 | 265.0 |
|  | Northern Region | 2.64 | 256.6 | 43.28 | 182.6 |
|  | North-.Eastern Region** | 0.68 | 133.8 | 10.54 | 90.8 |
|  | Eastern Region | 214.23 | 636.0 | 494.88 | 710.3 |
|  | Eastern Region* | 1.46 | 339.0 | 29.90 | 224.0 |
|  | Central Region | 1.64 | 294.0 | 24.08 | 186.9 |
|  | Western Region | 56.00 | 633.8 | 432.30 | 603.0 |
|  | Southern Region | 17.40 | 476.0 | 228.00 | 538.0 |
|  | ALL- INDIA | 46.70 | 1179.0 | 199.34 | 902.0 |
|  | ALL -INDIA | 14.32 | 1041.0 | 122.09 | 896.0 |

*Excluding Kolkata      ** Same as that of Assam

(i)    The number of bank branches, bank credit, credit to agriculture and small-scale industries The per 100 square k.m. increased considerably for All-India and for all States almost uniformly over the period 1972-1988;

(ii)   In general, the degree of variation in the measures for the districts continued to remain   as regards most of the States, particularly in the case of bank credit and credit to small -scale sector.

(iii)  In the case of agricultural credit, the degree of variation has tended to come down.

The next chapter presents empirical evidence.

# BRANCH BANKING – EMPIRICAL EVIDENCE

The present chapter deals with an empirical examination of the cause and effect relationship among critical variables of branch banking and some of the key development aspects experienced over the years. Single and multiple regression equations have been estimated and tested, using historical data since the beginning of the Five-Year Plan period (1950-51). The main objective of the analysis is an in-depth understanding of the structural changes that had taken place in the economy due to the increase in the number of bank branches and consequently by financial intermediation and the process of monetization and credit utilization. The aim is also to unravel whether there were noticeable inter-regional disparities as a result of the impact of increased branch banking facilities. In particular, attempt has also been made to identity whether a different pattern has emerged after the nationalization of major Indian banks in 1969 and its impact on the ultimate target variables, the fulfillment of which has been the aim of the implied policy frameworks.

All-India level analyses have been carried out for certain functions 19 years before and 19 years after 1969, using relevant data from 1950 to 1988. Taking into account the special interest of the empirical investigation the above period has thus, been divided equally into pre-nationalisation and post-nationalisation sub-periods. The division of the whole period, however, was based on Chows' 'F' test value of which was calculated for certain equations.

## Intermediation by Banks

Banks play a productive role as a catalyst in any capital-deficient economy. Banks mobilize primary deposits and create credit. They generate derivative deposits by increasing their intermediary efforts and by promoting growth which is an innate part of money supply. Saving and investment are closely related to national income. An increase in investment leads to provision of adequate linkages and social overheads to meet the growing social needs like public hospitals, public educational institutions and other public utilities for the benefit of the underprivileged sections of the community.

Banks create credit during the course of their business. Branch activities result in increased mobilization of deposits and consequent increase in credit creation. The functioning of the bank branches also establishes linkages with all productive sectors, thus, contributing to growth.

## Priority Sectors

One of the most important objectives of bank nationalisation was the extension of bank credit to the priority sectors and the weaker sections of the society in order to generate gainful employment in these areas. Since 1969, banks have made efforts to increase this type of lending through introduction of various novel methods.

Credit to priority sectors includes lending to agriculture, micro, medium and small enterprises small road and water transport operators, retail trade and professional and self-employed persons.

Industrialization also has its due share. An attempt was made to broaden the industrial base by stipulating flow of funds to the small-scale industrial sector and the sector was included under the priority sector lending. Small-scale industrial units were also earmarked for establishing district industrial centres at each district. The Lead Bank Scheme lends some support to this strategy.

The following questions have been taken up as part of the regression analysis.

(i) Has expansion of bank branches over the years significantly contributed to increase in national income? If so, how far the critical variables of banking operations have made their impact?

(ii) Are there a significant cause and effect relationship between number of bank branches on the one hand and aggregate deposits and aggregate credit (which are the critical banking variables) on the other?

(iii) How far trends in production of the primary and secondary sectors of the economy have been influenced and explained by growth in number of bank branches and growth in credit to their respective sectors?

(iv) Do aggregate deposits and the number of bank branches contribute sufficiently to gross saving as independent factors?

(v) To What extent the overall role of branch banking and credit have influenced variation in small-scale units and financing of them?

(vi) Equally importantly, are there identifiable differences among the different regions of the economy as regards the pattern of answers obtained for the above questions?

(vii) Finally and most crucially, has there been noticeable impact of nationalization of major banks in the results?

## Regression Models and Select Banking Variables

The empirical analysis encompasses growth in income, number of bank branches, indicators of banking performance, agricultural and industrial production, savings and most importantly growth and credit aspect of small-scale industries as a leading priority sector. The following list of variables has been considered for the study. Notations used are indicated along with the variables in brackets.

(i) (**BB**) – Number of scheduled commercial bank branches (No)

(ii) (**AD**) – Aggregate deposits of scheduled commercial banks(₹ cr.).

(iii) (**AC**) – Aggregate credit of scheduled commercial banks.(₹ cr.)

(iv) (**NI**) – Net national product at current prices (₹ cr.).

(v) (**AG**) – Total credit to agriculture by scheduled commercial banks (₹ cr.)

(vi) (**AP**) – Agricultural production (lakh tons).

(vi) (**IC**) – Credit to industry by scheduled commercial banks (₹ cr)

(vii) (**IP**) – Index number of Industrial Production – 1970=100.

(viii) (**GS**) – Gross domestic saving (₹ cr).

(ix)  (**SSU**)  –  Small-scale industrial units (No)

(x)  (**SSIC**)  –  Credit to small-scale industrial units by scheduled commercial banks (₹ cr)

(xi)  (**SDP**)  –  State domestic product at current prices (₹ cr).

At the All-India level, following equations have been estimated.

**Sr. No functions**

|       |       |                 |
|-------|-------|-----------------|
| I.    | NI    | – f[BB]         |
| II.   | NI    | – f[AD, BB]     |
| III.  | NI    | – f[AC, BB]     |
| IV.   | NI    | – f[AP , BB]    |
| V.    | AD    | – f[BB]         |
| VI.   | AC    | – f[BB]         |
| VII.  | AP    | – f[AG, BB]     |
| VIII. | IP    | – f[IC,BB]      |
| IX.   | GS    | – f[AD, BB]     |
| X.    | SSU   | – f[BB]         |
| XI.   | SSU   | – f[BB, AD]     |
| XII.  | SSU   | – f[BB, AC]     |
| XIII. | SSIC  | – f[BB]         |
| XIV.  | SSIC  | – f[BB,AD]      |
| XV.   | SSIC  | – f[BB,AC]      |

At the **State** level, the following equations have been considered.

**Sr. No. functions**

|       |                  |
|-------|------------------|
| i.    | SDP – f[BB]      |
| ii.   | SDP – f[BB, AD]  |
| iii.  | SDP – f[BB,AC]   |
| iv.   | AD  – f[BB]      |
| v.    | AC  – f[BB]      |
| vi.   | AP  – f[BB, AG]  |
| vii.  | SSIC – f[BB]     |
| viii. | SSIC – f[BB,AD]  |
| ix.   | SSIC – f[BB, AC] |
| x.    | SSU – f [BB]     |
| xi.   | SSU –f[BB, AD]   |
| xii.  | SSU – f[BB, AC]  |

**Twelve representative States** selected for the analyses are:

i.    Andhra Pradesh,

ii.   Bihar,

iii.  Gujarat,

iv.   Karnataka,

v.    Kerala,

vi.   Madhya Pradesh,

vii.  Maharashtra,

viii.    Punjab,
  ix.    Rajasthan,
    x.    Tamil Nadu,
  xi.    Uttar Pradesh and
 xii.    West Bengal.

[The criteria of selection of these states have been elaborated earlier]

## Period covered and data

All –India level analysis have been carried out for functions serially numbered from (i) to (ix) using the relevant data from 1950 to 1988 (19 years before and 19 years after 1969. Taking into account, the special interest of the empirical investigation as cited earlier, the above period has thus been divided equally into pre-nationalisation and post-nationalisation sub-periods. The division of the whole period, however, was based on chows' 'F' test value of which was calculated for equations serially numbered from (i) to (ix) Table 6.1 below presents the results of 'F' test.

### Table 5.1
### Chow's 'F' Test Results

| Sr.No. | Functions | 'f' value |
|--------|-----------|-----------|
| I. | NI – f[ BB] | 31.98* |
| II. | NI – f[AD, BB] | 64.75* |
| III. | NI – f[AC, BB] | 34.03* |
| IV. | NI –f[AP, BB] | 13.82* |
| V. | AD – f [BB] | 192.92* |
| VI. | AC – f [BB] | 103.95* |
| VII. | AP – f [AG, BB] | 0.15 |
| VIII. | IP – f [IC, BB] | 28.25* |
| IX. | GS – f [AD, BB] | 42.15* |

Note: * Above the critical value

It may be observed  that according to the results of chow's 'F' test, the division of the entire period into two sub-periods *viz.* period I (1950–1968) and period II (1969–1988) has been justified as indicated by the significant 'F' values, However, in the case of the function AP-f(BB, AC), the 'F' value is quite insignificant.

Therefore, as regards this function, analysis has been carried out only for the whole period (1950–1988).

For equations (x) to (xv), period of analysis corresponds to years from 1970–71 to 1985–86. These equations, it may be noted, pertain to small-scale industrial sector for which uniform and reliable data are available since 1970–71 only. This period, however, forms the major part of the post-nationalisation, period.

Thus, for All-India analyses, period I (1950–1968), period II (1969–1988) and period III (1950–1988), respectively indicate pre-nationlisation, post–nationalisation and the entire Plan period.

Time period for testing all the functions listed under State-level relate to the period from 1970–71 to 1985–86, which is also indicated as period III.

# Results and Discussion

All the regression equations were estimated for their double log functional form, using ordinary least square method. The results are presented in Table 5.2 corresponding to All-India and Tables from 5.3 to 5.14 to States.

The tables provide the elasticity coefficients (β's), t-test values ('t') along with their level of significance, the adjusted value of coefficient of determination ($\bar{R}^2$) and F-statistics.

## All-India level- Analysis

## 1) Branch Banking and National Income

Equations (i) to (iv) in Table 5.2 correspond to growth of national income traceable to number of bank branches and associated variables considered with different combinations, Equation (i) clearly indicates that bank branch expansion has had a positive and highly significant influence on national income during the entire period under study as well as in the two sub-periods (Period I and Period II). By and large, national income has tended to grow at a faster pace than bank branch expansion. 87 percent of variations in national income have been explained by bank branch expansion and the results are found to be significant.

Table 5.2
Results of Regression Analysis
(All India)

| Equation No. | Period | Equation | $\bar{R}^2$ | F-Statistics |
|:---:|:---:|:---|:---:|:---:|
| (1) | (2) | (3) | (4) | (5) |
| (i) | I | ln NI=0.35+1.04 ln BB<br>(2.15)** (23.21)* | 0.87 | 538.74 |
| | II | ln NI= -(0.29)+1.37 ln BB<br>(-1.35) (7.36) | 0.77 | 54.20 |
| | III | ln NI=(0.07)+1.04 lnBB<br>(1.40) (16.53)* | 0.88 | 273.33 |
| II | I | ln Ni = 0.14- 0.13 ln AD +1.21 ln BB<br>(0.35)-(0.59) (4.13)* | 06.97 | 259.27 |
| | II | ln NI=2.57+0.74. ln AD-0.21 ln BB<br>(6.23)* (7.64)* (-1.10) | 0.99 | 1087.82 |
| | III | ln NI= 0.54+0.46 ln AD+ 0.34 ln BB<br>(5.66)* (4.74)* (2.28)** | 0.98 | 753.32 |
| III | I | ln NI=-0.01-0.13 ln AC+1.26 ln BB<br>(-0.02)(-0.51) (4.13)* | 0.97 | 257.77 |
| | II | ln NI = 2.11+0.76 ln AC-0.09 ln BB<br>(4.11)* (5.22)* (-0.35) | 0.99 | 630.19 |
| | III | ln NI= 0.70+0.50 ln AC + 0.30 ln BB<br>(5.39)*+ (4.37)* (1.78) | 0.99 | 930.80 |
| IV | I | ln NI=0.47-0.34 ln AP+1.19 ln BB<br>(3.05)* (-2.32)** (16.10)* | 0.97 | 341.34 |

*Continued*

| | II | $\ln NI=0.37+0.18 \ln AP+1.33 \ln BB$ <br> $(-1.59)\ (0.79)\ (7.14)$ | 0.77 | 29.50 |
|---|---|---|---|---|
| | III | $\ln NI=0.05+0.14 \ln AP+1.01 \ln BB$ <br> $(0.75)\ (0.83)\ (15.55)\ *$ | 0.92 | 209.98 |
| V | I | $\ln AD=-1.69+1.36 \ln BB$ <br> $(-8.95)^*\ (26.16)^*$ | 0.97 | 684.27 |
| | II | $\ln AD=-1.26+2.09 \ln BB$ <br> $(-4.90)^*\ (9.60)^*$ | 0.84 | 92.22 |
| | III | $\ln AD=-0.21+1.50 \ln BB$ <br> $(-3.86)^*\ (11.83)^*$ | 0.87 | 139.91 |

Explanatory power of bank branches in determining national income is found to be almost same for the periods I and III (87 percent and 88 percent). However, it has decreased in the post-nationalisation period as evidenced by the value of $\bar{R}^2$ (77 percent).

Addition of the aggregate deposits variable increases the explanatory power noticeably and for all three periods, extremely high values of $\bar{R}^2$

| VI | I | $\ln AC=-2.73+1.60 \ln BB$ <br> $(-17.71)^*\ (37.76)^*$ | 0.99 | 1425.92 |
|---|---|---|---|---|
| | II | $\ln AC=-1.75+1.88 \ln BB$ <br> $(-6.99)^*\ (14.14)^*$ | 0.92 | 208.61 |
| | III | $\ln AC=-0.48+1.48 \ln BB$ <br> $(-7.83)^*\ (21.27)^*$ | 0.93 | 452.26 |
| VII | III | $\ln AP=-0.48+0.02 \ln AG+0.22$ <br> $\ln BB$ <br> $(-4.83)^*\ (0.66)\ (3.40)\ *$ | 0.73 | 49.62 |
| VIII | I | $\ln IP=-0.24+0.03 \ln IC+0.70 \ln BB$ <br> $(-1.78)\ (0.38)\ (3.79)^*$ | 0.89 | 68.72 |
| | II | $\ln IP=-0.68+0.16 \ln IC+0.19 \ln BB$ <br> $(5.84)^*(4.25)^*\ (3.29)^*$ | 0.99 | 670.35 |
| | III | $\ln IP=-0.08+0.13 \ln IC+0.28 \ln BB$ <br> $(3.09)^*(3.20)^*\ (4.40)^*$ | 0.92 | 198.62 |
| IX | I | $\ln GS=-2.70-0.32 \ln AD+1.94 \ln BB$ <br> $(-4.26)^*\ (-0.94)\ (4.13)^*$ | 0.96 | 211.21 |
| | II | $\ln GS=-0.01-0.51 \ln AD+0.47 \ln BB$ <br> $(0.02)\ (4.61)^*(2.19)^{**}$ | 0.99 | 1164.60 |
| | III | $\ln GS=-0.43+0.29 \ln AD+0.88 \ln BB$ <br> $(-3.83)^*\ (1.05)\ (10.92)^*$ | 0.98 | 829.40 |
| X | II | $\ln SSU = 3.20+0.95 \ln BB$ <br> $(3.25)^*(9.80)^*$ | 0.87 | 96.11 |
| XI | II | $\ln SSU = 14.43- 1.39 \ln BB+1.26 \ln AD$ <br> $(7.78)^*\ (-3.70)^*\ (6.28)^*$ | 0.97 | 210.01 |
| XII | II | $\ln SSU = 7.33- 1.17 \ln BB+0.57 \ln AC$ <br> $(14.81)^*\ (-1.25)^*\ (11.16)^*$ | 0.89 | 124.75 |
| XIII | II | $\ln SSIC = -7.22+ 1.91 \ln BB$ <br> $(-13.16)^*\ (35.51)^*$ | 0.99 | 1261.15 |

| XIV | II | ln SSIC = -2.42+ 0.91 ln BB+0.54 ln AD<br>(-1.53) (2.85)* (3.15)* | 0.99 | 1068.45 |
|-----|----|------------------------------------------------------------------|------|---------|
| XV | II | ln SSIC = 1.26+ 0.45 ln BB+1.14 ln AC<br>(4.22)* (1.57) (36.93)* | 0.99 | 1363.63 |

Note: (i) period II for equations 10 to 15 refers to the period from 1970-71 to 1984-85 only

(ii) Figures in parenthesis are t- statistic

*Significant at 1% level  **Significant at 5% level

Power of bank branches in determining national income is found to be almost same for the periods I and III (87 percent and 88 percent). However, it has decreased in the post-nationalisation period as evidenced by the value of $\bar{R}^2$ (77 percent).

Addition of the aggregate deposits variable increases the explanatory power noticeably and for all three periods, extremely high values of $\bar{R}^2$ are obtained.

Whereas the elasticity coefficient associated with the number of branches for period I is high (1.21) and which is also statistically significant at 1 percent, it is completely insignificant during the period II. For period III, it is significant at 5 percent level.  However for this period, the value is 0.34 only.

It may be further noted that for the periods II and III 'aggregate deposits' (AD) is a statistically significant variable at 1 percent level, the value of elasticity coefficient being 0.74 and 0.46, respectively (Equation II).

Almost identical results emerge in the case of equation (III) where the number of bank branches and aggregate credit are the independent variables.

Equation (IV) reveals that movement in national income has been explained to the extent of 97 percent by 'bank branches' and 'agricultural production' variables during period I, while the two variables are statistically significant at 1 percent and 5 percent, respectively. On the other hand, the explanatory power has decreased notably (77 percent) for period II. In this period, agricultural production has been statistically insignificant.

Results of equation (i), (ii) and (iv), thus, clearly indicate that bank branches expanded seemingly in a haphazard manner despite there being a licensing authority, without taking into account the real economic need for establishing a bank branch at a particular centre.

Concentration of bank branches is also noticed in the industrially developed cities and towns and it persists. For instance, at and June 1990, while the number of bank branches was 59, 632,18.8 percent of these were in India's 100 top major centres, which accounted for 59.2 percent of the total deposits mobilized in the entire country amounting to ₹ 1,73,612.80 crore and developed 65.7 percent of the total bank of credit amounting to ₹ 14,14,643.65 crore in the same countries. As a result, spread effects did not take place despite the herald of geographical expansion of Indian banks since 1969 in rural and under banked areas and charter of regional rural banks in the country.

The equations also indicate that during the post-nationalisation period, the growth of 'aggregate deposits' was faster than the expansion of bank branches, and thus, played a role to activate national income more dominantly than bank branches.

The equation (iii) indicates that aggregate credit has played a major role during the post-nationalisation period. The role played by bank credit outweighed that of number of bank branches.

## 2) Aggregate Deposits and Aggregate Credit

Equation (v) and (vi) pertain to aggregate credit function where bank branches is the sole explanatory variable. Both equations provide expected results. In both equations, the variable, 'bank branches' happens to be highly significant casual variable during both the pre and post-nationalisation periods. However, during the later period, the explanatory power is slightly where as the elasticity coefficients of the respective equations show increases in their values. This tendency is more noticeable in the case of elasticity of 'aggregate deposits' with relation to bank branches. Thus, over the period covered as compared to bank credit, deposits has tended to grow faster in relation to bank branches, However, the relevance of other variables- other than simply number of bank branches – is also indicated in this respect. At the same time, the absolute influence of the number of bank branches upon aggregate credit has also increased notably. Perhaps, bank credit to poverty alleviation programmes and government sponsored schemes found their way as deposits in the banks.

## 3.1 Agricultural Production

The result of function (vii) in Table 5.2 reveals that variation in agricultural production is explained to the extent of 73 percent by bank credit to the agricultural sector and the number of bank branches. While bank branches remain a statistically significant variable, bank credit to agriculture seems to have affected agricultural production only insignificantly. However, the value of elasticity coefficient associated with bank branches is very small. Thus, it is observed that although expansion of banking facilities has shown its influence on agricultural production, evidence indicates that its impact is not substantial. The agricultural sector which received substantial bank credit has failed to yield the desired results. It may be observed that result of chow's test does not justify demarcation of the plan period under reference into two periods *viz.* pre and post-nationalisation.

One of the objectives of giving priority to agriculture during the post-nationlisation period is to increase agricultural production and thereby increase national output/income. Bank credit to agricultural sector, though remains as crucial input, did not receive attention from the government in the formation of linkages. Credit to agriculture, inter alia, depends on expansion of the area under irrigation, power facilities, application of modern methods of cultivation, increased use of fertilizers, pesticides, high-yielding varieties of seeds and scientific farming. Sustained and simultaneous efforts have not been made to accelerate agricultural output by the departments connected with the agricultural sector. Perhaps the lack of linkages between bank credit to agriculture and other inputs or leakages in the process of reaching ultimately the targeted cultivators through a bank branch failed to provide significant impetus to agricultural production. Based on the above, it may be stated that the structural tendencies which have, evolved over the years as per tradition, have continued to stay during the post-nationalisation period also.

Though regional rural banks were chartered since 1975, small and marginal farmers who constituted the majority among the Indian agriculturists could not get adequate credit facilities. Table 5.7 indicated that 40.0 percent of the total agricultural credit disbursed by banks have been utilised by only 2.4 percent of farmers. In other words, 60.0 percent of was utilized 97.6 percent of bank credit amounting to around ₹ 25,000 Indirect finance which formed the major portion of bank credit to agriculture to boost output has never reached the ultimate beneficiary - the farmers. As a result agricultural output did not register any significant increase due to increased dosage of bank credit. Thus, it is difficult to observe that agricultural sector could notably boost the growth of gross national output through the instrument of bank credit.

Against the objectives of nationalization, bank credit has reached the richer sections among the farmers. Illiteracy among the poor farmers has also been exploited by the concerned authorities for denial of adequate credit.

Most borrowers of small means have availed of bank credit not for the purpose for which it was borrowed but diverted in to repay the earlier loans or meet wasteful expenditure.

Annexure IV and V reveal the latest trend on bank credit to farmers directly disbursed and the impact on irrigated area, sown area and food grains output, respectively over decades of deployment by various bank branches. Perhaps timely bank credit has not reached the deserving farmer at the right time to enable the sector to develop faster, using latest technology.

## 3.2 Industrial Production

From results of function (viii) in table 5.2 , it can be inferred that explanatory power of banking facility variable (BB) and industrial credit variable (IC) are notably increasing. In fact, the explanatory power is close to perfection in the post-nationalisation period ($\overline{R}^2$ 0.99). The bank branches variable is statistically significant only during the post-nationalisation period.

However, the absolute influence of bank branches substantially decreases. The result thus tends to support the view that in the post-nationalisation period banks have contributed to Industrialization.

It is observed that industrial credit formed 48.6 percent in total bank credit at end-June 1988. However 16 percent of the beneficiaries availed of 95.6 percent of bank credit during 1987-88.

It was observed from Table 5.2 (equation (vii)) that in the case of agricultural production, credit appeared to be an insignificant variable. In conjunction with this, it may be inferred that as compared to agricultural sector, industrial units have obtained timely and adequate assistance from banks.

Annexure – VI presents the credit granted to the SSI (SME) sector to improve their performance. However, considerable amount of bank credit has been locked in sick units, resulting in monetary loss and unemployment.

Annexure – III presents the quantum of housing loan disbursed across the country and also indicates the official data on housing shortage. There seems to be unknown reasons to bridge the gap between demand for and supply of this basic need of shelter to common citizen.

Another type of bank credit is indirect credit to agriculture. The same is granted to promote agriculture and allied activities to improve productivity or increase agricultural income. These loans are advanced by such institutions as co-operatives, Rural Electrification Corporation for power supply, fertilizer plants, or routed through some other agency/conduit/tier.

## 4) Gross Savings

The function (equation ix) in Table 5.2 fits very well for all periods of analysis. While widening their branches, banks have been instrumental for monetization of the economy. The function of branches was significant at 1 percent during the pre-nationalisation year. But after the post-nationalisation period, this was so at 5 percent. on the other hand aggregate deposits variable which has been statistically significant only at 5 percent during the pre- nationalization period with a negative sign along with its coefficient becomes a highly significant (statistically) variable as compared to bank branches.

Thus while bank branches were more influential in generating savings of the community during the pre-nationalisation period, its influence has declined and aggregate deposits tend to dominate the gross saving function.

Statistical evidence, therefore, supports the view that the spread of bank branches has not necessarily implied steady and uniform growth in saving. At the same time, all banks efforts put together as represented by aggregate deposits in mobilizing public saving has shown growing after nationalization.

## 5) Small-Scale Industrial Units and Bank Credit

Equation (x), (xi) and (XII) explain the variation in the growth of small-scale industrial unit with reference to the number of bank branches, aggregate deposits with banks and aggregate credit where as equations (xiii), (xiv) and (xv) throw light on the experience of priority sector lending (where bank credit to small – scale industries is stipulated). All these equations are tested as indicated earlier, only for the period 1971-1986. Equation (x) where small-scale industrial unit is the dependent variable and bank branches is the explanatory variable provides good results in terms of $\overline{R}^2$ value (0.87). The value of elasticity coefficient for bank branches however, is less than unity although statistically significant.

When we add aggregate deposits there is considerable improvement in $\overline{R}^2$ value (from 0.87 to 0.97). Also, statistically significant and economically meaningful elasticity coefficient is obtained in the case of aggregate deposits the value being 1.26. The results indicate complete perversion as far as the sign of elasticity coefficients of bank branches is concerned

(-1.39) which is statistically significant.

The same holds good in respect of results pertaining to function (xii), where aggregate credit is used instead of aggregate deposits. Here however the statically significant elasticity coefficients with reference to aggregate credit (AC) is much less than unity (0.57).

These results indicate that 'deposits' had played a major role in raising the number of small-scale industrial units. The results also tend to negate the role of bank branches in this regard.

The insistence on deposits by bank branches while lending to small- scale and other units, which have helped generate deposits but, evidence is wanting of economic activities being promoted. It may also, be due to the fact, existing units are not provided with adequate credit. However, new units have been established. As the impact of 'bank deposits' is more than the number of 'bank branches', one can infer that bank credit has been granted to procure deposits to meet their overall  targets in respect of deposit mobilization.

It is observed from Table 5.7 that 12 percent of total beneficiaries bank credit to small-scale industries development programme, have availed of 86 percent of total bank credit allotted, resulting not only in concentration but also misuse of bank resources by them. All functions (equations (xiii), (xiv) and (xv)) relating to small-scale industrial credit provide excellent goodness of fits ( $\overline{R}^2$ =0.99) and results obtained are sufficiently meaningful.

Equation (xiii) indicates, the lone explanatory variable *viz* ' bank branches' influences credit substantially which is very (elasticity coefficients = 1.91) highly significant statistically. When bank branches and aggregate deposits are considered as the two explanatory variables the elasticity coefficient associated with bank branches has declined from 1.91 to 0.91. Both the coefficient values are however statistically significant.

(insignificant value of elasticity coefficients 0.45). Replacing 'aggregate deposits' with 'aggregate credit', equation (xv) reveals the complete disappearance of the importance of 'bank branches'

Aggregate credit has elasticity coefficient which is more than I and is highly significant. Though bank credit deployed to small-scale industrial units has grown in size, the number of small-scale units did not increase proportionately as expected. Moreover, the role played by widening bank branches was less in the case of small-scale industrial units, when considered with aggregate deposits and aggregate credit. It may be mentioned that priority sector advances enjoyed concessional rate of interest and easy terms of refinance.

## State-wise Analysis

The results of the various functions fitted for each of the 12 major states are presented in Tables from 5.3 (i) to 5.3 (xii). For each of the equations, the results are shown in the tables for the states together in order to facilitate comparison. As mentioned earlier, these regression results are based on the period from 1970-71 to 1985-86. The analysis of the results also covers identical equations used at the All-India level (Table 5.2).

Table: 5.3. (i)

RESULTS OF STATE LEVEL ANALYSIS

| SN | States | Equation | RBAR | F-test |
|----|--------|----------|------|--------|
| 01 | Andhra Pradesh | ln SDP = 3.22 + 1.00 ln BB<br>(5.70)*    (13.58) | 0.93 | 184.5 |
| 02 | Bihar | ln SDP = 5.96 + 0.67 ln BB<br>(21.95)*    (17.88) | 0.96 | 319.7 |
| 03 | Gujarat | ln SDP = -2.07 + 1.70 ln BB<br>(-2.34)**    (14.51) | 0.94 | 210.5 |
| 04 | Karnataka | ln SDP = 0.73 + 1.28 ln BB<br>(1.17)    (15.91)* | 0.95 | 253.2 |
| 05 | Kerala | ln SDP = 1.96 + 1.10 ln BB<br>(2.79)*    (11.72)* | 0.91 | 137.5 |
| 06 | Madhya Pradesh | ln SDP = 4.68 + 0.83 ln BB<br>(14.73)*    (19.18)* | 0.96 | 367.9 |
| 07 | Maharashtra | ln SDP = 0.41 + 1.50 ln BB<br>(-1.09)*    (31.15)* | 0.99 | 970.3 |
| 08 | Punjab | ln SDP = 1.74 + 1.22 ln BB<br>(3.11)*    (15.49)* | 0.94 | 240.0 |
| 09 | Rajasthan | ln SDP = 3.32 + 1.01 ln BB<br>(7.41)*    (15.88)* | 0.95 | 251.3 |
| 10 | Tamil Nadu | ln SDP = 0.08 + 1.38 ln BB<br>(0.16)    (19.39)* | 0.96 | 376.0 |
| 11 | Uttar Pradesh | ln SDP = 4.41 + 0.88 ln BB<br>(14.71)*    (23.49)* | 0.98 | 551.9 |
| 12 | West Bengal | ln SDP = 4.31 + 0.93 ln BB<br>(10.30)*    (16.23)* | 0.95 | 263.3 |

Table: 5.3. (ii)

## RESULTS OF STATE LEVEL ANALYSIS

| SN | States | Equation | RBAR | F-test |
|----|--------|----------|------|--------|
| 01 | Andhra Pradesh | ln SDP = 13.09 - 1.37 ln BB +1.16 ln AD<br>(4.55)*    (-2.00)    (3.45)* | 0.96 | 176.5 |
| 02 | Bihar | ln SDP = 6.98 – 0.08 ln BB +0.64 ln AD<br>(22.42)*    (-0.40)    (4.06)* | 0.98 | 358.2 |
| 03 | Gujarat | ln SDP = 5.27 – 0.01 ln BB +0.74 ln AD<br>(3.82)*    (0.02)    (5.67)* | 0.98 | 373.2 |
| 04 | Karnataka | ln SDP = 5.18 – 0.08 ln BB +0.46 ln AD<br>(4.55)*    (0.86)    (3.14)* | 0.97 | 217.9 |
| 05 | Kerala | ln SDP = 7.99 – 0.27 ln BB +0.63 ln AD<br>(4.55)*    (-1.17)    (5.38)* | 0.97 | 231.5 |
| 06 | Madhya Pradesh | ln SDP = 2.74 – 1.47 ln BB – 0.41 ln AD<br>(4.55)*    (1.38)    (-0.59)* | 0.95 | 175.7 |
| 07 | Maharashtra | ln SDP = 1.01 – 1.08 ln BB +0.22 ln AD<br>(4.55)*    (2.22)    (0.08)* | 0.99 | 475.5 |
| 08 | Punjab | ln SDP = 5.13 – 0.28 ln BB +0.45 ln AD<br>(4.55)*    (2.60)    (8.99)* | 0.99 | 896.5 |
| 09 | Rajasthan | ln SDP = 5.66 – 0.37 ln BB +0.34 ln AD<br>(4.55)*    (0.40)    (0.68)* | 0.94 | 120.7 |
| 10 | Tamil Nadu | ln SDP = 11.44 – 0.99 ln BB +0.97 ln AD<br>(4.55)*    (-1.53)    (3.67)* | 0.98 | 375.6 |
| 11 | Uttar Pradesh | ln SDP = 8.08 – 0.35 ln BB +0.81 ln AD<br>(4.55)*    (-0.90)    (3.14)* | 0.99 | 468.7 |
| 12 | West Bengal | ln SDP = 6.25 – 0.15 ln BB +0.76 ln AD<br>(4.55)*    (-0.60)    (4.24)* | 0.98 | 312.9 |

## Table: 5.3. (iii)

## RESULTS OF STATE LEVEL ANALYSIS

| SN | States | Equation | RBAR | F-test |
|----|--------|----------|------|--------|
| 01 | Andhra Pradesh | ln SDP = 10.11 - 0.69 ln BB +0.89 ln AC<br>(5.45)*    (-1.54)    (3.80)* | 0.97 | 194.7 |
| 02 | Bihar | ln SDP = 6.99 + 0.33 ln BB +0.26 ln AC<br>(18.51)*    (2.91)    (3.25)* | 0.98 | 282.5 |
| 03 | Gujarat | ln SDP = 5.78 - 0.05 ln BB +0.79 ln AC<br>(4.11)*    (-0.18)    (5.91)* | 0.98 | 397.2 |
| 04 | Karnataka | ln SDP = 3.46 + 0.65 ln BB +0.31 ln AC<br>(1.11)*    (1.53)    (1.48) | 0.98 | 139.4 |
| 05 | Kerala | ln SDP = 7.42 - 0.12 ln BB +0.57 ln AC<br>(6.87)*    (-0.53)    (5.43)* | 0.97 | 234.4 |
| 06 | Madhya Pradesh | ln SDP = 6.90 + 0.20 ln BB +0.40 ln AC<br>(3.47)*    (0.36)    (1.13) | 0.96 | 188.3 |
| 07 | Maharashtra | ln SDP = 1.12 - 1.06 ln BB +0.23 ln AC<br>(1.11)    (3.92)*    (1.63) | 0.99 | 548.0 |
| 08 | Punjab | ln SDP = 6.33 + 0.19 ln BB +0.45 ln AC<br>(12.74)*    (1.74)    (9.99)* | 0.99 | 1082.0 |
| 09 | Rajasthan | ln SDP = 5.39 - 0.52 ln BB +0.24 ln AC<br>(2.11)*    (0.89)    (0.83)* | 0.95 | 122.9 |
| 10 | Tamil Nadu | ln SDP = 7.91 - 0.41 ln BB +0.83 ln AC<br>(4.52)*    (-1.04)    (4.56)* | 0.99 | 485.2 |
| 11 | Uttar Pradesh | ln SDP = 6.07 + 0.42 ln BB +0.29 ln AC<br>(5.87)*    (1.51)    (1.68)* | 0.98 | 315.14 |
| 12 | West Bengal | ln SDP = 4.62 + 0.24 ln BB +0.63 ln AC<br>(15.79)*    (1.38)    (4.06)* | 0.98 | 297.0 |

## Table: 5.3. (iv)

## RESULTS OF STATE LEVEL ANALYSIS

| SN | States | Equation | RBAR | F-test |
|----|--------|----------|------|--------|
| 01 | Andhra Pradesh | ln AD = -8.44 + 2.03 ln BB<br>(-24.63)* (45.38)* | 0.99 | 2060.0 |
| 02 | Bihar | ln AD = -1.57 + 1.17 ln BB<br>(-4.94)* (26.49)* | 0.98 | 701.9 |
| 03 | Gujarat | ln AD = -9.91 + 2.29 ln BB<br>(-9.72)* (16.93)* | 0.95 | 286.6 |
| 04 | Karnataka | ln AD = -9.58 + 2.16 ln BB<br>(-10.71)* (18.52)* | 0.96 | 342.9 |
| 05 | Kerala | ln AD = -9.64 + 2.20 ln BB<br>(-10.24)* (17.48)* | 0.96 | 305.71 |
| 06 | Madhya Pradesh | ln AD = -4.72 + 1.54 ln BB<br>(-37.41)* (86.47)* | 0.99 | 8006.5 |
| 07 | Maharashtra | ln AD = -6.46 + 1.87 ln BB<br>(-15.67)* (36.00)* | 0.99 | 1296.0 |
| 08 | Punjab | ln AD = -7.21 + 2.00 ln BB<br>(-6.50)* (12.77)* | 0.92 | 163.1 |
| 09 | Rajasthan | ln AD = -6.72 + 1.43 ln BB<br>(-27.19)* (52.00)* | 0.99 | 2703.9 |
| 10 | Tamil Nadu | ln AD = -11.61 + 2.43 ln BB<br>(-28.22)* (45.87)* | 0.99 | 2104.4 |
| 11 | Uttar Pradesh | ln AD = -4.48 + 1.52 ln BB<br>(-18.23)* (49.14)* | 0.99 | 2415.5 |
| 12 | West Bengal | ln AD = -2.54 + 1.42 ln BB<br>(-5.97)* (24.40)* | 0.98 | 595.6 |

## Table: 5.3. (v)

## RESULTS OF STATE LEVEL ANALYSIS

| SN | States | Equation | RBAR | F-test |
|----|--------|----------|------|--------|
| 01 | Andhra Pradesh | $\ln AC = -7.73 + 1.90 \ln BB$ <br> $(-16.49)^*$    $(31.10)^*$ | 0.98 | 967.2 |
| 02 | Bihar | $\ln AC = -4.09 + 1.40 \ln BB$ <br> $(-5.53)^*$    $(17.37)^*$ | 0.93 | 184.1 |
| 03 | Gujarat | $\ln AC = -9.85 + 2.05 \ln BB$ <br> $(-11.22)^*$    $(19.74)^*$ | 0.96 | 301.7 |
| 04 | Karnataka | $\ln AC = -8.93 + 2.05 \ln BB$ <br> $(-11.22)^*$    $(19.74)^*$ | 0.97 | 389.7 |
| 05 | Kerala | $\ln AC = -9.51 + 2.13 \ln BB$ <br> $(-9.24)^*$    $(15.17)^*$ | 0.94 | 239.51 |
| 06 | Madhya Pradesh | $\ln AC = -5.52 + 1.57 \ln BB$ <br> $(-23.33)^*$    $(48.65)^*$ | 0.99 | 2367.3 |
| 07 | Maharashtra | $\ln AC = -6.63 + 1.86 \ln BB$ <br> $(-9.51)^*$    $(21.27)^*$ | 0.97 | 452.4 |
| 08 | Punjab | $\ln AC = -10.11 + 2.28 \ln BB$ <br> $(-8.68)^*$    $(13.90)^*$ | 0.93 | 193.0 |
| 09 | Rajasthan | $\ln AC = -8.76 + 2.05 \ln BB$ <br> $(-19.96)^*$    $(32.79)^*$ | 0.99 | 1073.9 |
| 10 | Tamil Nadu | $\ln AC = -9.36 + 2.14 \ln BB$ <br> $(-17.77)^*$    $(31.56)^*$ | 0.99 | 996.2 |
| 11 | Uttar Pradesh | $\ln AC = -5.55 + 1.55 \ln BB$ <br> $(-12.76)^*$    $(28.36)^*$ | 0.99 | 804.5 |
| 12 | West Bengal | $\ln AC = -0.49 + 1.08 \ln BB$ <br> $(-0.97)^*$    $(15.81)^*$ | 0.95 | 249.8 |

## Table: 5.3. (vi)

## RESULTS OF STATE LEVEL ANALYSIS

| SN | States | Equation | RBAR | F-test |
|----|--------|----------|------|--------|
| 01 | Andhra Pradesh | ln AP = 3.24 + 0.10 ln BB+ 0.99 ln AG<br>(1.46)    (0.23) (0.49) | 0.80 | 28.46 |
| 02 | Bihar | ln AP = 3.88 + 0.12 ln BB+ 0.27 ln AG<br>(10.95)*    (-0.23) (1.41) | 0.07 | 1.6 |
| 03 | Gujarat | ln AP = -15.91 + 2.73 ln BB+ 0.11 ln AG<br>(-8.95)*    (16.97)* (0.37) | 0.95 | 145.2 |
| 04 | Karnataka | ln AP = -1.95 + 1.07 ln BB- 0.39 ln AG<br>(-0.87)    (2.68)* (-2.43)* | 0.39 | 5.4 |
| 05 | Kerala | ln AP = 1.17 + 0.26 ln BB- 0.11 ln AG<br>(1.79)    (2.36)* (-2.90)* | 0.39 | 5.6 |
| 06 | Madhya Pradesh | ln AP = 0.86 + 0.72 ln BB- 0.30 ln AG<br>(0.37)    (1.61) (-1.35) | 0.22 | 3.0 |
| 07 | Maharashtra | ln AP = -0.75 + 0.71 ln BB-0.08 ln AG<br>(-0.17)    (0.88) (-0.22) | 0.77 | 25.0 |
| 08 | Punjab | ln AP = 6.96 - 0.56 ln BB+ 0.35 ln AG<br>(4.51)*    (-0.29) (4.32)* | 0.94 | 104.4 |
| 09 | Rajasthan | ln AP = 4.20 + 0.06 ln BB+ 0.07 ln AG<br>(1.85)    (0.16) (-0.45) | 0.02 | 1.1 |
| 10 | Tamil Nadu | ln AP = -1.30 + 1.00ln BB- 0.41 ln AG<br>(-0.41)    (1.85) (-2.16) | 0.29 | 3.8 |
| 11 | Uttar Pradesh | ln AP = 3.33 + 0.28 ln BB- 0.04 ln AG<br>(1.22)    (0.51) (-0.13) | 0.43 | 6.34 |
| 12 | West Bengal | ln AP = 0.82 + 0.65 ln BB-0.28 ln AG<br>(0.23)    (1.03) (-1.03) | 0.08 | 0.5 |

## Table: 5.3. (vii)

## RESULTS OF STATE LEVEL ANALYSIS

| SN | States | Equation | RBAR | F-test |
|----|--------|----------|------|--------|
| 01 | Andhra Pradesh | $\ln SSU = 4.27 + 0.74 \ln BB$<br>(3.47)    (4.63)* | 0.59 | 21.4 |
| 02 | Bihar | $\ln SSU = 4.20 + 0.77 \ln BB$<br>(13.02)    (7.87)* | 0.95 | 292.4 |
| 03 | Gujarat | $\ln SSU = 1.38 + 1.15 \ln BB$<br>(1.25)    (7.87)* | 0.81 | 62.0 |
| 04 | Karnataka | $\ln SSU = 2.17 + 0.99 \ln BB$<br>(1.66)    (5.78)* | 0.70 | 33.4 |
| 05 | Kerala | $\ln SSU = 2.68 + 0.92 \ln BB$<br>(3.17)*    (8.11)* | 0.82 | 65.9 |
| 06 | Madhya Pradesh | $\ln SSU = 1.32 + 1.22 \ln BB$<br>(1.58)    (10.98)* | 0.88 | 114.1 |
| 07 | Maharashtra | $\ln SSU = 6.81 + 0.43 \ln BB$<br>(10.14)*    (5.11)* | 0.64 | 26.1 |
| 08 | Punjab | $\ln SSU = 6.52 + 0.55 \ln BB$<br>(4.48)*    (2.70)* | 0.31 | 7.3 |
| 09 | Rajasthan | $\ln SSU = 2.57 + 1.04 \ln BB$<br>(7.38)*    (21.05)* | 0.97 | 443.2 |
| 10 | Tamil Nadu | $\ln SSU = 4.26 + 0.78 \ln BB$<br>(4.72)*    (6.74)* | 0.76 | 45.5 |
| 11 | Uttar Pradesh | $\ln SSU = 4.90 + 0.70 \ln BB$<br>(3.88)*    (4.40)* | 0.57 | 19.3 |
| 12 | West Bengal | $\ln SSU = 2.08 + 1.22 \ln BB$<br>(4.19)*    (18.06)* | 0.95 | 326.5 |

## Table: 5.3. (viii)

## RESULTS OF STATE LEVEL ANALYSIS

| SN | States | Equation | RBAR | F-test |
|----|--------|----------|------|--------|
| 01 | Andhra Pradesh | lnSSU = 28.31-5.04 ln BB+2.85 ln AD<br>(5.24)*(-3.90)* (4.50)* | 0.83 | 36.8 |
| 02 | Bihar | lnSSU = 4.58- 0.50 ln BB+0.23 ln AD<br>(8.23)*(1.46)* (0.82)* | 0.95 | 142.0 |
| 03 | Gujarat | lnSSU = 11.96-1.28 ln BB +1.06 ln AD<br>(19.79)*(-9.61)* (18.66)* | 0.99 | 1034.6 |
| 04 | Karnataka | lnSSU = 12.16-1.29 ln BB +1.06 ln AD<br>(4.08)*(-1.95)* (3.54)* | 0.84 | 37.8 |
| 05 | Kerala | lnSSU = 10.73-0.92 ln BB +0.83 ln AD<br>(10.86)*(-4.22)* (8.63)* | 0.97 | 256.6 |
| 06 | Madhya Pradesh | lnSSU = -4.97 + 3.28 ln BB -1.33 ln AD<br>(-0.58)*(1.18)* (-0.74)* | 0.88 | 55.4 |
| 07 | Maharashtra | lnSSU = 15.49-2.091 ln BB +1.34 ln AD<br>(8.78)*(-4.16)* (5.05)* | 0.88 | 50.5 |
| 08 | Punjab | lnSSU = 15.73-2.00 ln BB +1.27 ln AD<br>(22.53)*(-11.36)* (15.05)* | 0.96 | 180.9 |
| 09 | Rajasthan | lnSSU = 9.15-01.74 ln BB +0.98 ln AD<br>(4.61)*(-1.39)* (3.34)* | 0.98 | 400.8 |
| 10 | Tamil Nadu | lnSSU = 11.07-0.64 ln BB +0.56 ln AD<br>(1.55)*(-0.43)* (0.96)* | 0.76 | 23.0 |
| 11 | Uttar Pradesh | lnSSU = 23.54-5.63 ln BB +4.15 ln AD<br>(5.93)*(-4.24)* (4.79)* | 0.84 | 37.54 |
| 12 | West Bengal | lnSSU = 1.72 + 1.42 ln BB -0.14 ln AD<br>(1.72)*(2.97)* (-0.16)* | 0.96 | 152.9 |

## Table: 5.3. (ix)
## RESULTS OF STATE LEVEL ANALYSIS

| SN | States | Equation | RBAR | F-test |
|----|--------|----------|------|--------|
| 01 | Andhra Pradesh | lnSSU = 21.98-3.62 ln BB+2.29 ln AC<br>(7.49)*(-5.08)* (6.18)* | 0.89 | 60.5 |
| 02 | Bihar | lnSSU = 4.43+ 0.69 ln BB+ 0.05 ln AC<br>(9.56)*(-4.82)* (0.44)* | 0.95 | 137.2 |
| 03 | Gujarat | lnSSU = 12.01-1.22 ln BB +1.07 ln AC<br>(9.56)*(-4.51)* (8.96)* | 0.97 | 260.8 |
| 04 | Karnataka | lnSSU = 9.70-0.74 ln BB +0.84 ln AC<br>(2.54)*(-0.87)* (2.07)* | 0.76 | 23.1 |
| 05 | Kerala | lnSSU = 9.87-0.69 ln BB +0.75 ln AC<br>(10.41)*(-3.40)* (8.14)* | 0.97 | 231.5 |
| 06 | Madhya Pradesh | lnSSU = 10.56-1.42 ln BB +1.67 ln AC<br>(2.19)*(-1.03)* (1.94)* | 0.90 | 70.2 |
| 07 | Maharashtra | lnSSU = 12.30-1.161 ln BB +0.82 ln AC<br>(8.78)*(-4.16)* (5.05)* | 0.90 | 62.7 |
| 08 | Punjab | lnSSU = 18.57-2.17 ln BB +1.19 ln AC<br>(15.96)*(-8.56)* (11.22)* | 0.93 | 101.6 |
| 09 | Rajasthan | lnSSU = 5.65+0.32 ln BB +0.35 ln AC<br>(3.08)*(0.77)* (1.71)* | 0.97 | 255.7 |
| 10 | Tamil Nadu | lnSSU = 14.99-1.67 ln BB +1.14 ln AC<br>(4.26)*(-2.10)* (3.11)* | 0.86 | 42.1 |
| 11 | Uttar Pradesh | lnSSU = 14.22-1.91 ln BB +1.68 ln AC<br>(3.61)*(-1.78)* (2.46)* | 0.69 | 16.4 |
| 12 | West Bengal | lnSSU = 2.00 + 1.39 ln BB -0.16 ln AC<br>(3.79)*(4.48)* (-0.58)* | 0.96 | 155.1 |

## Table: 5.3. (x)

## RESULTS OF STATE LEVEL ANALYSIS

| SN | States | Equation | RBAR | F-test |
|----|--------|----------|------|--------|
| 01 | Andhra Pradesh | lnSSIC-4.09+1.77 ln BB<br>(-4.08)*(14.45)* | 0.94 | 208.6 |
| 02 | Bihar | lnSSIC-1.01+1.33 ln BB<br>(-4.16)*(39.38)* | 0.99 | 1551.0 |
| 03 | Gujarat | lnSSIC-7.64+2.32 ln BB<br>(-7.42)*(16.99)* | 0.95 | 288.5 |
| 04 | Karnataka | lnSSIC-7.51+2.22 ln BB<br>(-11.34)*(25.75)* | 0.98 | 663.4 |
| 05 | Kerala | lnSSIC-3.44+1.69 ln BB<br>(-3.25)*(11.94)* | 0.91 | 142.6 |
| 06 | Madhya Pradesh | lnSSIC-3.15+1.64 ln BB<br>(-16.40)*(62.25)* | 0.99 | 3875.5 |
| 07 | Maharashtra | lnSSIC-5.86+2.08 ln BB<br>(-14.16)*(39.85)* | 0.99 | 1588.4 |
| 08 | Punjab | lnSSIC-5.28+2.10 ln BB<br>(-12.90)*(36.48)* | 0.99 | 1330.8 |
| 09 | Rajasthan | lnSSIC-5.35+1.97 ln BB<br>(-24.66)*(63.77)* | 0.99 | 4067.1 |
| 10 | Tamil Nadu | lnSSIC-8.57+2.39 ln BB<br>(-14.55)*(31.59)* | 0.99 | 998.1 |
| 11 | Uttar Pradesh | lnSSIC-3.96+1.73 ln BB<br>(-19.21)*(27.68)* | 0.99 | 4423.5 |
| 12 | West Bengal | lnSSIC-2.29+1.63 ln BB<br>(-5.28)*(27.68)* | 0.98 | 766.3 |

## Table: 5.3. (xi)

## RESULTS OF STATE LEVEL ANALYSIS

| SN | States | Equation | RBAR | F-test |
|----|--------|----------|------|--------|
| 01 | Andhra Pradesh | lnSSIC = 15.07-3.84 ln BB+2.27 ln AD<br>(4.00)* (-3.16)* (5.14)* | 0.98 | 321.9 |
| 02 | Bihar | lnSSIC = -0.59+ 1.02 ln BB+0.26 ln AD<br>(-1.48) (4.18)* (1.26) | 0.99 | 811.8 |
| 03 | Gujarat | lnSSIC = 1.64+0.17 ln BB+0.10 ln AD<br>(1.42) (0.68)(8.55)* | 0.99 | 982.6 |
| 04 | Karnataka | lnSSIC = 1.51+0.87 ln BB+0.63 ln AD<br>(-1.31) (3.48)* (5.51)* | 0.99 | 1097.7 |
| 05 | Kerala | lnSSIC = 6.80-0.65 ln BB+1.06 ln AD<br>(6.35)*(-2.76)* (10.13)* | 0.99 | 680.8 |
| 06 | Madhya Pradesh | lnSSIC = -2.24+1.34 ln BB+0.19 ln AD<br>(-1.13) (2.07)(0.46) | 0.99 | 1828.4 |
| 07 | Maharashtra | lnSSIC = -2.84+ 1.20 ln BB+0.46 ln AD<br>(-1.67) (2.49)* (1.82) | 0.99 | 937.2 |
| 08 | Punjab | lnSSIC = -3.97 + 1.75 ln BB+0.18 ln AD<br>(-5.19)*(9.05)* (1.96) | 0.99 | 812.9 |
| 09 | Rajasthan | lnSSIC = -4.27 + 1.68 ln BB+0.16 ln AD<br>(-2.52)*(3.66)* (0.64) | 0.99 | 1942.5 |
| 10 | Tamil Nadu | lnSSIC = 4.11 – 0.26 ln BB+1.09 ln AD<br>(1.31) (-0.39)(4.09)* | 0.99 | 1112.3 |
| 11 | Uttar Pradesh | lnSSIC = -2.61+ 1.27 ln BB+0.30 ln AD<br>(-2.53)*(3.68)* (1.32) | 0.99 | 2341.2 |
| 12 | West Bengal | lnSSIC = 0.22 + 0.23 ln BB+0.98 ln AD<br>(1.15) (2.40)* (14.73)* | 0.99 | 6860.9 |

## Table: 5.3. (xii)

## RESULTS OF STATE LEVEL ANALYSIS

| SN | States | Equation | RBAR | F-test |
|----|--------|----------|------|--------|
| 01 | Andhra Pradesh | lnSSIC = 10.38– 1.79 ln BB+1.87 ln AC<br>(6.46)* (-4.62)* (9.22)* | 0.99 | 821.5 |
| 02 | Bihar | lnSSIC = -0.45+ 1.14 ln BB+0.13 ln AC<br>(-1.06) (9.15)* (1.57) | 0.99 | 864.6 |
| 03 | Gujarat | lnSSIC = 2.25+0.10 ln BB+0.11 ln AC<br>(1.94) (0.42)(9.04)* | 0.99 | 1081.9 |
| 04 | Karnataka | lnSSIC = -2.93+1.17 ln BB+0.51 ln AC<br>(-1.65) (2.97)* (2.71)* | 0.99 | 497.2 |
| 05 | Kerala | lnSSIC = 6.11-0.45 ln BB+1.00 ln AC<br>(9.64)*(-3.32)* (16.17)* | 0.99 | 1632.7 |
| 06 | Madhya Pradesh | lnSSIC = -2.98+1.59 ln BB+0.03 ln AC<br>(-2.37) (4.48)(0.14) | 0.99 | 1801.9 |
| 07 | Maharashtra | lnSSIC = -3.53+ 1.42 ln BB+0.35 ln AC<br>(-3.60) (5.43)* (2.54) | 0.99 | 1131.9 |
| 08 | Punjab | lnSSIC = -3.73 + 1.42 ln BB+0.15 ln AC<br>(-3.75)*(8.15)* (1.66) | 0.99 | 758.1 |
| 09 | Rajasthan | lnSSIC = -5.03 + 1.90 ln BB+0.04 ln AC<br>(-3.96)*(6.46)* (0.26) | 0.99 | 1887.7 |
| 10 | Tamil Nadu | lnSSIC = -1.95 + 0.88 ln BB+0.70 ln AC<br>(-0.82) (1.63)(2.83)* | 0.99 | 771.7 |
| 11 | Uttar Pradesh | lnSSIC = -3.51+ 1.60 ln BB+0.08 ln AC<br>(-4.51)*(7.58)* (0.60) | 0.99 | 2103.6 |
| 12 | West Bengal | lnSSIC = -2.01 + 1.01 ln BB+0.57 ln AC<br>(-5.72) (4.90)* (3.05)* | 0.99 | 633.2 |

## 1) State Domestic Product (SDP)

Equations (i), (ii) and (iii) (Tables 5.3 (i), 5.3 (ii) and 5.3 (iii)) relate to state domestic product as functions of (a) bank branches, (b) bank branches and aggregate deposits and bank branches and bank credit as explanatory variables.

(a) All the selected 12 states invariably provide high value of $\bar{R}^2$ (Table 5.3 (i)), the value ranging between 0.91 and 0.99. The influence of bank branches upon variation in state domestic product is clearly indicated in each of the states through significant values of t-statistic associated with respective elasticity coefficients. The value of elasticity coefficient ranges between 0.67 in the case of Bihar and 1.70 in the case of Gujarat, Bihar, Madhya Pradesh, Uttar Pradesh and West Bengal have elasticity coefficients less than 1. The states of Gujarat, Maharashtra and Tamil Nadu have their elasticity coefficients whose values are more than that of the All-India values of 1.37.

(b) The results of this function presented in Table 5.3 (ii) reveal that only in the case of Punjab, both variables are statistically significant. 'Bank branches' variable alone is significant at 5 percent for Maharashtra. On the other hand, 'aggregate deposits' alone is significant in the case of Andhra Pradesh, Bihar, Gujarat, Karnataka, Kerala, Tamil Nadu and West Bengal, which indicate the more dominant role of aggregate deposits than the number of bank branches in explaining the variation in state domestic product in these states. In the case of Madhya Pradesh and Rajasthan, both variables are insignificant. It may be noted that similar results are also obtained at the national level where the significance of 'aggregate deposits', while considered along with bank branches was dominant.

(c) The results of this equation are presented in Table 5.3 (iii). They indicate that in majority of the States, bank credit is the only statistically significant variable, the States being Andhra Pradesh, Gujarat, Kerala, Punjab, Tamil Nadu and West Bengal. Here also, Maharashtra is the state where 'bank branch' (BB) is the lone statistically significant variable. In the case of Bihar, both variables are statistically insignificant whereas in Karnataka, Madhya Pradesh, Rajasthan and Uttar Pradesh, both variables are significant.

2) Bank Branches, Deposits and Credit

Here, two equations are fitted viz. (a) 'aggregate deposits' and (b) 'bank credit'.

a) Bank branches have explained variation in 'aggregate deposits' more prominently as indicated by the notably higher value of $\bar{R}^2$ (Table 5.3 (iv)). Elasticity coefficients of bank branches in all states are significant at 1 percent. In comparison with the all-India value (2.1), Gujarat, Karnataka, Kerala and Tamil Nadu have higher values. The elasticity value lies between 1.17 in Bihar and 2.29 in Gujarat.

(b) Table 5.3 (v) suggests the same picture as $\bar{R}^2$ follows an identical behavior just as function 4 (Table 5.3 (iv)). The elasticity coefficients for all States are statistically significant. Gujarat, Karnataka, Kerala, Punjab, Rajasthan and Tamil Nadu had a higher value than the all-India level in respect of the elasticity coefficient (1.9) provided in Table 5.2. In this case, Punjab has the highest value 2.29 and West Bengal has the lowest at 1.08.

## 3) Agricultural Production

The estimated equation where agricultural production and agricultural credit provide at extremely poor value of goodness of fit (Table 5.3 (vi)) in the states of Bihar (0.08), Madhya Pradesh (0.22), Rajasthan (0.02), Tamil Nadu (0.29) and West Bengal (-0.08). In Maharashtra, although the $\bar{R}^2$ is high, both 'bank branches' and 'agricultural credit' variables are statistically insignificant.

The results in Gujarat reveal that 'bank branches' is a statistically significant variable. On the other hand, in Punjab, bank credit to agriculture appears to be significant. In Gujarat and Punjab, $\overline{R}^2$ values are 0.94 and 0.95, respectively. Since all-India results pertain to the period from 1950-51 to 1987-88 for the analysis (Table 5.2) an attempt to compare the present results has been avoided.

## 4) Small-Scale Industrial Units and Credit

Six equations are estimated under this aspect. They are:

(i)   Small-scale units as a function of bank branches.
(ii)  Small-scale units as a function of bank branches and deposits.
(iii) Small-scale units as a function of bank branches and credit.
(iv)  Small-scale industrial credit as a function of bank branches.
(v)   Small-scale industrial credit as a function of bank branches and deposits.
(vi)  Small-scale industrial credit as a function of bank branches and credit.

   (a)   The analysis as regards growth of small-scale industrial units with reference to the number of 'bank branches' reveals (Table 5.3 (vii)) that (i) as compared to all-India results, the role of bank branches is of declining significance in the states of Punjab, Uttar Pradesh, Andhra Pradesh and Maharashtra in that order as indicated by $\overline{R}^2$ value.

   In Bihar, Rajasthan and West Bengal, the $\overline{R}^2$ value is very high. In other States, they are in and around the all-India value; (ii) the least value of the elasticity coefficient is obtained in the case of Maharashtra (0.43). This is followed by Punjab, Uttar Pradesh, Bihar, Tamil Nadu and Kerala in that order in whose cases, the value is less than that of all-India analysis (0.95). West Bengal, Madhya Pradesh and Gujarat have the elasticity value which is higher than 1.

   (b)   As was observed earlier, for all-India analysis in Table 5.2, the inclusion of 'aggregate deposits' along with 'bank branches' reveals a substantial increase in the value of $\overline{R}^2$ for all states (Table 5.3 (viii)). In all the states, except West Bengal, Bihar and Madhya Pradesh, the relevance of 'bank branches' becomes economically meaningless with negative signs associated with their respective elasticity coefficients of bank branches. In the case of West Bengal, the elasticity coefficient is not only meaningful but also statistically significant, while in Bihar and Madhya Pradesh, the elasticity coefficient is not statistically significant. The 'Aggregate deposits' variable is not statistically significant for the States of Bihar, Madhya Pradesh and West Bengal.

   (c)   The same observations can be made as regards results of this equation (Table 5.3 (ix)).The 'Bank branches' variable is statistically significant in Bihar and West Bengal, the coefficient value having a meaningful sign. For Rajasthan also, it is meaningful, but, not statistically significant. But the 'credit' variable is statistically not significant in Bihar, Rajasthan and West Bengal.

   (d)   Bank credit to small-scale industries has been very highly and uniformly explained by the variation in bank branches in all States as was the case at the national level (Table 5.3 (x)). The elasticity coefficients associated with the number of bank branches are statistically significant in each of the States varying between 1.33 in Bihar and 2.39 in Tamil Nadu. Gujarat also has a very high value which is 2.32. Bihar, West Bengal, Madhya Pradesh, Kerala and Andhra Pradesh have small values of elasticity coefficients as compared to the all-India value (1.91).

(e) In Table 5.3 (xi), where the variation in credit to small-scale industries is studied with reference to bank branches and deposits and bank branches and bank credit, a high value for $\overline{R}^2$ is obtained in all states. The 'Bank branches' variable has a negative sign in the case of Andhra Pradesh, Kerala and Tamil Nadu. But it is positive and statistically significant in Bihar, Karnataka, Maharashtra, Punjab, Rajasthan, Uttar Pradesh and West Bengal. The role of the 'aggregate deposits' variable is statistically and strongly vindicated in the case of Andhra Pradesh, Kerala, Tamil Nadu and to a certain extent in West Bengal. Although the coefficients are significant, their absolute values are very small in Gujarat and Karnataka. In other states, it is statistically insignificant. The same can be said for the national level where the role of aggregate deposits was more dominant than 'bank branches'.

(f) Table 5.3 (xii) indicates that the fits are almost perfect in all states for this equation. Andhra Pradesh and Kerala have negative signs for the elasticity value corresponding to bank branches.

Meaningful sign and statistically significant elasticity values are obtained in the case of Bihar, Karnataka, Madhya Pradesh, Maharashtra, Punjab, Rajasthan, Uttar Pradesh and West Bengal.

Bank credit is not statistically significant in states of Bihar, Madhya Pradesh, Punjab, Rajasthan, and Uttar Pradesh. It can be noted that the most ideal results are obtained in the case of Maharashtra, where both banking variables 'bank branches' and 'bank credit' are statistically significant and economically meaningful.

The examination of various results pertaining to the State-level analysis for the post-nationalisation period reveals the following:

(1) As was in the case of All-India, the influence of number of bank branches upon state domestic product has been noticeable. Particularly in States of Gujarat, Maharashtra and Tamil Nadu, this phenomenon has been quite above the All-India situation. Bihar, Madhya Pradesh, Uttar Pradesh and West Bengal lag behind others. At one can also inter from this that in many of the non-selected states, the impact of the number of bank branches would have been substantially of a lesser degree,

The role played by deposits and credit variables is more dominant than the number of bank branches in explaining movements in state domestic product. In all the States except Maharashtra, the influence of the number of bank branches is brought down to a noticeable extent by aggregate deposits or the bank credit variable.

Although results tally with the observations pertaining to All-India, 'bank credit' dominates number of 'bank branches' in a few states.

(2) As at the national level in almost all the States, there is a considerable aggravating effect of number of bank branches on deposits mobilization. Gujarat, Karnataka, Kerala and Tamil Nadu are the States which need special mention especially in comparison with the All-India position. However, in a few States, the effect is not so evident.

The same holds good in the case of bank credit too. Here, the States where the number of bank branches influence bank credit include Gujarat, Karnataka, Kerala, Rajasthan and Tamil Nadu. In a few States like West Bengal, the results are not worth-mentioning.

(3) In many States, the results do not seem to indicate any noticeable effect of bank branches and bank credit to agriculture on agricultural production. Extremely poor results were obtained in West Bengal, closely followed by the States of Bihar, Madhya Pradesh, Rajasthan and Tamil Nadu.

Gujarat testifies to the role of bank branches whereas in Punjab, bank credit to agriculture appears to be an instrumental variable that generates growth in agricultural production.

(4) The results pertaining to growth of small-scale industrial units and bank finance reveal the following:

   (i)   In the states of Punjab, Uttar Pradesh, Andhra Pradesh and Maharashtra, the impact of the number of branches is less felt compare to the all-India picture.

         In particular, Maharashtra deserves special mention in this regard. On the other hand, in Bihar, Rajasthan, Madhya Pradesh, Gujarat and West Bengal, the impact is more significant and pronouncedly felt. Among these States, the impact of growth in bank branches upon the number of small-scale industrial units is the highest in Gujarat.

   (ii)  The inclusion of aggregate deposits along with bank branches exhibits that are identical to those of All-India. It was found that the influence of the number of bank branches is suppressed by the 'aggregate deposits' variable, though West Bengal is an exception to a certain extent.

   (iii) The behavior of 'bank credit' is found to be similar to that of 'aggregate deposits' variable when it is included with the number of bank branches in explaining the number of units. It may be noted that at the all-India level, a similar observation was made. Here, West Bengal and Bihar seem to be exceptions.

   (iv)  Movements in credit disbursal are well-explained by the number of bank branches in all the States. On the one hand in Tamil Nadu, and closely followed by Gujarat, the responsiveness of credit to number of bank branches is very high as compared to All –India. On the other Bihar, West Bengal, Madhya Pradesh and Kerala, this impact is below the all-India level.

   (v)   'Aggregate deposits' variable assumes considerable dominance over the number of bank branches in explaining bank credit to small industrial units which was the case with the all-India results as well. However, in Bihar, Maharashtra, Punjab, Karnataka, Uttar Pradesh and West Bengal, the 'bank branch' variable is significant.

   (vi)  Similar results are obtained in the case of the equation where the number of bank branches and bank credit are considered to explain the variation in credit to small-scale industrial units. As regards the state of Maharashtra, we obtain the most ideal results.

# CHAPTER

# 6

# CONCLUSION

In this chapter, the findings of the study are briefly enumerated. It has three sections. Section I highlights the major findings obtained through different chapters. Section II reveals the probable theoretical and policy implications of the findings and Section III is devoted to an examination of the nature of various findings in relation to the objectives of the study. A list of suggestions is also provided for furtherance of research in this area.

## SECTION I

Chapter 1 explained the role of money and subsequently banking in the economy, the part played by bank branches and their intermediary role, credit creation, capital and investments. While banks were expected to promote the national interest, priorities of which were stipulated by the planning authority from time to time, they were also expected to be economically viable and efficient micro-level institutions.

Over a period of six decades, of planned growth, the contribution of banks has been substantial although (i) whether growth of banks has been uniform upon all regions of the Indian economy? (ii) Whether the spread effect of banking has reached the grass root level? (iii) How far some of the quantifiable socio-economic variables have reflected gains of widening and deepening banking activities?

Chapter 2 surveyed a few studies already made on the subject. It was seen that, in those studies, less emphasis has been attached to the region-specific context to evaluate the implications of development banking in India with special reference to the branch banking concept. Further, in strict sense, attempts have not been made to comprehensively analyse the causal relationship between growth of bank branches and other socio-economic indicators from a historic perspective.

Chapter 3 outlined the evolution of branch banking in India with special reference to the policy perspectives pursued. The need to assign an enhanced role to commercial banking was strongly felt on the eve of nationalisation in 1969 and, consequently, one of the main objectives nationalisation was innovative schemes to promote expansion of bank branches by fixing new targets for geographical and population coverage. Some of the most important aspects like (i) Lead Bank Scheme, (ii) priority sector lending and (iii) poverty alleviation programmes were evolved to achieve specific goals of social welfare and justice. This background of practical banking was used, in the present study, as important points, to take up certain descriptive and quantitative analysis in Chapters 4, 5 and 6 to analyse the issue cited earlier.

Chapter 4 deals with a few aspects of basic needs to highlight deficiencies observed while evaluating a common citizen's necessities of life. An elaborate analysis of economic growth was made in the chapter by attempting a cross sectional analysis pertaining to some key development indicators on the one hand and the measure of branch banking on the other.

A few major States were considered for the analysis. Socio-economic indicators like per capita income, literacy rate, poverty ratio, calorie intake and index of urbanization were used for analysis. The following observations emerged from the analysis:

(i)    Disparities in population coverage by banks have narrowed down disparities considerably since 1977;

(ii)   Disparities among the states in terms of calorie intake had been reduced though expansion of bank branches had no impact on the living standards of the underprivileged citizens measured in terms of calorie intake.

(iii)  The existing tendency of wide disparities in terms of per capita income persisted.

(iv)   The existing disparities had widened in major states in terms of rural poverty ratio.

(v)    Disparities among states in terms of urbanization have narrowed down.

(vi)   Though education was included under priority sector lending, bank branches could not bring about much change in the literacy rates in a few states.

Concentration  bank offices, concentration of economic power, migration of bank funds and leakages in the system; an in-depth analysis of branch banking at the district level to examine the inter-regional disparities as regards selected indicators of developmental banking.

The main points emerging from the analysis, *inter alia,* are as follows:

Disparities in terms of bank branch per thousand population among the various districts have considerably declined. However, in respect of credit deployment per thousand population, states situated in western and southern regions were found to have an edge over the rest of the states. Disparities among the states, therefore, in this respect persist. Perhaps, the urban – rural characteristics dictate this feature. The high variation among districts in Maharashtra and West Bengal substantiated this point.

Chapter 5 dealt with the empirical examination of the cause and effect relationship among critical variables of branch banking and some of the key developmental aspects experienced over the Plan period. The chapter also unraveled the noticeable inter-regional disparities as a result of the impact of branch banking in India. The major observations as indicated by the findings are:

(i)    There appeared to be an element of haphazardness in the expansion programme of banks in relation to national income. In particular, during the post-nationalisation period, the growth of aggregate deposits and aggregate credit has played a more important role as compared to the number of bank branches to induce national income.

(ii)   As regards 'aggregate deposits', 'aggregate credit' and 'savings' function, expected results were obtained. However, 'savings' were determined more dominantly by 'aggregate deposits' than number of bank branches.

(iii)  Estimation of agricultural production function provided unsatisfactory levels, indicating that number of bank branches had no real say, in promoting growth of agricultural production. Industrial production, on the other hand, revealed satisfactory results, which convey the positive role of number of bank branches.

(iv)   In Bihar, Madhya Pradesh, Uttar Pradesh and West Bengal, the influence of number of bank branches upon state domestic product was less during the nationalization period. Except

Maharashtra, in all other states, 'bank deposits' played a major role in explaining the movements in state domestic product. There are some states where 'bank credit' had not influenced growth in national income.

(v)   Branch expansion in Bihar, Madhya Pradesh, Rajasthan, Tamil Nadu and West Bengal had not caused any increase in agricultural production.

(vi)  As regards 'aggregate deposits' and 'aggregate credit', the same results as were noted at the all - India level were achieved in respect of states.

(vii) The results pertaining to growth of small-scale industrial units and bank finance for the same revealed the following:

In the states of Punjab, Uttar Pradesh, Andhra Pradesh and Maharashtra, the impact of the 'number of branches' was less felt compared to at the all-India level. In particular, Maharashtra deserved special mention. In contrast, Bihar, Rajasthan, Madhya Pradesh, Gujarat and West Bengal, the impact was more significant and pronouncedly felt.

The impact of growth in 'bank branches' upon 'small- scale industrial units' was more felt in Gujarat.

Inclusion of 'aggregate deposits' along with 'bank branches' exhibited identical results as at the all-India level. In general, it was found that the influence of number of bank branches was suppressed by the aggregate deposits variable. However, West Bengal was an exception to a certain extent.

The behavior of bank credit was found to be similar to that of the aggregate deposits variable, when it was included with the number of bank branches in explaining the number of units. It may be noted that at the all-India level also, a similar observation was made. Here, West Bengal and Bihar were the exceptions.

Movements in credit disbursal were well explained by the number of bank branches in all the states. In Tamil Nadu, which was closely followed by Gujarat, the responsiveness of credit to number of bank branches was very high as compared to the all-India average. Bihar, West Bengal, Madhya Pradesh and Kerala had this impact below the national average.

The 'aggregate deposits' variable assumed considerable dominance over the number of bank branches in explaining bank credit to small industrial units which was the case with results at the all-India level too. However, in Bihar, Maharashtra, Punjab, Karnataka, Uttar Pradesh and West Bengal, 'bank branch' variable was significant.

Similar results were obtained when the number of bank branches and bank credit were considered to explain the variation in credit to small-scale industrial units. As regards Maharashtra, ideal results were obtained.

The theoretical and policy implications of the major findings of the study are presented in Section II.

## SECTION II

### Theoretical implications:

Evidence indicates that banking system was still to reach the vulnerable sections of the community. In all probabilities, certain branches have attempted window-dressing. Bank credit also helped create new bank deposits.

The primary vehicle of monetary expansion in India, however, has been the Reserve Bank's credit to Government. Everything connected to evidence that deposits had increased at a faster rate than the expansion of bank branches.

Spread effects have not taken place. The 'demonstration effect' continued and the monetization by the banks through new bank branches could not have the desired results.

There is evidence that the resources of the banking system had been diverted to non-banking institutions, pawn shops and money lenders even after the nationalisation of banks, seriously impeding the ability of the banking system to deploy their resource for productive use.

Bank branches have tended to expand, as per the findings, in a haphazard manner, aiding concentration of bank branches at a particular centre, but also concentration of economic power. Bank branches also have transferred mobilized funds from the undeveloped rural sector to the developed centres, widening disparities in the process. Though banks have played both supply-leading and demand-following roles, they could not establish forward and backward linkages. One of the reasons could have been that their registered office or head office was situated at another part of the country.

There are indications that selected sections of the borrowers had been repeatedly granted advances by the commercial banks.

The beneficiaries could have been the richer sections of the community. For instance, small and marginal farmers who cultivated one fifth of the total harvested area and contributed one fourth of the total agricultural output in the country were, thus, ignored to a larger extent, even by the regional rural banks, to grant adequate farm loans at the appropriate time. This also indicated that, in general, banks have favoured richer sections of the community who cornered bank resources, utilised the concessional finance for diversified activities and, thus, avoided the productive purpose for which the loans were granted.  For instance, number of small-scale industrial units did not grow in accordance with the rate of growth of bank credit to the small-scale industries. Similarly, in a few states, agricultural output did not improve. Data on finance to agriculture also show that the share of indirect loans to the sector has always been more, throughout the period, indicating that bank credit did not reach the target.

The results of the findings also indicate the misuse of resources under priority sectors and weaker sections of the community. Even the priority sector advances to transport operators did not increase the fleet of public transport buses and other modes of travel for the common citizens.

The vicious circle, cited earlier, needs further elaboration. When a bank announces a new scheme of deposit, targets are fixed for zonal, regional and branch level to achieve the targets. The branch managers at the micro level are compelled to reach the unrealistic targets by indulging in various methods to improve their rating. One of the methods adopted by branches with the knowledge of the controlling authorities was to lend advances under the stipulated/Government – sponsored schemes. Branches are normally encouraged to reach the targets by the controlling offices. To reach the targets under each eligible category, bank branches trace a few beneficiaries who are neither interested in bank loans nor interested in investing these for productive purposes. While advancing such loans, a margin is demanded as deposits from the borrowers. Branches manage to achieve, in the process, both the targets – advances and deposits – with ease.

As a result, a mere creation of funds had taken place within the branch premises. The empirical results, therefore, point out that financial intermediation by banks could not bring about the required growth rate of the Indian economy during the period covered by the study.

Though a particular bank has, say, thirty types of deposit schemes all carry the same interest. Giving a new name to an existing deposit scheme has added deposits to a bank. This view is strengthened because the recovery of bank loans is poor.

Large loans are, generally, approved by the board which was not made accountable, and a few politically powerful individuals have, perhaps, availed of these. For these lapses, a small branch manager was not at all responsible, but, often is made a scapegoat to fix accountability.

Loans for weaker sections are reduced to a leak since the widening or deepening banking activities could not lift the rural poor from below the poverty line.

The Reserve Bank of India has given powers to write off loans up to a certain limit. Bad and doubtful debts are not published by the RBI.

Loan melas and other poverty alleviation programmes pursued by banks also failed to uplift the rural poor.

The spread effects could not outweigh the backwash effects as the laggard sectors were not developed by banks.

It seems, in a nutshell, that banks have treated equals as unequally while performing its role to promote growth with justice by imposing reservations based on criteria –other than economic - while pursuing social justice.

In view of the above, the following policy aspects are briefly outlined, which need careful consideration.

Banks in the post-nationalisation period have failed to provide adequate support to the planning authority.

Future policy certainly, *inter alia*, calls for consolidation of bank branches, selection of personnel, restructuring of their administrative machinery, more direct control from the RBI, abolition of targets under priority sectors, communication with bank customers in their own languages  and fixing accountability at all levels for efficient functioning of branch officials.

Branch managers have to be given wider powers, necessary freedom to identify the potential productive activity. Priority should be region-specific, based on local requirements to bring about growth.

Branch managers may also be allowed to submit a limited number of specific periodic returns to their own offices.

All vulnerable bank branches need to be provided with adequate security arrangements.

## SECTION III

In the following lines, an attempt is made to evaluate the findings in relation to the objectives with which the study began.

(i)    As regards monetization of the economy, widening and deepening of banking facilities did not show the desired results uniformly; urban – rural dimensions on the one hand, weaker – richer sections of the population on the other, had its say in this regard.

(ii)   (a) Industrial growth has been amply promoted by growth of banking activity in the country despite a deliberate policy to provide credit increasingly to other areas.

In contrast, growth in agricultural sector has not been faster despite a sharp rise in bank lending for the purpose.

(ii)   (b) Growth of small-scale industries does not seem to be significantly influenced by number of bank branches, though bank credit to this sector should have grown along with the number of bank branches and scale of activity in the branches.

(iii) It is extremely difficult to answer in the affirmative about the positive role of lead banks and the relative schemes in the promotion of development in the districts.

(iv) There is evidence to nullify the argument that banks in India played a major role in uplifting the weaker sections of the society.

(v) Inter-state disparities in number of bank branches and agricultural credit had undoubtedly narrowed down. But, this pattern does not emerge as regards to other indicators of banking facilities viz. total bank credit and credit to small-scale industries. Thus, although banking as a concept, has tended to get incorporated as a cultural element, the fruits of its operation do not tend to get distributed to all.

(vi) Statistical evidence has indicated that the structural aspects of the economy where banking variables played a pivotal role have undergone a noticeable change after nationalisation.

## Suggestions

The following are the suggestions for future research:

(i) Removal of multi-collinearity and auto-correlation in the multiple regression analysis which may enhance the reliability and usefulness of the analysis.

(ii) An attempt should be made to uncover more intricate aspects of bidirectional causality between banking and economic development i.e. supply-leading and demand-following roles of banks.

(iii) Concerted and integrated approach is necessary *i.e.* an inter-disciplinary research design incorporating banks and development on the one hand and public administration on the other can fetch sound results which can help in more accurate and probable policy formulations.

# ANNEXURES

## ANNEXURE – I

## District-wise Lead Banks in India and  Development Indicators

| State/Union Territory/ District | Lead Bank | Branches (No.) | Sex- Ratio | Literacy (%) | Density (No. of Persons per sq. Km) |
|---|---|---|---|---|---|
| 1 | 2 | 3 | 4 | 5 | 6 |
| NORTHERN REGION | | 23843 | | | |
| HARYANA | PUNJAB NATIONAL BANK | 4407 | 877 | 75.6 | 573 |
| Ambala | Punjab National Bank | 132 | 885 | 81.8 | 722 |
| Bhiwani | Punjab National Bank | 109 | 886 | 75.2 | 341 |
| Faridabad | Syndicate Bank | 141 | 873 | 81.7 | 2298 |
| Fatehabad | Punjab National Bank | 68 | 902 | 67.9 | 371 |
| Gurgaon | Syndicate Bank | 259 | 854 | 84.7 | 1241 |
| Hissar | Punjab National Bank | 130 | 872 | 72.9 | 438 |
| Jhajjar | Punjab National Bank | 71 | 862 | 80.7 | 522 |
| Jind | Punjab National Bank | 77 | 871 | 71.4 | 493 |
| Kaithal | Punjab National Bank | 73 | 881 | 69.2 | 467 |
| Karnal | Punjab National Bank | 128 | 887 | 74.7 | 598 |
| Kurukshetra | Punjab National Bank | 85 | 888 | 76.3 | 630 |
| Mahendragarh | Punjab National Bank | 56 | 895 | 77.7 | 485 |
| Mewat | Syndicate Bank | 35 | 907 | 54.1 | 729 |
| Palwal | Oriental Bank of Commerce | 57 | 880 | 69.3 | 761 |
| Panchkula | Punjab National Bank | 103 | 873 | 81.9 | 622 |
| Panipet | Punjab National Bank | 109 | 864 | 75.9 | 949 |
| Rewari | Punjab National Bank | 75 | 898 | 81.1 | 562 |
| Rohtak | Punjab National Bank | 113 | 867 | 80.2 | 607 |
| Sirsa | Punjab National Bank | 103 | 897 | 68.8 | 303 |
| Sonipat | Punjab National Bank | 119 | 856 | 79.1 | 697 |
| Yamunanagar | Punjab National Bank | 106 | 877 | 78.1 | 687 |
| HIMACHAL PRADESH | UCO BANK | 1466 | 974 | 82.8 | 123 |
| Bilaspur | UCO Bank | 53 | 981 | 84.6 | 327 |
| Champa | State Bank of India | 57 | 986 | 72.2 | 80 |
| Hamirpur | Punjab National Bank | 63 | 1095 | 88.2 | 406 |

*Continued*

| | | | | | |
|---|---|---|---|---|---|
| Kangra (Dharamshala) | Punjab National Bank | 180 | 1012 | 85.7 | 263 |
| Kinnaur (Peo) | Punjab National Bank | 22 | 819 | 80.1 | 13 |
| Kullu | Punjab National Bank | 56 | 942 | 79.4 | 79 |
| Lahul & Spiti (Kelyong) | State Bank of India | 10 | 903 | 76.8 | 2 |
| Mandi | Punjab National Bank | 114 | 1007 | 81.5 | 253 |
| Shimla | UCO Bank | 157 | 915 | 83.6 | 159 |
| Sirmaur | UCO Bank | 56 | 918 | 78.8 | 188 |
| Solan | UCO Bank | 119 | 880 | 83.7 | 298 |
| Una | Punjab National Bank | 63 | 976 | 86.5 | 328 |
| **JAMMU & KASHMIR** | **THE JAMMU & KASHMIR BANK LTD** | **1634** | **883** | **67.2** | **124** |
| Anantnag | Jammu & kashmir Bank Ltd | 64 | 927 | 62.7 | 375 |
| Badgam | Jammu & Kashmir Bank Ltd | 36 | 894 | 56.1 | 128 |
| Bandipora | Jammu & kashmir Bank Ltd | 16 | 889 | 56.3 | 128 |
| Baramulla | Jammu & Kashmir Bank Ltd | 92 | 885 | 64.6 | 305 |
| Doda | State Bank of India | 19 | 919 | 64.7 | 79 |
| Ganderbal | Jammu & Kashmir Bank Ltd | 23 | 874 | 58.0 | 1151 |
| Jammu | State Bank of India | 200 | 880 | 83.5 | 596 |
| Kargil | State Bank of India | 11 | 810 | 71.3 | 10 |
| Kathua | State Bank of India | 51 | 890 | 73.1 | 232 |
| Kishtwar | State Bank of India | 8 | 920 | 56.2 | 125 |
| Kulgam | Jammu & Kashmir Bank Ltd | 27 | 951 | 59.2 | 925 |
| Kupwara | Jammu & Kashmir Bank Ltd | 44 | 835 | 64.5 | 368 |
| Ladakh (Leh) | State Bank of India | 16 | 690 | 77.2 | 3 |
| Poonch | Jammu & Kashmir Bank Ltd | 20 | 893 | 66.7 | 285 |
| Pulwama | Jammu & Kashmir Bank Ltd | 35 | 912 | 63.5 | 598 |
| Rajouri | Jammu & Kashmir Bank Ltd | 40 | 860 | 68.2 | 235 |
| Ramban | State Bank of India | 16 | 902 | 54.3 | 213 |
| Reasi | State Bank of India | 23 | 890 | 58.2 | 184 |
| Samba | State Bank of India | 28 | 886 | 81.4 | 318 |
| Shupiyan | Jammu & Kashmir Bank Ltd | 16 | 951 | 60.8 | 852 |
| Srinagar | Jammu & Kashmir Bank Ltd | 149 | 900 | 69.4 | 703 |
| Udhampur | State Bank of India | 39 | 870 | 68.5 | 211 |
| **PUNJAB** | **PUNJAB NATIONAL BANK** | **6024** | **893** | **75.8** | **550** |
| Amritsar | Punjab National Bank | 298 | 889 | 76.3 | 932 |
| Barnala | State Bank of patiala | | 876 | 67.8 | 419 |
| Bathinda | State Bank of Patiala | 133 | 868 | 68.3 | 414 |
| Faridkot | Punjab & Sind Bank | 63 | 890 | 70.1 | 424 |
| Fatehgarh Sahib | State Bank of Patiala | 70 | 871 | 79.4 | 508 |
| Fazilka | Punjab National Bank | | | | |
| Ferozpur | Oriental Bank of Commerce | 152 | 893 | 68.9 | 380 |

| | | | | | |
|---|---|---|---|---|---|
| Gurdaspur | Punjab National Bank | 212 | 895 | 80.1 | 649 |
| Hoshiarpur | Punjab National Bank | 193 | 961 | 84.6 | 466 |
| Jalandhar | UCO Bank | 423 | 915 | 82.5 | 831 |
| Kapurthala | Punjab National Bank | 143 | 912 | 79.1 | 501 |
| Ludhiana | Punjab & Sind Bank | 481 | 873 | 82.2 | 975 |
| Mansa | State Bank of Patiala | 62 | 883 | 61.8 | 350 |
| Moga | Punjab & Sind Bank | 104 | 893 | 70.7 | 444 |
| Mohali (Sahibzada Ajit Singh Nagar) | Punjab National Bank | | 879 | 84.0 | |
| Sri Muktsar Sahib | State Bank of Patiala | 78 | 896 | 65.8 | 348 |
| Pathankot | Punjab National Bank | | | | |
| Patiala | State Bank of Patiala | 239 | 891 | 75.3 | 596 |
| Rupnagar | UCO Bank | 82 | 915 | 82.2 | 488 |
| Sangrur | State Bank of Patiala | 141 | 885 | 68.1 | 449 |
| Shahid Bhagat Singh Nagar | Punjab National Bank | | 954 | 79.8 | 479 |
| Tarn Taran | Punjab National Bank | | 900 | 67.8 | 464 |
| **RAJASTHAN** | **BANK OF BARODA** | **6426** | **926** | **66.1** | **201** |
| Ajmer | Bank of Baroda | 190 | 951 | 69.3 | 305 |
| Alwar | Punjab National Bank | 193 | 895 | 70.7 | 438 |
| Banswara | Bank of Baroda | 93 | 980 | 56.3 | 399 |
| Baran | Central Bank of India | 60 | 929 | 66.7 | 175 |
| Barmer | State Bank of Bikaner and Jaipur | 81 | 902 | 56.5 | 92 |
| Bharatpur | Punjab National Bank | 117 | 880 | 70.1 | 503 |
| Bhilwara | Bank of Baroda | 144 | 973 | 61.4 | 230 |
| Bikaner | State Bank of Bikaner and Jaipur | 155 | 905 | 65.1 | 78 |
| Bundi | Bank of Baroda | 68 | 925 | 61.5 | 193 |
| Chittaurgarh | Bank of Baroda | 94 | 972 | 61.7 | 193 |
| Churu | Bank of Baroda | 117 | 940 | 66.8 | 148 |
| Dausa | UCO Bank | 72 | 905 | 68.2 | 476 |
| Dholpur | Punab National Bank | 38 | 846 | 69.1 | 398 |
| Dungarpur | Bank of Baroda | 66 | 994 | 59.5 | 368 |
| Ganganagar | Oriental Bank of Commerce | 157 | 887 | 69.6 | 179 |
| Hanumangarh | State Bank of Bikaner and Jaipur | 109 | 906 | 67.1 | 184 |
| Jaipur | UCO Bank | 548 | 910 | 75.5 | 598 |
| Jaisalmer | State Bank of Bikaner and Jaipur | 39 | 852 | 57.2 | 17 |
| Jalore | State Bank of Bikaner and Jaipur | 70 | 952 | 54.9 | 172 |

*Continued*

| | | | | | |
|---|---|---|---|---|---|
| Jhalawar | Central Bank of India | 67 | 946 | 61.5 | 227 |
| Jhunjhunun | Bank of Baroda | 110 | 950 | 74.1 | 361 |
| Jodhpur | UCO Bank | 203 | 916 | 65.9 | 161 |
| Karauli | Bank of Baroda | 48 | 861 | 66.2 | 264 |
| Kota | Central Bank of India | 153 | 911 | 76.6 | 374 |
| Nagaur | UCO Bank | 136 | 950 | 62.8 | 187 |
| Pali | State Bank of Bikaner and Jaipur | 131 | 987 | 62.4 | 165 |
| Pratapgarh | Bank of Baroda | | 983 | 56.0 | 211 |
| Rajsamand | State Bank of Bikaner and Jaipur | 68 | 990 | 63.1 | 302 |
| Sawai Madhopur | Bank of Baroda | 73 | 897 | 65.4 | 257 |
| Sikar | Punjab National Bank | 134 | 747 | 71.9 | 346 |
| Sirohi | State Bank of Bikaner and Jaipur | 64 | 940 | 55.3 | 202 |
| Tonk | Bank of Baroda | 75 | 952 | 61.6 | 198 |
| Udaipur | State Bank of Bikaner and Jaipur | 190 | 958 | 61.8 | 242 |
| **CHANDIGARH** | **PUNJAB NATIONAL BANK** | **439** | **818** | **86.1** | **9252** |
| Chandigarh | Punjab National Bank | 439 | 818 | 86.1 | 9252 |
| **NCT OF DELHI** | **ORIENTAL BANK OF COMMERCE** | **3447** | **866** | **88.3** | **11297** |
| Central Delhi | Canara Bank | | | | |
| East Delhi | Punjab National Bank | | | | |
| New Delhi | Canara Bank | | | | |
| North Delhi | Oriental Bank of Commerce | | | | |
| North East Delhi | Punjab National Bank | | | | |
| North West Delhi | Punjab National Bank | | | | |
| Shahdara | Bank of Baroda | | | | |
| South Delhi | State Bank of India | | | | |
| South East Delhi | State Bank of India | | | | |
| South west Delhi | State Bank of India | | | | |
| West Delhi | Canara Bank | | | | |
| **NORTH - EASTERN REGION** | | 3345 | | | |
| **ARUNACHAL PRADESH** | **STATE BANK OF INDIA** | **135** | **920** | **65.4** | **17** |
| Anjaw | State Bank of India | 1 | 839 | 56.5 | 3 |
| Chunglang | State Bank of India | 4 | 926 | 59.8 | 32 |
| Dibang Valley | State Bank of India | 1 | 813 | 64.1 | 1 |
| East Kameng | State Bank of India | 2 | 980 | 72.5 | 19 |

| | | | | | |
|---|---|---|---|---|---|
| East Siang | State Bank of India | 9 | 1029 | 60.1 | 27 |
| Kurung Kumey | State Bank of India | 1 | 1032 | 48.8 | 15 |
| Lohit | State Bank of India | 5 | 912 | 68.2 | 28 |
| Longding | State Bank of India | | | | |
| Lower Dibang Valley | State Bank of India | 1 | 928 | 69.1 | 14 |
| Lower Subansiri | State Bank of India | 5 | 984 | 74.4 | 24 |
| Papum Pure | State Bank of India | 21 | 980 | 80.1 | 51 |
| Tawang | State Bank of India | 3 | 714 | 59.1 | 23 |
| Tirap | State Bank of India | 4 | 944 | 52.2 | 47 |
| Upper Siang | State Bank of India | 2 | 889 | 60.1 | 5 |
| Upper Subansiri | State Bank of India | 3 | 998 | 63.8 | 12 |
| West Kameng | State Bank of India | 7 | 819 | 67.1 | 12 |
| West Siang | State Bank of India | 7 | 930 | 66.5 | 23 |
| <u>ASSAM</u> | **STATE BANK OF INDIA** | <u>2103</u> | <u>954</u> | <u>72.2</u> | <u>397</u> |
| Baksa | State Bank of India | 22 | 974 | 69.3 | 475 |
| Barpeta | UCO Bank | 55 | 953 | 63.8 | 632 |
| Bongaigaon | State Bank of India | 30 | 966 | 69.7 | 425 |
| Cachar | United Bank of India | 80 | 959 | 79.3 | 459 |
| Chirang | State Bank of India | 14 | 969 | 63.6 | 244 |
| Darrang | UCO Bank | 25 | 954 | 63.1 | 491 |
| Dhemaji | United Bank of India | 18 | 953 | 72.7 | 213 |
| Dhubri | UCO Bank | 43 | 953 | 58.3 | 683 |
| Dibrugarh | United Bank of India | 87 | 961 | 76.1 | 393 |
| Dima Hasao (North Cachar Hills) | State Bank of India | | 932 | 77.5 | 44 |
| Goalpara | UCO Bank | 31 | 964 | 67.4 | 553 |
| Golaghat | United Bank of India | 51 | 964 | 77.4 | 302 |
| Hailakandi | United Bank of India | 19 | 951 | 74.3 | 497 |
| Jorhat | United Bank of India | 73 | 962 | 82.2 | 383 |
| Kakrojhar | UCO Bank | 22 | 959 | 65.2 | 280 |
| Kamrup | UCO Bank | 82 | 949 | 75.6 | 436 |
| Kamrup Metropolitan | UCO Bank | 159 | 936 | 88.7 | 2010 |
| Karbi Anglong | State Bank of India | 50 | 951 | 69.3 | 93 |
| Karimganj | United Bank of India | 50 | 963 | 78.2 | 673 |
| Lakhimpur | United Bank of India | 47 | 968 | 77.2 | 457 |
| Morigaon | United Bank of India | 27 | 967 | 68.1 | 618 |
| Nagaon | United Bank of India | 92 | 962 | 72.4 | 711 |
| Nalbari | UCO Bank | 37 | 949 | 78.6 | 763 |
| Sivasagar | United Bank of India | 62 | 954 | 80.4 | |
| Sonitpur | UCO Bank | 85 | 956 | 67.3 | |
| Tinsukia | United Bank of India | 76 | 952 | 70.1 | |

*Continued*

| | | | | | |
|---|---|---|---|---|---|
| Udalguri | State Bank of India | 25 | 973 | 65.4 | |
| **MANIPUR** | **STATE BANK OF INDIA** | **138** | **987** | **76.9** | **122** |
| Bishenpur | United Bank of India | 6 | 999 | 75.9 | 485 |
| Chandel | State Bank of India | 5 | 933 | 71.1 | 43 |
| Churachandpur | State Bank of India | 4 | 975 | 82.8 | 59 |
| Imphal (East) | United Bank of India | 10 | 1017 | 82.0 | 638 |
| Imphal (West) | State Bank of India | 27 | 1031 | 86.1 | 992 |
| Senapati | State Bank of India | 12 | 937 | 63.6 | 109 |
| Tamenglong | United Bank of India | 4 | 943 | 70.1 | 32 |
| Thoubal | State Bank of India | 8 | 1002 | 74.5 | 818 |
| Ukhrul | United Bank of India | 4 | 943 | 81.4 | 40 |
| **MEGHALAYA** | **STATE BANK OF INDIA** | **294** | **986** | **74.4** | **132** |
| East Garo Hills | State Bank of India | 16 | 972 | 74.1 | 121 |
| East Jaintia Hills | State Bank of India | | | | |
| East Khasi Hills | State Bank of India | 92 | 1011 | 84.2 | 292 |
| Jaintia Hills | State Bank of India | 26 | 1013 | 61.6 | |
| North Garo Hills | State Bank of India | | | | |
| Ri Bhoi | State Bank of India | 15 | 953 | 75.7 | 109 |
| South Garo Hills | State Bank of India | | | | |
| South West Garo Hills | State Bank of India | 3 | 945 | 71.7 | 77 |
| South West Khasi Hills | State Bank of India | | | | |
| West garo Hills | State Bank of India | 29 | 984 | 67.6 | 173 |
| West Khasi Hills | State Bank of India | 20 | 980 | 77.9 | 73 |
| **MIZORAM** | **STATE BANK OF INDIA** | **151** | 975 | **91.3** | **52** |
| Aizawal | State Bank of India | 40 | 1009 | 97.9 | 113 |
| Champhai | State Bank of India | 9 | 984 | 95.9 | 39 |
| Kolasib | State Bank of India | 8 | 956 | 93.5 | 60 |
| Lawngtlai | State Bank of India | 3 | 945 | 65.9 | 46 |
| Lunglei | State Bank of India | 11 | 947 | 88.9 | 34 |
| Mamit | State Bank of India | 10 | 927 | 84.9 | 28 |
| Saiha | State Bank of India | 4 | 979 | 90.1 | 40 |
| Serchhip | State Bank of India | 8 | 979 | 90.1 | 46 |
| **NAGALAND** | **STATE BANK OF INDIA** | **145** | **931** | **79.6** | **119** |
| Dimapur | State Bank of India | 28 | 919 | 84.8 | 410 |
| Kiphire | State Bank of India | | 956 | 69.5 | 66 |
| Kohima | State Bank of India | 18 | 928 | 85.2 | 213 |
| Longleng | State Bank of India | | 905 | 72.2 | 89 |
| Mokokchung | State Bank of India | 10 | 925 | 91.6 | 120 |
| Peren | State Bank of India | | 915 | 78 | 55 |
| Mon | State Bank of India | 3 | 899 | 57.1 | 145 |

| | | | | | |
|---|---|---|---|---|---|
| Phek | State Bank of India | 6 | 951 | 78.1 | 81 |
| Tuensang | State Bank of India | 4 | 929 | 73.1 | 98 |
| Wokha | State Bank of India | 7 | 968 | 87.7 | 120 |
| Zunheboto | State Bank of India | 6 | 976 | 85.3 | 112 |
| **TRIPURA** | **UNITED BANK OF INDIA** | **379** | **961** | **87.2** | **350** |
| Dhalai | United Bank of India | 15 | 944 | 85.7 | 157 |
| Gomati | United Bank of India | | | | |
| Khowai | United Bank of India | | | | |
| North Tripura | United Bank of India | 35 | 967 | 87.5 | 288 |
| Sepahijala | United Bank of India | | | | |
| South Tripura | United Bank of India | 48 | 957 | 84.7 | 283 |
| Unakoti | United Bank of India | | | | |
| West Tripura | United Bank of India | 115 | 962 | 88.7 | 973 |
| EASTERN REGION | | 20893 | | | |
| **BIHAR** | **STATE BANK OF INDIA** | **6210** | **916** | **61.8** | **1102** |
| Araria | State Bank of India | 72 | 921 | 53.5 | 992 |
| Arwal | Punjab National Bank | 27 | 928 | 67.4 | 1098 |
| Aurangabad | Punjab National Bank | 85 | 926 | 70.3 | 760 |
| Banka | UCO Bank | 54 | 907 | 58.2 | 672 |
| Begusarai | UCO Bank | 109 | 895 | 63.9 | 1540 |
| Bhagalpur | UCO Bank | 129 | 880 | 63.1 | 1180 |
| Bhojpur ( Arrah) | Punjab National Bank | 112 | 907 | 70.5 | 1136 |
| Buxar | Punjab National Bank | 74 | 922 | 70.1 | 1003 |
| Darbhanga | Central Bank of India | 160 | 911 | 56.6 | 1721 |
| Gaya | Punjab National Bank | 173 | 937 | 63.7 | 880 |
| Gopalganj | Central Bank of India | 97 | 1021 | 65.5 | 1258 |
| Jamui | State Bank of India | 56 | 922 | 59.8 | 567 |
| Jehanabad | Punjab National Bank | 41 | 922 | 66.8 | 1206 |
| Kaimur (Bhabua) | Punjab National Bank | 66 | 920 | 69.3 | 488 |
| katihar | Central Bank of India | 100 | 919 | 52.2 | 1004 |
| khagaria | Union Bank of India | 50 | 886 | 57.9 | 1115 |
| kishanganj | State Bank of India | 53 | 950 | 55.5 | 898 |
| Lakhisarai | Punjab National Bank | 36 | 902 | 62.4 | 815 |
| Madhepura | State Bank of India | 58 | 911 | 52.3 | 1116 |
| Madhubani | Central Bank of India | 150 | 926 | 58.6 | 1279 |
| Munger | UCO Bank | 60 | 876 | 70.5 | 958 |
| Muzaffarpur | Central Bank of India | 195 | 900 | 63.4 | 1506 |
| Nalanda | Punjab National Bank | 115 | 922 | 64.4 | 1220 |
| Nawada | Punjab National Bank | 68 | 939 | 59.8 | 889 |
| Paschim Champaran | Central Bank of India | 120 | 909 | 55.7 | 753 |

*Continued*

| | | | | | |
|---|---|---|---|---|---|
| Patna | Punjab National Bank | 393 | 897 | 70.7 | 1803 |
| Purbi Champaran | Central Bank of India | 158 | 902 | 55.8 | 1281 |
| Purnia | State Bank of India | 95 | 921 | 51.1 | 1014 |
| Rohtas (Sasaram) | Punjab National Bank | 110 | 918 | 73.4 | 763 |
| Saharsa | State Bank of India | 59 | 906 | 53.2 | 1125 |
| samastipur | Union Bank of India | 148 | 911 | 61.9 | 1465 |
| saran | Central Bank of India | 143 | 954 | 66.1 | 1493 |
| sheikhpura | Canara Bank | 22 | 930 | 63.9 | 922 |
| Sheohar | Bank of Baroda | 17 | 893 | 53.8 | 1882 |
| Sitamarhi | Bank of Baroda | 101 | 899 | 52.1 | 1491 |
| Siwan | Central Bank of India | 133 | 988 | 69.5 | 1495 |
| Supaul | State Bank of India | 68 | 929 | 57.7 | 919 |
| Vaishali | Central Bank of India | 118 | 895 | 66.6 | 1717 |
| **JHARKHAND** | **BANK OF INDIA** | **2763** | **947** | **66.4** | **414** |
| Bokaro | Bank of India | 127 | 922 | 72.1 | 716 |
| Chatra | Bank of India | 36 | 953 | 60.2 | 275 |
| Deoghar | State Bank of India | 81 | 925 | 64.9 | 602 |
| Dhanbad | Bank of India | 151 | 909 | 74.5 | 1284 |
| Dumka | Allahabad Bank | 77 | 977 | 61.1 | 300 |
| Garhwa | State Bank of India | 40 | 935 | 60.3 | 327 |
| Giridih | Bank of India | 99 | 944 | 63.1 | 497 |
| Godda | Allahabad Bank | 62 | 938 | 56.4 | 622 |
| Gumla | Bank of India | 46 | 993 | 65.7 | 193 |
| Hazaribag | Bank of India | 83 | 947 | 70.1 | 403 |
| Jamtara | State Bank of India | 35 | 954 | 64.6 | 439 |
| Khunti | Bank of India | 27 | 997 | 63.9 | 215 |
| Koderma | Bank of India | 31 | 950 | 66.8 | 427 |
| Latehar | State Bank of India | 23 | 967 | 59.5 | 200 |
| Lohardagga | Bank of India | 19 | 985 | 67.6 | 310 |
| Pakur | State Bank of India | 39 | 989 | 48.8 | 498 |
| Palamau | State Bank of India | 85 | 928 | 44.2 | 381 |
| Paschimi Slnghbhum | Bank of India | 79 | 1005 | 58.6 | 209 |
| Purbi Singhbhum | Bank of India | 179 | 949 | 75.5 | 648 |
| Ramgarh | Bank of India | 49 | 921 | 73.2 | 684 |
| Ranchi | Bank of India | 207 | 949 | 76.1 | 557 |
| Sahebganj | State Bank of India | 50 | 952 | 52.1 | 719 |
| Seraikela-Kharsawan | Bank of India | 53 | 956 | 67.7 | 390 |
| Simdega | Bank of India | 27 | 997 | 63.9 | 160 |
| **ODISHA** | **UCO BANK** | **4410** | **978** | **72.9** | **269** |
| Anugul | UCO Bank | 89 | 943 | 77.5 | 199 |
| Balangir | State Bank of India | 80 | 987 | 64.7 | 251 |

| | | | | | |
|---|---|---|---|---|---|
| Baleshwar | UCO Bank | 130 | 957 | 79.8 | 609 |
| Bargarh | State Bank of India | 78 | 977 | 74.6 | 253 |
| Bhadrak | UCO Bank | 72 | 981 | 82.8 | 601 |
| Boudh | State Bank of India | 21 | 991 | 71.6 | 142 |
| Cuttack | UCO Bank | 205 | 940 | 85.5 | 666 |
| Deogarh | State Bank of India | 20 | 975 | 72.6 | 106 |
| Dhenkanal | UCO Bank | 72 | 947 | 78.8 | 268 |
| Gajapati | Andhra Bank | 34 | 1043 | 53.5 | 133 |
| Ganjam | Andhra Bank | 231 | 983 | 71.1 | 429 |
| Jagatsinghpur | UCO Bank | 88 | 968 | 86.6 | 681 |
| Jajapur | State Bank of India | 98 | 973 | 80.1 | 630 |
| Jharsuguda | State Bank of India | 51 | 953 | 78.9 | 274 |
| Kalahandi | State Bank of India | 87 | 1003 | 59.2 | 199 |
| Kandhamal | State Bank of India | 42 | 1037 | 64.1 | 91 |
| Kendrapara | State Bank of India | 74 | 1007 | 85.2 | 545 |
| Kendnjhar | Bank of India | 118 | 988 | 68.2 | 217 |
| Khurdha | State Bank of India | 290 | 929 | 86.9 | 799 |
| Koraput | State Bank of India | 73 | 1032 | 49.2 | 156 |
| Malkangiri | State Bank of India | 20 | 1020 | 48.5 | 106 |
| Mayurbhanj | Bank of India | 155 | 1006 | 63.2 | 241 |
| Nawapara | State Bank of India | 30 | 1021 | 57.4 | 157 |
| Nawrangpur | State Bank of India | 34 | 1019 | 46.4 | 230 |
| Nayagarh | State Bank of India | 58 | 915 | 80.4 | 247 |
| Puri | UCO Bank | 116 | 963 | 84.7 | 488 |
| Rayagada | State Bank of India | 57 | 1051 | 49.8 | 136 |
| Sambalpur | State Bank of India | 95 | 976 | 76.2 | 158 |
| Sonepur (Subarnapur) | State Bank of India | 29 | 960 | 74.4 | 279 |
| Sundargarh | State Bank of India | 142 | 973 | 73.3 | 214 |
| **SIKKIM** | **STATE BANK OF INDIA** | **122** | | | |
| East Sikkim | State Bank of India | 44 | 873 | 83.9 | 295 |
| North sikkim | State Bank of India | 7 | 967 | 78.1 | 10 |
| South Sikkim | State Bank of India | 11 | 915 | 81.4 | 196 |
| West Sikkim | State Bank of India | 9 | 942 | 77.4 | 117 |
| **WEST BENGAL** | **UNITED BANK OF INDIA** | **7327** | **947** | **76.3** | **1029** |
| Bankura | United Bank of India | 174 | 957 | 70.3 | 523 |
| Barddhaman | UCO Bank | 438 | 945 | 76.2 | 1100 |
| Birbhum | UCO Bank | 183 | 956 | 70.7 | 771 |
| Dakshin Dinajpur | United Bank of India | 67 | 956 | 72.8 | 753 |
| Darjiling | Central Bank of India | 141 | 970 | 80.1 | 585 |
| Haora | UCO Bank | 251 | 939 | 83.3 | 3300 |
| Hugli | UCO Bank | 293 | 961 | 81.8 | 1751 |

*Continued*

| | | | | | |
|---|---|---|---|---|---|
| Jalpaiguri | Central Bank of India | 146 | 953 | 73.3 | 621 |
| Koch Bihar | Central Bank of India | 119 | 942 | 74.8 | 833 |
| Kolkata | State Bank of India | 1121 | 908 | 86.3 | 24252 |
| Maldah | United Bank of India | 154 | 944 | 61.7 | 1071 |
| Paschim Medinipur | United Bank of India | 518 | 966 | 78.1 | 1076 |
| Purba Medinipur | United Bank of India | | 938 | 87.1 | 923 |
| Murshidabad | United Bank of India | 235 | 958 | 66.6 | 1334 |
| Nadia | United Bank of India | 200 | 947 | 75.1 | 1316 |
| North 24 Parganas | Allahabad Bank | 493 | 955 | 84.1 | 2463 |
| Puruliya | United Bank of India | 121 | 957 | 64.5 | 468 |
| South 24 Parganas | United Bank of India | 280 | 956 | 77.5 | 819 |
| Uttara Dinajpur | United Bank of India | 89 | 939 | 59.1 | 956 |
| **ANDAMAN & NICOBAR ISLANDS** | **STATE BANK OF INDIA** | **61** | **878** | **86.6** | **46** |
| Nicobar  Islands | State Bank of India | 3 | 777 | 78.1 | |
| North and Middle Andaman | State Bank of India | 5 | 925 | 83.9 | |
| South Andaman | State Bank of India | 29 | 871 | 89.1 | |
| **CENTRAL REGION** | | 25926 | | | |
| **CHHATTISGARH** | **STATE BANK OF INDIA** | **1217** | **991** | **70.3** | **189** |
| Balod | Dena Bank | | | | |
| Baloda Bazar | State Bank of India | | | | |
| Balrampur | Central Bank of India | | | | |
| Bastar (Jagdalpur) | State Bank of India | 59 | 1023 | 54.1 | 87 |
| Bemetara | State Bank of India | | | | |
| Bijapur | State Bank of India | | 984 | 4039 | 69 |
| Bilaspur | State Bank of India | 115 | 971 | 70.8 | 337 |
| Dantewada | State Bank of India | 24 | 1020 | 42.1 | 59 |
| Dhamtari | Dena Bank | 37 | 1010 | 78.4 | 394 |
| Durg | Dena Bank | 184 | 988 | 79.1 | 391 |
| Gariaband | Dena Bank | | | | |
| Jangir-Champa | State Bank of India | 59 | 986 | 73.1 | 421 |
| Jashpur | State Bank of India | 42 | 1005 | 67.9 | 146 |
| Kabirdham (Kawardha) | State Bank of India | 23 | 996 | 60.9 | 195 |
| Kanker | State Bank of India | 26 | 1006 | 70.3 | 115 |
| Korba | State Bank of India | 65 | 969 | 72.4 | 183 |
| Koria | Central Bank of India | 42 | 968 | 70.6 | 100 |
| Mahasamund | Dena Bank | 45 | 1017 | 71.1 | 216 |
| Mungeli | State Bank of India | | | | |
| Narayanpur | State Bank of India | 5 | 994 | 48.6 | 20 |

| | | | | | |
|---|---|---|---|---|---|
| Raigarh | State Bank of India | 84 | 984 | 75.6 | 211 |
| Raipur | Dena Bank | 210 | 991 | 73.3 | 310 |
| Rajnandgaon | Dena Bank | 77 | 1015 | 76.1 | 191 |
| Surguja | Central Bank of India | 111 | 978 | 60.1 | 150 |
| Sukma | State Bank of India | | | | |
| Surajpur | Central Bank of India | | | | |
| **MADHYA PRADESH** | **CENTRAL BANK OF INDIA** | <u>5997</u> | <u>930</u> | <u>69.3</u> | <u>236</u> |
| Agar-Malwa | Bank of India | | | | |
| Alirajpur | Bank of Baroda | 19 | 1011 | 36.1 | 229 |
| Anuppur | Central Bank of India | 36 | 976 | 67.9 | 200 |
| Ashok Nagar | State Bank of India | 38 | 904 | 66.4 | 181 |
| Balaghat | Central Bank of India | 81 | 1021 | 77.1 | 184 |
| Barwani | Bank of India | 59 | 982 | 49.1 | 256 |
| Betul | Central Bank of India | 76 | 971 | 68.9 | 157 |
| Bhind | Central Bank of India | 57 | 837 | 75.3 | 382 |
| Bhopal | Bank of India | 272 | 918 | 80.4 | 854 |
| Burhanpur | Bank of India | 39 | 883 | 63.7 | 221 |
| Chhatarpur | State Bank of India | 73 | 951 | 64.4 | 203 |
| Chhindwara | Central Bank of India | 113 | 964 | 71.2 | 177 |
| Damoh | State Bank of India | 61 | 910 | 69.7 | 173 |
| Datia | Punjab National Bank | 41 | 873 | 72.6 | 292 |
| Dewas | Bank of India | 92 | 942 | 69.4 | 223 |
| Dharwad | Bank of India | 118 | 964 | 59.1 | 268 |
| Dindori | Central Bank of India | 25 | 1002 | 63.9 | 94 |
| East Nimar (Khandwa) | Bank of India | 71 | 943 | 66.4 | 178 |
| Guna | State Bank of India | 59 | 912 | 63.2 | 194 |
| Gwalior | Central Bank of India | 149 | 864 | 76.7 | 445 |
| Harda | State Bank of India | 36 | 935 | 72.5 | 171 |
| Hoshangabad | Central Bank of India | 87 | 914 | 75.3 | 785 |
| Indore | Bank of India | 319 | 928 | 80.9 | 839 |
| Jabalpur | Central Bank of India | 190 | 929 | 81.1 | 472 |
| Jhabua | Bank of Baroda | 33 | 990 | 43.3 | 285 |
| Katni | State Bank of India | 68 | 952 | 72.1 | 261 |
| Mandla | Central Bank of India | 49 | 1008 | 66.9 | 182 |
| Mandsaur | Central Bank of India | 63 | 963 | 71.8 | 242 |
| Morena | Central Bank of India | 63 | 840 | 71.1 | 394 |
| Narsimhapur | Central Bank of India | 67 | 920 | 75.7 | 213 |
| Neemuch | State Bank oF India | 53 | 954 | 70.8 | 194 |
| Panna | State Bank of India | 38 | 905 | 64.8 | 142 |
| Raisen | Central Bank of India | 69 | 901 | 73.1 | 157 |

*Continued*

| | | | | | |
|---|---|---|---|---|---|
| Rajgarh | Bank of India | 79 | 956 | 61.2 | 251 |
| Ratlam | Central Bank of India | 85 | 971 | 66.8 | 299 |
| Rewari | Union Bank of India | 123 | 931 | 71.6 | 374 |
| Sagar | Central Bank of India | 121 | 893 | 76.5 | 272 |
| Satna | Allahabad Bank | 127 | 926 | 72.3 | 297 |
| Sehore | Bank of India | 71 | 918 | 70.1 | 199 |
| Seoni | Central Bank of India | 65 | 982 | 72.1 | 157 |
| Shahdol | Central Bank of India | 47 | 974 | 66.7 | 172 |
| Shajapur | Bank of India | 72 | 938 | 69.1 | 244 |
| Sheopur | State Bank of India | 20 | 901 | 57.4 | 104 |
| Shivpuri | State Bank of India | 66 | 877 | 62.6 | 168 |
| Sidhi | Union Bank of India | 45 | 957 | 64.4 | 232 |
| Singrauli | Union Bank of India | | 920 | 75.7 | 208 |
| Tikamgarh | State Bank of India | 56 | 901 | 61.4 | 286 |
| Ujjain | Bank of India | 135 | 955 | 72.3 | 356 |
| Umaria | State Bank of India | 26 | 950 | 65.9 | 158 |
| Vidisha | State Bank of Indore | 70 | 896 | 70.5 | 198 |
| West Nimar (Khargone) | Bank of India | 90 | 965 | 62.7 | 233 |
| **UTTAR PRADESH** | **BANK OF BARODA** | **15773** | **908** | **67.7** | **828** |
| Agra | Canara Bank | 284 | 868 | 71.6 | 1084 |
| Aligarh | Canara Bank | 179 | 882 | 67.5 | 1007 |
| Allahabad | Bank of Baroda | 311 | 901 | 72.3 | 1087 |
| Ambedkar Nagar | Bank of Baroda | 80 | 978 | 72.2 | 1021 |
| Auraiya | Central Bank of India | 57 | 864 | 79.1 | 681 |
| Azamgarh | Union Bank of India | 202 | 1019 | 70.9 | 1139 |
| Baghpat | Syndicate Bank | 56 | 861 | 72.1 | 986 |
| Bahraich | Allahabad Bank | 110 | 892 | 49.4 | 415 |
| Balia | Central Bank of India | 143 | 937 | 70.9 | 1081 |
| Balrampur | Allahabad Bank | 77 | 928 | 49.5 | 642 |
| Banda | Allahabad Bank | 86 | 863 | 66.7 | 404 |
| Barabanki | Bank of India | 155 | 910 | 61.8 | 739 |
| Bareilly | Bank of Baroda | 225 | 887 | 58.5 | 1084 |
| Basti | State Bank of India | 97 | 963 | 67.2 | 916 |
| Bijnor | Punjab National Bank | 158 | 917 | 68.5 | 808 |
| Badaun | Punjab National Bank | 125 | 871 | 51.3 | 718 |
| Bulandshahr | Punjab National Bank | 152 | 896 | 68.9 | 788 |
| Chandauli | Union Bank of India | 66 | 918 | 71.5 | 768 |
| Chhtrapati Sahuji Maharaj Nager | Bank of Baroda | | | | |
| Chitrakoot | Allahabad Bank | 44 | 879 | 65.1 | 315 |
| Dooria | Central Bank of India | 117 | 1017 | 71.1 | 1220 |

| | | | | | |
|---|---|---|---|---|---|
| Etah | Canara Bank | 73 | 873 | 70.8 | 717 |
| Etawah | Central Bank of India | 71 | 870 | 78.4 | 683 |
| Faizabad | Bank of Baroda | 101 | 962 | 68.7 | 1054 |
| Farrukhabad | Bank of India | 87 | 874 | 69.1 | 865 |
| Fatepur | Bank of Baroda | 104 | 901 | 67.4 | 634 |
| Firozabad | State Bank of India | 97 | 875 | 71.9 | 1044 |
| Gautam Buddha Nagar | Syndicate Bank | 206 | 851 | 80.1 | 1252 |
| Ghaziabad | Syndicate Bank | 314 | 881 | 78.1 | 3967 |
| Ghazipur | Union Bank of India | 163 | 952 | 71.8 | 1072 |
| Gonda | Allahabad Bank | 130 | 921 | 58.7 | 857 |
| Gorakhpur | State Bank of India | 219 | 950 | 70.8 | 1336 |
| Hamirpur | Allahabad Bank | 59 | 861 | 68.8 | 268 |
| Hardoi | Bank of India | 144 | 868 | 64.6 | 683 |
| Jalaun | Allahabad Bank | 87 | 865 | 73.8 | 366 |
| Jaunpur | Union Bank of India | 192 | 1024 | 71.6 | 1108 |
| Jhansi | Punjab National Bank | 127 | 890 | 75.1 | 398 |
| Jyotiba Phule Nagar (Amroha) | Syndicate Bank | 84 | 910 | 63.8 | 818 |
| Kanauj | Bank of India | 61 | 879 | 72.7 | 792 |
| Kanpur Dehat (Ramabai Nagar) | Bank of Baroda | 134 | 865 | 75.8 | 594 |
| Kanpur Nagar (Chhatrpati S.M. Nagar) | Bank of Baroda | 372 | 862 | 79.7 | 1515 |
| Kanshiram Nagar (Kasganj) | Canara Bank | | 880 | 61.0 | 736 |
| Kaushambi | Bank of Baroda | 52 | 908 | 61.3 | 897 |
| Lakhimpur Kheri | Allahabad Bank | 150 | 894 | 60.6 | 523 |
| Kushi Nagar (Padrauna) | Central Bank of India | 109 | 961 | 65.3 | 1226 |
| Lalitpur | Punjab National Bank | 48 | 906 | 63.5 | 242 |
| Lucknow | Bank of India | 507 | 917 | 77.3 | 1815 |
| Mahamaya Nagar (Hathras) | Canara Bank | | 871 | 71.6 | 851 |
| Maharajganj | State Bank of India | 83 | 943 | 62.8 | 903 |
| Mahoba | Allahabad Bank | 37 | 878 | 65.3 | 288 |
| Mainpuri | Bank of India | 74 | 881 | 76.1 | 670 |
| Mathura | Syndicate Bank | 173 | 863 | 70.4 | 761 |
| Mau (Mau Nath Bahnjan) | Union Bank of India | 85 | 979 | 73.1 | 1287 |
| Meerut | Syndicate Bank | 251 | 886 | 72.8 | 1342 |
| Mirzapur | Allahabad Bank | 106 | 903 | 68.5 | 761 |
| Moradabad | Syndicate Bank | 233 | 906 | 56.8 | 1281 |
| Muzaffarnagar | Punjab National Bank | 214 | 889 | 69.1 | 1033 |

*Continued*

| | | | | | |
|---|---|---|---|---|---|
| Panchsheel Nager | Syndicate Bank | | | | |
| Pilibhit | Bank of Baroda | 84 | 895 | 61.5 | 567 |
| Prabudh Nagar(Shamli) | Punjab National Bank | | | | |
| Pratapgarh | Bank of Baroda | 138 | 998 | 70.1 | 854 |
| Ramabai Nagar (Kanpur Dehat) | Bank of Baroda | 134 | 865 | 75.8 | 594 |
| Rai Bareli | Bank of Baroda | 153 | 943 | 67.3 | 739 |
| Rampur | Bank of Baroda | 116 | 909 | 53.3 | 987 |
| Saharanpur | Punjab National Bank | 181 | 890 | 70.5 | 939 |
| Sant Kabir Nagar | State Bank of India | 61 | 972 | 66.7 | 1014 |
| Sant Ravidas Nagar (Bhadohi) | Union Bank of India | 59 | 955 | 69.1 | 1531 |
| Shahjahanpur | Bank of Baroda | 136 | 872 | 59.5 | 673 |
| Shravasti | Allahabad Bank | 57 | 881 | 46.7 | 572 |
| Sidharthan Nagar | State Bank of India | 86 | 976 | 59.3 | 882 |
| Sitapur | Allahabad Bank | 176 | 888 | 61.1 | 779 |
| Sonbhadra | Allahabad Bank | 72 | 918 | 64.1 | 274 |
| Sultanpur | Bank of Baroda | 159 | 983 | 69.3 | 855 |
| Unnao | Bank of India | 123 | 907 | 66.4 | 682 |
| Varanasi | Union Bank of India | 253 | 913 | 75.6 | 2399 |
| **UTTARAKHAND** | **STATE BANK OF INDIA** | **1903** | **963** | **78.8** | **189** |
| Almora | State Bank of India | 76 | 1139 | 80.5 | 198 |
| Bageshwar | State Bank of India | 29 | 690 | 80.1 | 116 |
| Chamoli | State Bank of India | 40 | 1019 | 82.7 | 49 |
| Champawat | State Bank of India | 27 | 980 | 79.8 | 147 |
| Dehra Dun | Punjab National Bank | 244 | 902 | 84.3 | 550 |
| Garhwal (Pauri) | State Bank of India | 116 | 1103 | 82 | 129 |
| Haridwar | Punjab National Bank | 144 | 880 | 73.4 | 817 |
| Nainital | Bank of Baroda | 105 | 934 | 83.9 | 225 |
| Pithoragarh | State Bank of India | 54 | 1020 | 82.3 | 69 |
| Rudraprayag | State Bank of India | 25 | 1114 | 81.3 | 119 |
| Tehri Garhwal | State Bank of India | 68 | 1077 | 76.4 | 169 |
| Udham Singh Nagar | Bank of Baroda | 129 | 920 | 73.1 | 648 |
| Uttar Kashi | State Bank of India | 26 | 958 | 75.8 | 41 |
| **WESTERN REGION** | | 19821 | | | |
| **GOA** | **STATE BANK OF INDIA** | **670** | **968** | **88.7** | **394** |
| North Goa | State Bank of India | 242 | 963 | 89.6 | 471 |
| South Goa | State Bank of India | 165 | 986 | 87.6 | 326 |
| **GUJARAT** | **DENA BANK** | **7241** | **918** | **78** | **308** |
| Ahmedabad | Dena Bank | 727 | 904 | 85.3 | 890 |
| Amreli | State Bank of India | 97 | 964 | 74.3 | 205 |

| Anand | Bank of Baroda | 185 | 925 | 84.4 | 711 |
|---|---|---|---|---|---|
| Aravalli | Dena Bank | | | | |
| Banaskantha | Dena Bank | 103 | 938 | 65.3 | 290 |
| Bharuch | Bank of Baroda | 136 | 925 | 81.5 | 238 |
| Bhavnagar | State Bank of India | 169 | 933 | 75.5 | 288 |
| Botad | Dena Bank | | | | |
| Chhotaudepur | Bank of Baroda | | | | |
| Dahod | Bank of Baroda | 69 | 990 | 58.8 | 582 |
| The Dangs | Bank of Baroda | 8 | 1006 | 75.2 | 129 |
| Devbhumi Dwarka | Dena Bank | | | | |
| Gandhinagar | Dena Bank | 119 | 923 | 84.2 | 660 |
| Gir Somnath | State Bank of India | | | | |
| Jamnagar | State Bank of India | 170 | 939 | 73.7 | 153 |
| Junagadh | State Bank of India | 164 | 953 | 75.8 | 310 |
| Kachchh (Bhuj) | Dena Bank | 208 | 908 | 70.6 | 46 |
| Mahisagar | Bank of Baroda | | | | |
| Kheda | Bank of Baroda | 149 | 940 | 82.7 | 541 |
| Mahesana | Dena Bank | 150 | 926 | 83.6 | 462 |
| Morbi | State Bank of India | | | | |
| Narmada | Bank of Baroda | 28 | 961 | 72.3 | 214 |
| Navsari | Bank of Baroda | 155 | 961 | 83.9 | 602 |
| Panch Mahal (Godhra) | Bank of Baroda | 96 | 949 | 71.1 | 458 |
| Patan | Dena Bank | 69 | 935 | 72.3 | 234 |
| Porbandar | State Bank of India | 55 | 950 | 75.8 | 255 |
| Rajkot | State Bank of India | 298 | 927 | 81.1 | 282 |
| Sabarkantha | Dena Bank | 137 | 952 | 75.8 | 328 |
| Surat | Bank of Baroda | 369 | 787 | 85.5 | 653 |
| Surendranagar | State Bank of India | 108 | 930 | 72.1 | 167 |
| Tapi | Bank of Baroda | | 1007 | 68.3 | 249 |
| Vadodara (Baroda) | Bank of Baroda | 415 | 934 | 78.9 | 467 |
| Valsad | Bank of Baroda | 127 | 922 | 78.6 | 561 |
| **MAHARASHTRA** | **BANK OF MAHARASHTRA** | **11810** | **946** | **82.3** | **365** |
| Ahmednagar | Central Bank of India | 236 | 939 | 79.1 | 266 |
| Akola | Central Bank of India | 118 | 946 | 88.1 | 321 |
| Amravati | Central Bank of India | 159 | 951 | 87.4 | 237 |
| Aurangabad | Bank of Maharashtra | 196 | 923 | 79.1 | 365 |
| Bhandara | Bank of India | 68 | 982 | 83.8 | 293 |
| Bidar | State Bank of India | 105 | 916 | 77.1 | 242 |
| Buldhana | Central Bank of India | 112 | 934 | 83.4 | 268 |

*Continued*

| | | | | | |
|---|---|---|---|---|---|
| Chandrapur | Bank of india | 161 | 961 | 80.1 | 192 |
| Dhule | Central Bank of India | 82 | 946 | 72.8 | 285 |
| Gadchiroli | Bank of India | 45 | 982 | 74.4 | 74 |
| Gondia | Bank of India | 67 | 999 | 85.1 | 253 |
| Mumbai City | Bank of India | 859 | 832 | 89.2 | 20038 |
| Mumbai Suburban | Bank of India | 950 | 860 | 89.9 | 20925 |
| Hingoli | State Bank of India | 40 | 942 | 78.2 | 244 |
| Jalgaon | Central Bank of India | 189 | 925 | 78.2 | 359 |
| Jalna | Bank of Maharashtra | 84 | 937 | 71.5 | 255 |
| Kolhapur | Bank of India | 252 | 957 | 81.5 | 504 |
| Latur | State Bank of India | 105 | 928 | 77.3 | 343 |
| Nagpur | Bank of India | 353 | 951 | 88.4 | 470 |
| Nanded | State Bank of India | 141 | 943 | 75.5 | 319 |
| Nandurbar | State Bank of India | 51 | 978 | 64.4 | 276 |
| Nashik | Bank of Maharashtra | 294 | 934 | 82.3 | 393 |
| Osmanabad | State Bank of India | 75 | 924 | 78.4 | 219 |
| Parbhani | State Bank of India | 78 | 947 | 73.3 | 295 |
| Pune | Bank of Maharashtra | 743 | 915 | 86.2 | 603 |
| Raigad | Bank of India | 189 | 959 | 83.1 | 368 |
| Ratnagiri | Bank of India | 151 | 1122 | 82.2 | 196 |
| Sangli | Bank of India | 194 | 966 | 81.5 | 329 |
| Satara | Bank of Maharashtra | 176 | 988 | 82.9 | 287 |
| Sindhudurg | Bank of India | 92 | 1036 | 85.6 | 163 |
| Solapur | Bank of India | 233 | 938 | 77.1 | 290 |
| Thane | Bank of Maharashtra | 688 | 886 | 84.5 | 1157 |
| Wardha | Bank of India | 88 | 946 | 87.1 | 205 |
| Washim | State Bank of India | 52 | 930 | 83.3 | 244 |
| Yavatmal | Central Bank of India | 129 | 952 | 82.8 | 204 |
| **DADRA & NAGAR HAVELI** | **DENA BANK** | **53** | **775** | **76.2** | **698** |
| Dadra & Nagar Haveli | Dena Bank | 24 | 774 | 76.2 | 698 |
| **DAMAN & DIU** | **DENA BANK** | **47** | **618** | **87.1** | **2169** |
| Daman | State Bank of India | 13 | 534 | 88.1 | 2651 |
| Diu | State Bank of India | 5 | 1031 | 83.5 | 1301 |
| **SOUTHERN REGION** | | 36654 | | | |
| **ANDHRA PRADESH** | **ANDHRA BANK** | **6290** | **993** | **67** | **308** |
| Anantapur | Syndicate Bank | 260 | 977 | 63.6 | 213 |
| Chittoor | Indian Bank | 289 | 997 | 71.5 | 275 |
| Cuddapah (YSR) | Syndicate Bank | 203 | 985 | 67.3 | 188 |
| East Godavari | Andhra Bank | 398 | 1006 | 71.1 | 477 |
| Guntur | Andhra Bank | 387 | 1003 | 67.4 | 429 |

| Krishna | Indian Bank | 451 | 992 | 73.7 | 519 |
|---|---|---|---|---|---|
| Kurnool | Syndicate Bank | 248 | 988 | 60.1 | 229 |
| Nellore (Sri Potti Sriram-ulu Nellore) | Syndicate Bank | 235 | 985 | 68.9 | 227 |
| Prakasam | Syndicate Bank | 254 | 981 | 63.1 | 192 |
| Srikakulam | Andhra Bank | 161 | 1015 | 61.7 | 462 |
| Vishakhapatnam | State Bank of India | 389 | 1006 | 66.9 | 384 |
| Vizianagaram | State Bank of India | 151 | 1019 | 58.9 | 358 |
| West Godavari | Andhra Bank | 321 | 1004 | 74.6 | |
| **KARNATAKA** | **SYNDICATE BANK** | **9365** | **968** | **78.4** | **319** |
| Bagalkote | Syndicate Bank | 143 | 989 | 68.8 | 288 |
| Bangalore (Rural) | Canara Bank | 91 | 946 | 77.9 | 441 |
| Bangalore (Urban) | Canara Bank | 1292 | 916 | 87.7 | 4378 |
| Belgaum | Syndicate Bank | 366 | 973 | 73.5 | 356 |
| Bellary | Syndicate Bank | 177 | 983 | 67.4 | 300 |
| Bidar | State Bank of India. | 97 | 956 | 70.5 | 312 |
| Bijapur | Syndicate Bank | 132 | 960 | 67.2 | |
| Chamarajanagar | State Bank of Mysore | 61 | 993 | 61.4 | 200 |
| Chikkaballapura | Canara Bank | 86 | 972 | 70.0 | 298 |
| Chikmagaluru | Corporation Bank | 150 | 1008 | 79.3 | 158 |
| Chitradurga | Canara Bank | 123 | 974 | 73.7 | 197 |
| Dakshina Kannada | Syndicate Bank | 362 | 1020 | 88.6 | 457 |
| Devangere | Canara Bank | 134 | 972 | 75.7 | 329 |
| Dharwad | Vijaya Bank | 230 | 971 | 80.1 | 434 |
| Gadag | State Bank of India | 88 | 982 | 75.1 | 229 |
| Gulbarga | State Bank of India | 207 | 971 | 64.9 | 233 |
| Hassan | Canara Bank | 181 | 1010 | 76.1 | 261 |
| Haveri | Vijaya Bank | 108 | 950 | 77.4 | 331 |
| Kodagu | Corporation Bank | 114 | 1019 | 82.6 | 135 |
| Kolar | Canara Bank | 103 | 979 | 74.4 | 384 |
| Koppal | State Bank of Hyderabad | 88 | 986 | 68.1 | 250 |
| Mandya | Vijaya Bank | 138 | 995 | 70.4 | 365 |
| Mysore | State Bank of Mysore | 291 | 985 | 72.8 | 437 |
| Raichur | State Bank of Hyderabad | 129 | 1000 | 59.6 | 228 |
| Ramanagara | Corporation Bank | 78 | 976 | 69.2 | 303 |
| Shimoga | Canara Bank | 178 | 998 | 80.5 | 207 |
| Tumkur | State Bank of Mysore | 194 | 984 | 75.1 | 253 |
| Udupi | Syndicate Bank | 238 | 1094 | 86.2 | 304 |
| Uttara Kannada | Syndicate Bank | 189 | 979 | 84.1 | 132 |
| Yadgir | State Bank of India | | 989 | 51.8 | 224 |
| **KERALA** | **CANARA BANK** | **6190** | **1084** | **94** | **859** |

*Continued*

| Alappuzha | State Bank of Travancore | 251 | 1100 | 95.7 | 1501 |
|---|---|---|---|---|---|
| Ernakulam | Union Bank of India | 634 | 1027 | 95.9 | 1069 |
| Idukki | Union Bank of India | 112 | 1006 | 92.1 | 254 |
| Kannur | Syndicate Bank | 243 | 1136 | 95.1 | 852 |
| Kasaragod | Syndicate Bank | 135 | 1080 | 90.1 | 654 |
| Kollam | Indian Bank | 231 | 1113 | 94.1 | 1056 |
| kottayam | State Bank of Travancore | 324 | 1039 | 97.2 | 896 |
| Kozhikode | Canara Bank | 287 | 1098 | 95.1 | 1318 |
| Malapuram | Canara Bank | 291 | 1098 | 93.6 | 1058 |
| Palakkad | Canara Bank | 281 | 1067 | 89.3 | 627 |
| Pathanamthitta | State Bank of Travancore | 275 | 1132 | 96.6 | 453 |
| Thiruvananthapuram | Indian Overseas Bank | 448 | 1087 | 93.1 | 1509 |
| Thrissur | Canara Bank | 460 | 1108 | 95.1 | 1026 |
| Wayanad (Kalepetta) | Canara Bank | 81 | 1035 | 89.1 | 383 |
| **TAMIL NADU** | **INDIAN OVERSEAS BANK** | **9847** | **995** | **80.1** | **555** |
| Ariyalur | State Bank of India | 42 | 1015 | 71.3 | 387 |
| Chennai | Indian Overseas Bank | 1028 | 989 | 90.2 | 26903 |
| Coimbatore | Canara Bank | 533 | 1000 | 84.1 | 748 |
| Cuddalore | Indian Bank | 163 | 987 | 78.1 | 702 |
| Dharmapuri | Indian Bank | 71 | 946 | 68.5 | 332 |
| Dindigul | Canara Bank | 157 | 998 | 76.3 | 357 |
| Erode | Canara Bank | 251 | 993 | 72.6 | 397 |
| Kancheepuram | Indian Bank | 310 | 986 | 84.5 | 927 |
| Kanniyakumari | Indian Overseas Bank | 149 | 1019 | 91.8 | 1106 |
| Karur | Indian Overseas Bank | 95 | 1015 | 75.6 | 371 |
| Krishnagiri | Indian Bank | | 958 | 71.5 | 370 |
| Madurai | Canara Bank | 245 | 990 | 83.5 | 823 |
| Nagapattinam | Indian Overseas Bank | 107 | 1025 | 83.6 | 668 |
| Namakkal | Indian Bank | 127 | 986 | 74.6 | 506 |
| Nilgiris | Canara Bank | 82 | 1042 | 85.2 | 288 |
| Perambalur | Indian overseas Bank | 35 | 1003 | 74.3 | 323 |
| Pudukkottai | Indian Overseas Bank | 111 | 1015 | 77.2 | 348 |
| Ramanathapuram | Indian Overseas Bank | 87 | 983 | 80.7 | 320 |
| Salem | Indian Bank | 206 | 954 | 72.9 | 663 |
| Sivaganga | Indian Overseas Bank | 141 | 1003 | 80.1 | 324 |
| Thanjavur | Indian Overseas Bank | 184 | 1035 | 82.6 | 691 |
| Theni | Canara Bank | 91 | 991 | 77.3 | 433 |
| Thiruvallur | Indian Bank | 222 | 987 | 84.1 | 1049 |
| Thirupur | Canara Bank | | 989 | 78.7 | 476 |
| Thiruvarur | Indian Overseas Bank | 85 | 1017 | 82.9 | 533 |

| | | | | | |
|---|---|---|---|---|---|
| Thiruchirapalli | Indian Overseas Bank | 231 | 1013 | 83.2 | 602 |
| Thirunelveli | Indian Overseas Bank | 234 | 1023 | 82.5 | 458 |
| Thiruvannamalai | Indian Bank | 110 | 994 | 74.2 | 399 |
| Thoothukudi | State Bank of India | 147 | 1023 | 86.2 | 378 |
| Vellore | Indian Bank | 226 | 1007 | 79.2 | 646 |
| Vizhupuram | Indian Bank | 167 | 987 | 71.9 | 462 |
| Virudhunagar | Indian Overseas Bank | 146 | 1007 | 80.2 | 454 |
| **TELANGANA** | **STATE BANK OF HYDERABAD** | **4721** | **988** | | **307** |
| Adilabad | State Bank of Hyderabad | 163 | 1001 | 61.1 | 170 |
| Hyderabad | State Bank of Hyderabad | 763 | 954 | 83.3 | 18480 |
| Karimnagar | State Bank of Hyderabad | 214 | 1008 | 64.2 | 322 |
| Khammam | State Bank of Hyderabad | 191 | 1011 | 64.8 | 175 |
| Mahbubnagar | State Bank of India | 226 | 977 | 55.1 | 219 |
| Medak | State Bank of India | 199 | 992 | 61.4 | 313 |
| Nalgonda | State Bank of Hyderabad | 206 | 983 | 64.2 | 245 |
| Nizamabad | State Bank of Hyderabad | 184 | 1019 | 58.9 | 321 |
| Rangareddy | State Bank of Hyderabad | 416 | 961 | 75.9 | 707 |
| Warangal | State Bank of India | 227 | 997 | 65.1 | 274 |
| **LAKSHADWEEP** | **SYNDICATE BANK** | **13** | **946** | **91.9** | **2013** |
| Lakshadweep | Syndicate Bank | 13 | 946 | 91.9 | 2013 |
| **PUDUCHERRY** | **INDIAN BANK** | **228** | **1038** | **85.9** | **2598** |
| Karaikal | Indian Bank | 26 | 1047 | 87.1 | 1252 |
| Mahe | Indian Bank | 5 | 1184 | 97.9 | 4659 |
| Puducherry | Indian Bank | 88 | 1029 | 85.4 | 3231 |
| Yanam | Indian Bank | 5 | 1038 | 79.5 | 3272 |
| ALL- INDIA | | 130482 | | | |

# ANNEXURE – II

## DEPOSITS AND CREDIT OF SCHEDULED COMMERCIAL BANKS – MARCH 2015

(Amount in ₹ Million)

| REGION/STATE/ UNION TERRITORY | No. of Bank branches | DEPOSITS | | CREDIT | |
|---|---|---|---|---|---|
| | | No. of Accounts | Amount | No. of Accounts | Amount Outstanding |
| | 1 | 2 | 3 | 4 | 5 |
| **NORTHERN REGION** | **23843** | **211816683** | **17935498.0** | **14909185** | **15867500.7** |
| Haryana | 4407 | 3,63,32,023 | 2226845.1 | 2488066 | 1688930.9 |
| Himachal Pradesh | 1466 | 1,04,97,958 | 598764.8 | 677064 | 211148.2 |
| Jammu & Kashmir | 1634 | 1,53,92,547 | 737205.0 | 1139925 | 310963.6 |
| Punjab | 6024 | 4,59,69,344 | 2619723.4 | 2869022 | 1966442.3 |
| Rajasthan | 6426 | 5,88,78,306 | 2354794.7 | 5035976 | 2029555.2 |
| Chandigarh | 439 | 34,77,529 | 554331.3 | 200453 | 586988.4 |
| Nct Of Delhi | 3447 | 4,12,68,976 | 8843833.6 | 2498679 | 9073472.2 |
| **NORTH-EASTERN REGION** | **3345** | **38432313** | **1554802.0** | **3299465** | **536061.6** |
| Arunachal Pradesh | 135 | 10,61,508 | 80085.6 | 81091 | 21456.0 |
| Assam | 2103 | 2,71,55,896 | 973814.4 | 2242675 | 357149.1 |
| Manipur | 138 | 17,97,773 | 57300.7 | 110783 | 19466.9 |
| Meghalaya | 294 | 20,32,101 | 166439.4 | 188443 | 43081.9 |
| Mizoram | 151 | 8,93,508 | 53152.5 | 105017 | 20076.8 |
| Nagaland | 145 | 10,63,026 | 69382.7 | 114582 | 22685.7 |
| Tripura | 379 | 44,28,501 | 154626.7 | 456874 | 52145.0 |
| **EASTERN REGION** | **20893** | **242920667** | **11113496.6** | **16908155** | **5173267.8** |
| Bihar | 6210 | 6,66,30,466 | 2168098.5 | 5819560 | 728622.4 |
| Jharkhand | 2763 | 2,91,93,954 | 1421112.8 | 2219490 | 420294.7 |
| Odisha | 4410 | 4,34,53,751 | 1900738.8 | 3804200 | 796964.0 |
| Sikkim | 122 | 7,29,561 | 57144.3 | 40322 | 14651.2 |
| West Bengal | 7327 | 10,23,90,287 | 5536916.1 | 4985390 | 3200914.4 |
| Andaman & Nicobar Islands | 61 | 5,22,648 | 29486.2 | 39193 | 11821.2 |
| **CENTRAL REGION** | **25926** | **307069833** | **11396700.1** | **20064326** | **5501695.9** |
| Chhattisgarh | 2253 | 2,46,97,313 | 991656.2 | 1210010 | 610622.4 |
| Madhya Pradesh | 5997 | 7,09,73,036 | 2793419.1 | 5286838 | 1530340.6 |
| Uttar Pradesh | 15773 | 19,70,19,991 | 6725295.6 | 12649277 | 3054626.8 |

| | | | | | |
|---|---|---|---|---|---|
| Uttarakhand | 1903 | 1,43,79,493 | 886329.2 | 918201 | 306106.2 |
| **WESTERN REGION** | **19821** | **236006719** | **26853629.8** | **24185241** | **23399305.2** |
| Goa | 670 | 51,96,070 | 515442.3 | 286281 | 137474.5 |
| Gujarat | 7241 | 7,53,74,658 | 4777581.9 | 4341296 | 3471167.6 |
| Maharashtra | 11810 | 15,43,81,415 | 21500095.1 | 19524152 | 19772979.7 |
| Dadra & Nagar Haveli | 53 | 6,08,887 | 27172.8 | 21313 | 9582.2 |
| Daman & Diu | 47 | 4,45,689 | 33337.8 | 12199 | 8101.2 |
| **SOUTHERN REGION** | **36654** | **403646068** | **20366985.5** | **64873264** | **18306894.1** |
| Andhra Pradesh | 6290 | 8,21,97,725 | 1933489.3 | 11383208 | 1986138.7 |
| Karnataka | 9365 | 9,67,59,817 | 6342916.2 | 9652281 | 4292248.4 |
| Kerala | 6190 | 5,75,83,486 | 3283993.6 | 8813485 | 2121607.8 |
| Tamil Nadu | 9847 | 11,16,12,470 | 5453170.4 | 27956406 | 6491637.0 |
| Lakshadweep | 13 | 87,176 | 7618.0 | 5782 | 693.1 |
| Puducherry | 228 | 22,87,327 | 110639.3 | 394711 | 79101.4 |
| Telangana | 4721 | 5,31,18,067 | 3235158.7 | 6667391 | 3335467.7 |
| **ALL-INDIA** | **130482** | **1439892283** | **89221112.1** | **144239636** | **68784725.2** |

# ANNEXURE – III

## BANK CREDIT TO HOUSING & HOUSING SHORTAGE

| REGION/STATE/UNION TERRITORY | Total Deposits (₹ Mn) | Total Credit (₹ Mn) | Credit to Agriculture (₹ Mn) | Credit to Housing (₹ Mn) | Housing shortage (in Mn) |
|---|---|---|---|---|---|
| 1 | 2 | 3 | 4 | 5 | 6 |
| **NORTHERN REGION** | 17935498 | 16467382 | 1517200 | 403532 | |
| HARYANA | 2226845 | 1898210 | 319772 | 56868 | 0.42 |
| HIMACHAL PRADESH | 598764 | 219182 | 43700 | 17289 | 0.04 |
| JAMMU & KASHMIR | 737205 | 313648 | 61466 | 16644 | 0.13 |
| PUNJAB | 2619723 | 2013210 | 501088 | 60785 | 0.39 |
| RAJASTHAN | 2354795 | 2121822 | 410409 | 107103 | 1.15 |
| CHANDIGARH | 554331 | 611150 | 21969 | 12426 | 0.02 |
| NCT OF DELHI | 8843834 | 9290159 | 158805 | 132417 | 0.49 |
| **NORTH-EASTERN REGION** | 1554802 | 547264 | 74503 | 34741 | |
| ARUNACHAL PRADESH | 80085 | 23335 | 1751 | 467 | 0.03 |
| ASSAM | 973814 | 361886 | 53728 | 22994 | 0.28 |
| MANIPUR | 57301 | 19788 | 3878 | 2386 | 0.08 |
| MEGHALAYA | 166439 | 44782 | 3893 | 2023 | 0.03 |
| MIZORAM | 53152 | 21207 | 1429 | 3420 | 0.02 |
| NAGALAND | 69383 | 23636 | 2853 | 1078 | 0.21 |
| TRIPURA | 154627 | 52629 | 6971 | 2373 | 0.03 |
| **EASTERN REGION** | 11113497 | 5384329 | 667244 | 237494 | |
| BIHAR | 2168098 | 743701 | 209425 | 30224 | 1.19 |
| JHARKHAND | 1421113 | 434333 | 47307 | 22691 | 0.63 |
| ODISHA | 1900739 | 835233 | 103743 | 41612 | 0.41 |
| SIKKIM | 57144 | 21115 | 1219 | 3813 | 0.01 |
| WEST BENGAL | 5536916 | 3338366 | 304925 | 137913 | 1.33 |
| ANDAMAN & NICOBAR ISLANDS | 29486 | 11582 | 625 | 1241 | |
| **CENTRAL REGION** | 11396700 | 5842506 | 1158666 | 326863 | |
| CHHATTISGARH | 991656 | 628768 | 59470 | 33990 | 0.35 |
| MADHYA PRADESH | 2793419 | 1610042 | 382809 | 105626 | 1.10 |
| UTTAR PRADESH | 6725296 | 3291402 | 646562 | 160984 | 3.07 |
| UTTARAKHAND | 886329 | 312294 | 69824 | 26262 | 0.16 |
| **WESTERN REGION** | 26853630 | 21717730 | 2099071 | 1120651 | |

| | | | | | |
|---|---|---|---|---|---|
| GOA | 515442 | 145379 | 8101 | 12924 | 0.06 |
| GUJARAT | 4777582 | 3774923 | 340079 | 224722 | 0.99 |
| MAHARASHTRA | 21500095 | 17776399 | 1750103 | 880956 | 1.94 |
| DADRA & NAGAR HAVELI | 27173 | 9842 | 358 | 1126 | 0.05 |
| DAMAN & DIU | 33338 | 11187 | 430 | 923 | 0.01 |
| **SOUTHERN REGION** | 20366986 | 18825514 | 3397772 | 1030514 | |
| ANDHRA PRADESH | 1886280 | 2043338 | 1121819 | 1034322 | 1.27 |
| KARNATAKA | 6342916 | 4606693 | 687724 | 309045 | 1.02 |
| KERALA | 3283993 | 2147499 | 498049 | 239574 | 0.54 |
| TAMIL NADU | 5453170 | 6406312 | 1075561 | 1888255 | 1.25 |
| TELANGANA | 3282367 | 3538633 | | | |
| LAKSHADWEEP | 7618 | 694 | 113 | 17 | 0.01 |
| PUDUCHERRY | 110639 | 82345 | 14506 | 17971 | 0.07 |
| **ALL-INDIA** | 89221112 | 68784725 | 8914465 | 3153795 | 18.78 |

Note: Data on banking variables relate to 31st March 2015 of the RBI

Data on Housing Shortage pertain to the year 2012 of the Government of India.

# ANNEXURE – IV

## Direct Disbursement of Bank Credit to FARMERS by Scheduled Commercial banks as per Size of Land Holdings

| Year | Upto 2.5 acres | | Between 2.5 & 5 acres | | Above 5 acres | | Total | |
|---|---|---|---|---|---|---|---|---|
| | No of accounts in '000 | Amount ₹ Bn | No of accounts in '000 | Amount ₹ Bn | No of accounts in '000 | Amount ₹ Bn | No of accounts in '000 | Amount ₹ Bn |
| 1 | 2 | 3 | 4 | 5 | 6 | 7 | 8 | 9 |
| 1982–83 | 1304 | 2.90 | 652 | 2.11 | 616 | 4.76 | 2571 | 9.77 |
| 1983–84 | 1831 | 4.04 | 1072 | 3.72 | 835 | 7.43 | 3738 | 15.19 |
| 1984–85 | 1829 | 5.06 | 1241 | 4.82 | 903 | 9.51 | 3972 | 19.38 |
| 1985–86 | 1950 | 6.17 | 1232 | 5.89 | 988 | 10.37 | 4170 | 22.43 |
| 1986–87 | 2045 | 7.58 | 1386 | 7.08 | 1044 | 12.78 | 4475 | 27.44 |
| 1987–88 | 2236 | 8.24 | 1442 | 7.60 | 1038 | 13.60 | 4716 | 29.45 |
| 1988–89 | 2191 | 8.81 | 1453 | 8.35 | 990 | 14.71 | 4634 | 31.87 |
| 1989–90 | 2057 | 10.33 | 1337 | 8.90 | 947 | 16.07 | 4341 | 35.30 |
| 1990–91 | 1960 | 11.81 | 1219 | 9.52 | 899 | 17.82 | 4078 | 39.15 |
| 1991–92 | 1862 | 11.72 | 1289 | 10.13 | 949 | 18.87 | 4100 | 40.72 |
| 1992–93 | 1871 | 11.71 | 1336 | 10.33 | 1000 | 20.03 | 4206 | 42.06 |
| 1993–94 | 1886 | 13.12 | 1341 | 11.76 | 1192 | 20.70 | 4419 | 45.58 |
| 1994–95 | 2032 | 16.92 | 1518 | 14.74 | 1261 | 29.70 | 4812 | 61.37 |
| 1995–96 | 2024 | 20.01 | 1689 | 19.52 | 1703 | 37.03 | 5416 | 76.57 |
| 1996–97 | 2076 | 21.76 | 1676 | 22.89 | 1745 | 45.11 | 5496 | 89.76 |
| 1997–98 | 2104 | 22.88 | 1811 | 24.13 | 1420 | 48.27 | 5336 | 95.28 |
| 1998–99 | 2308 | 27.87 | 1878 | 31.81 | 1659 | 58.62 | 5845 | 118.29 |
| 1999–2000 | 2342 | 33.38 | 1871 | 34.67 | 1581 | 72.09 | 5784 | 140.14 |
| 2000–01 | 2382 | 37.40 | 1860 | 36.42 | 1599 | 71.35 | 5841 | 145.16 |
| 2001–02 | 2679 | 43.52 | 1933 | 43.71 | 2359 | 75.78 | 6970 | 163.00 |
| 2002–03 | 2494 | 48.34 | 1934 | 55.78 | 1983 | 114.45 | 6411 | 218.57 |
| 2003–04 | 3711 | 79.53 | 2695 | 73.40 | 2259 | 165.92 | 8665 | 318.85 |
| 2004–05 | 4478 | 108.33 | 3172 | 105.50 | 2535 | 197.35 | 10185 | 411.19 |
| 2005–06 | 5004 | 168.23 | 3670 | 176.19 | 3670 | 326.82 | 12344 | 671.24 |
| 2006–07 | 5963 | 232.46 | 4008 | 215.88 | 4379 | 493.35 | 14350 | 941.69 |
| 2007–08 | 6605 | 253.52 | 4463 | 232.15 | 4932 | 484.40 | 16000 | 967.07 |
| 2008–09 | 8544 | 342.67 | 6641 | 332.80 | 6811 | 727.53 | 21996 | 1403.00 |
| 2009–10 | 8127 | 426.26 | 7175 | 443.31 | 6385 | 730.61 | 21687 | 1600.18 |
| 2010–11 | 9253 | 460.19 | 9690 | 574.36 | 6044 | 854.55 | 24987 | 1889.10 |
| 2011–12 | 13735 | 897.14 | 10021 | 829.19 | 6782 | 990.37 | 30538 | 2716.70 |

Note: Number of accounts in Thousands and Amount is in ₹ Crore      Billion

Source: Reserve Bank of India -

ANNEXURE – V

DATA BASE: ALL-INDIA - Population and other Macro - Economic Aggregates.

| Year | Credit to Agriculture (₹ Bn) | Gross Irrigated area (Mn He) | Net sown area (Mn He) | Area under foodgrains cultivation (Mn He) | Foodgrains Output (Mn Ton) | Yield per He (Foodgrains) Kg/He | Area under Oilseeds cultivation (Mn He) | Oilseeds Output (Mn Ton) | Yield per He (Oilseeds) Kg/He |
|---|---|---|---|---|---|---|---|---|---|
| 1 | 2 | 3 | 4 | 5 | 6 | 7 | 8 | 9 | 10 |
| 1950-51 | | | | | | | | | 481 |
| 1951-52 | | | | | | | | | 430 |
| 1952-53 | | 23.31 | 123.44 | | 59.2 | | | | 424 |
| 1953-54 | | 24.36 | 126.81 | 109.07 | 69.82 | 640 | | | 488 |
| 1954-55 | | 24.95 | 127.85 | 107.86 | 68.03 | 631 | 12.52 | 6.41 | 511 |
| 1955-56 | | 25.64 | 129.16 | 110.56 | 66.85 | 605 | 12.09 | 5.73 | 474 |
| 1956-57 | | 25.71 | 130.85 | 111.14 | 69.86 | 629 | 12.49 | 6.36 | 509 |
| 1957-58 | | 26.63 | 129.08 | 109.48 | 64.31 | 587 | 12.66 | 6.35 | 502 |
| 1958-59 | | 26.95 | 131.83 | 114.76 | 77.14 | 672 | 13.01 | 7.31 | 561 |
| 1959-60 | | 27.45 | 132.94 | 115.82 | 76.67 | 662 | 13.95 | 6.56 | 470 |
| 1960-61 | | 27.98 | 133.21 | 115.58 | 82.02 | 710 | 13.77 | 6.98 | 507 |
| 1961-62 | | 28.46 | 135.41 | 117.23 | 82.71 | 706 | 14.77 | 7.28 | 493 |
| 1962-63 | | 29.45 | 136.34 | 117.84 | 80.15 | 680 | 15.34 | 7.39 | 482 |
| 1963-64 | | 29.71 | 136.48 | 117.42 | 80.64 | 687 | 14.82 | 7.13 | 481 |
| 1964-65 | | 30.71 | 138.12 | 118.11 | 89.36 | 757 | 15.26 | 8.56 | 561 |
| 1965-66 | | 30.91 | 136.21 | 115.11 | 72.35 | 629 | 15.25 | 6.41 | 419 |
| 1966-67 | | 32.68 | 137.23 | 115.31 | 74.23 | 644 | 15.01 | 6.43 | 428 |
| 1967-68 | | 33.21 | 139.88 | 121.42 | 95.05 | 783 | 15.67 | 8.31 | 530 |
| 1968-69 | | 35.48 | 137.31 | 120.43 | 94.01 | 781 | 14.47 | 6.85 | 473 |
| 1969-70 | | 36.97 | 138.77 | 123.57 | 99.51 | 805 | 14.81 | 7.73 | 522 |
| 1970-71 | | 38.21 | 140.27 | 124.32 | 108.42 | 872 | 16.64 | 9.63 | 579 |
| 1971-72 | | 38.43 | 139.72 | 122.62 | 105.17 | 858 | 17.27 | 9.08 | 526 |
| 1972-73 | | 39.06 | 137.14 | 119.28 | 97.03 | 813 | 15.79 | 7.14 | 452 |
| 1973-74 | | 40.28 | 142.42 | 126.54 | 104.67 | 827 | 16.91 | 9.39 | 555 |
| 1974-75 | | 41.74 | 137.79 | 121.08 | 99.83 | 824 | 17.31 | 9.15 | 529 |
| 1975-76 | | 43.36 | 141.65 | 128.18 | 121.03 | 944 | 16.92 | 10.61 | 627 |
| 1976-77 | | 43.55 | 139.48 | 124.35 | 111.17 | 894 | 16.47 | 8.43 | 512 |
| 1977-78 | 13.40 | 46.08 | 141.95 | 127.52 | 126.41 | 991 | 17.17 | 9.66 | 563 |
| 1978-79 | 18.25 | 48.31 | 142.98 | 129.01 | 131.91 | 1022 | 17.71 | 10.11 | 570 |
| 1979-80 | 23.64 | 49.21 | 138.91 | 125.21 | 109.71 | 876 | 16.94 | 8.74 | 516 |
| 1980-81 | 30.43 | 49.78 | 140.01 | 126.67 | 129.59 | 1023 | 17.61 | 9.37 | 532 |
| 1981-82 | 35.41 | 51.41 | 141.93 | 129.14 | 133.31 | 1032 | 18.91 | 12.08 | 639 |

*Continued*

| Year | | | | | | | | | |
|---|---|---|---|---|---|---|---|---|---|
| 1982-83 | 41.43 | 51.83 | 140.22 | 125.09 | 129.52 | 1035 | 17.76 | 10.01 | 563 |
| 1983-84 | 52.80 | 53.82 | 142.84 | 131.16 | 152.37 | 1162 | 18.69 | 12.69 | 679 |
| 1984-85 | 66.13 | 54.53 | 140.89 | 126.67 | 145.54 | 1149 | 18.92 | 12.95 | 684 |
| 1985-86 | 84.16 | 54.28 | 140.91 | 128.03 | 150.44 | 1175 | 19.02 | 10.83 | 570 |
| 1986-87 | 93.55 | 55.76 | 139.58 | 127.21 | 143.42 | 1128 | 18.63 | 11.27 | 605 |
| 1987-88 | 114.24 | 56.04 | 134.09 | 119.69 | 140.35 | 1173 | 20.13 | 12.65 | 629 |
| 1988-89 | 128.40 | 61.13 | 141.89 | 127.67 | 169.92 | 1331 | 21.91 | 18.03 | 824 |
| 1989-90 | 152.83 | 61.85 | 142.34 | 126.77 | 171.04 | 1349 | 22.81 | 16.92 | 742 |
| 1990-91 | 170.32 | 63.21 | 143.01 | 127.84 | 176.39 | 1380 | 24.15 | 18.61 | 771 |
| 1991-92 | 169.81 | 65.68 | 141.63 | 121.87 | 168.38 | 1382 | 25.89 | 18.61 | 719 |
| 1992-93 | 182.88 | 66.76 | 142.72 | 123.15 | 179.48 | 1457 | 25.24 | 20.11 | 797 |
| 1993-94 | 191.13 | 68.26 | 142.34 | 122.76 | 184.26 | 1501 | 26.91 | 21.51 | 799 |
| 1994-95 | 209.20 | 70.65 | 142.96 | 123.71 | 191.51 | 1546 | 25.31 | 21.34 | 843 |
| 1995-96 | 234027 | 71.35 | 142.21 | 121.01 | 180.42 | 1491 | 25.96 | 22.11 | 851 |
| 1996-97 | 263.27 | 76.03 | 142.93 | 123.58 | 199.43 | 1614 | 26.34 | 24.38 | 926 |
| 1997-98 | 284.45 | 75.67 | 141.95 | 123.85 | 193.12 | 1552 | 26.12 | 21.32 | 816 |
| 1998-99 | 298.19 | 78067 | 142.75 | 125.16 | 203.61 | 1627 | 26.23 | 24.75 | 944 |
| 1999-2000 | 334.42 | 79.22 | 141.06 | 123.11 | 209.81 | 1704 | 24.28 | 20.71 | 853 |
| 2000-01 | 382.70 | 76.19 | 141.36 | 121.05 | 196.81 | 1626 | 22.77 | 18.44 | 810 |
| 2001-02 | 451.06 | 78.42 | 140.73 | 122.77 | 212.85 | 1734 | 22.64 | 20.66 | 913 |
| 2002-03 | 538.04 | 73.41 | 132.47 | 113.87 | 174.78 | 1535 | 21.49 | 14.84 | 691 |
| 2003-04 | 681.03 | 78.15 | 140.76 | 123.45 | 213.19 | 1727 | 23.66 | 25.19 | 1064 |
| 2004-05 | 955.19 | 81.18 | 141.17 | 120.08 | 198.36 | 1652 | 27.52 | 24.35 | 885 |
| 2005-06 | 1536.03 | 83.94 | 141.49 | 121.61 | 208.59 | 1715 | 27.86 | 27.98 | 1004 |
| 2006-07 | 1690.18 | 86.51 | 139.95 | 123.71 | 217.28 | 1756 | 26.51 | 24.29 | 916 |
| 2007-08 | 2027.96 | 87.26 | 140.86 | 124.06 | 230.78 | 1860 | 26.69 | 29.76 | 1115 |
| 2008-09 | 2561.19 | | | 122.83 | 234.47 | 1909 | 27.56 | 27.72 | 1006 |
| 2009-10 | 3154.36 | | | 121.12 | 218.11 | 1798 | 26.22 | 24.88 | 955 |
| 2010-11 | 3575.84 | | | 125.73 | 241.56 | 1921 | 26.82 | 31.11 | 1159 |
| 2011-12 | 4432.98 | | | | | | | | |
| 2012-13 | 5224.78 | | | | | | | | |
| 2013-14 | 5035.32 | | | | | | | | |
| 2014-15 | | | | | | | | | |

Source 1: Reserve Bank of India - Handbook of Statistics on the Indian Economy
Ministry of Agriculture, Government of India

# ANNEXURE – VI

## Bank credit to Small Scale Industries & Output

| Year | Credit to SSI Sector (₹ Bn) | No of SSI units | Employed in SSI Units | No of sick units | Credit locked in sick units (₹ cr) |
|------|------|------|------|------|------|
| 1 | 2 | 3 | 4 | 5 | 6 |
| 1975–76 | | 0.55 | 4.59 | | |
| 1976–77 | | 0.59 | 4.98 | | |
| 1977–78 | | 0.67 | 5.41 | | |
| 1978–79 | | 0.73 | 6.38 | | |
| 1979–80 | | 0.81 | 6.71 | | |
| 1980–81 | | 0.87 | 7.11 | | |
| 1981–82 | 3901 | 0.96 | 7.51 | | |
| 1982–83 | 4486 | 1.06 | 7.91 | | |
| 1983–84 | 5447 | 1.06 | 8.42 | | |
| 1984–85 | 6612 | 1.24 | 9.01 | | |
| 1985–86 | 7816 | 1.35 | 9.61 | | |
| 1986–87 | 9108 | 1.46 | 10.14 | | |
| 1987–88 | 10820 | 1.58 | 10.71 | 219351 | 6927 |
| 1988–89 | 13135 | 1.71 | 11.31 | 188622 | 8684 |
| 1989–90 | 15543 | 1.82 | 11.96 | 221097 | 9553 |
| 1990–91 | 17181 | 6.79 | 15.83 | 223809 | 10768 |
| 1991–92 | 18150 | 7.06 | 16.61 | 247924 | 11533 |
| 1992–93 | 20026 | 7.35 | 17.48 | 240700 | 13134 |
| 1993–94 | 22617 | 7.65 | 18.26 | 258952 | 13696 |
| 1994–95 | 27638 | 7.96 | 19.14 | 271206 | 13739 |
| 1995–96 | 31884 | 8.28 | 19.79 | 264750 | 13748 |
| 1996–97 | 35944 | 8.62 | 20.59 | 237400 | 13787 |
| 1997–98 | 43508 | 8.97 | 21.32 | 224012 | 15682 |
| 1998–99 | 48483 | 9.34 | 22.06 | 309013 | 19464 |
| 1999–2000 | 52814 | 9.72 | 22.91 | 307399 | 23656 |
| 2000–01 | 56002 | 10.11 | 24.09 | 252947 | 25776 |
| 2001–02 | 57199 | 10.52 | 24.93 | 180597 | 26065 |
| 1002–03 | 60394 | 10.95 | 26.02 | 171376 | 34816 |
| 2003–04 | 65855 | 11.41 | 27.14 | 144432 | 40982 |
| 2004–05 | 74588 | 11.86 | 28.26 | 143293 | 39807 |
| 2005–06 | 91212 | 12.34 | 29.49 | 131364 | 37970 |
| 2006–07 | 117910 | 26.11 | 59.46 | 118124 | 30333 |
| 2007–08 | 132698 | 27.28 | 62.63 | 89641 | 35366 |

*Continued*

| Year | | | | | |
|---|---|---|---|---|---|
| 2008–09 | 168997 | 28.52 | 65.94 | | |
| 2009–10 | 206401 | 29.81 | 69.54 | | |
| 2010–11 | 229101 | | | | |
| 2011–12 | | | | | |
| 2012–13 | | | | | |
| 2013–14 | | | | | |
| 2014–15 | | | | | |
| Note: Data upto 2006–07 is SSI & since then Micro & Small Enterprises (MSEs) | | | | | |
| Source: RBI Handbook of Statistics on the Indian Economy | | | | | |

# ANNEXURE – VII

# URBANISATION AND EMPLOYMENT

| REGION/STATE/UNION TERRITORY | No. of Bank Branches | Urbanisation (%) | Per capita income (₹) | Unemployed (%) | | HDI |
|---|---|---|---|---|---|---|
| | | | | Rural | Urban | |
| 1 | 2 | 3 | 4 | 5 | 6 | 7 |
| **NORTHERN REGION** | 23843 | | | | | |
| HARYANA | 4407 | 24.2 | 147076 | 18 | 25 | 0.641 |
| HIMACHAL PRADESH | 1466 | 10 | | 16 | 49 | 0.837 |
| JAMMU & KASHMIR | 1634 | 27.2 | 58888 | | | 0.626 |
| PUNJAB | 6024 | 37.5 | 99578 | 26 | 48 | 0.734 |
| RAJASTHAN | 6426 | 24.9 | 72156 | 4 | 22 | 0.318 |
| CHANDIGARH | 439 | 97.3 | | | | |
| NCT OF DELHI | 3447 | 97.5 | 240849 | | | |
| **NORTH-EASTERN REGION** | 3345 | | | | | |
| ARUNACHAL PRADESH | 135 | 22.7 | 96199 | | | 0.402 |
| ASSAM | 2103 | 14.1 | 49480 | 39 | 52 | |
| MANIPUR | 138 | 20.2 | | | | |
| MEGHALAYA | 294 | 20.1 | 69516 | | | |
| MIZORAM | 151 | 51.5 | | | | |
| NAGALAND | 145 | 29 | 85544 | | | |
| TRIPURA | 379 | 26.2 | | | | |
| **EASTERN REGION** | 20893 | | | | | |
| BIHAR | 6210 | 11.3 | 36143 | 20 | 73 | 0.108 |
| JHARKHAND | 2763 | 24.1 | 52147 | | | 0.218 |
| ODISHA | 4410 | 16.7 | 59229 | 30 | 42 | 0.268 |
| SIKKIM | 122 | 25 | | | | |
| WEST BENGAL | 7327 | 31.9 | 78903 | 19 | 40 | 0.483 |
| ANDAMAN & NICOBAR ISLANDS | 61 | 35.7 | | | | |
| **CENTRAL REGION** | 25926 | | | | | |
| CHHATTISGARH | 2253 | 23.2 | 64442 | | | 0.291 |
| MADHYA PRADESH | 5997 | 27.6 | 59770 | 7 | 29 | 0.252 |
| UTTAR PRADESH | 15773 | 22.3 | 40373 | 10 | 29 | 0.214 |
| UTTARAKHAND | 1903 | 30.6 | 115632 | | | 0.641 |
| **WESTERN REGION** | 19821 | | | | | |
| GOA | 670 | 62.2 | | | | |

*Continued*

| | | | | | | |
|---|---|---|---|---|---|---|
| GUJARAT | 7241 | 42.6 | | 7 | 18 | 0.526 |
| MAHARASHTRA | 11810 | 45.2 | 129235 | 6 | 32 | 0.627 |
| DADRA & NAGAR HAVELI | 53 | 46.6 | | | | |
| DAMAN & DIU | 47 | 75.2 | | | | |
| **SOUTHERN REGION** | 36654 | | | | | |
| ANDHRA PRADESH | 6290 | | 90517 | 12 | 31 | 0.466 |
| KARNATAKA | 9365 | 38.6 | 101594 | 5 | 27 | 0.507 |
| KERALA | 6190 | 47.7 | | 76 | 73 | 0.981 |
| TAMIL NADU | 9847 | 48.5 | 128366 | 15 | 32 | 0.761 |
| TELANGANA | 4721 | 38.7 | | | | |
| LAKSHADWEEP | 13 | 68.3 | | | | |
| PUDUCHERRY | 228 | 78.1 | 175006 | | | |
| **ALL-INDIA** | 130482 | 31.2 | | 16 | 34 | 0.411 |

Note:  1.  Urbanization is as per National Census, 2011; per capita income refers to

2.  Net State Domestic Product -2014–15 at current prices (₹);

3.  Unemployed statistics relate to the 66th round National Sample Survey of Government of

4.  India - last modified on 1st February, 2016 - by Ministry of Statistics and Programme

5.  Implementation. Human development Index (HDI) as per the published Special Article

in EPW dated 29th September, 2012 (Vol.XLVII No.39)

# ANNEXURE - VIII

# LITERACY LEVEL AND BANK CREDIT

| REGION/STATE/UNION TERRITORY | No. of Bank Branches | Literacy Levels (%) | | |
|---|---|---|---|---|
| | | Male | Female | Combined |
| 1 | 2 | 3 | 4 | 5 |
| **NORTHERN REGION** | 23843 | | | |
| HARYANA | 4407 | 85.4 | 66.8 | 75.6 |
| HIMACHAL PRADESH | 1466 | 90.8 | 76.6 | 82.8 |
| JAMMU & KASHMIR | 1634 | 78.3 | 58 | 67.2 |
| PUNJAB | 6024 | 81.5 | 71.3 | 75.8 |
| RAJASTHAN | 6426 | 80.5 | 52.7 | 66.1 |
| CHANDIGARH | 439 | 90.5 | 81.4 | 86.1 |
| NCT OF DELHI | 3447 | 91 | 80.9 | 86.2 |
| **NORTH-EASTERN REGION** | 3345 | | | |
| ARUNACHAL PRADESH | 135 | 73.7 | 59.6 | 65.4 |
| ASSAM | 2103 | 78.8 | 67.3 | 72.2 |
| MANIPUR | 138 | 86.5 | 73.2 | 76.9 |
| MEGHALAYA | 294 | 77.2 | 73.8 | 74.4 |
| MIZORAM | 151 | 93.7 | 89.4 | 91.3 |
| NAGALAND | 145 | 83.3 | 76.7 | 79.6 |
| TRIPURA | 379 | 92.2 | 83.2 | 87.2 |
| **EASTERN REGION** | 20893 | | | |
| BIHAR | 6210 | 73.4 | 53.3 | 61.8 |
| JHARKHAND | 2763 | 78.5 | 56.2 | 66.4 |
| ODISHA | 4410 | 82.4 | 64.4 | 72.9 |
| SIKKIM | 122 | 87.3 | 76.4 | 81.4 |
| WEST BENGAL | 7327 | 82.7 | 71.2 | 76.3 |
| ANDAMAN & NICOBAR ISLANDS | 61 | 90.1 | 81.8 | 86.6 |
| **CENTRAL REGION** | 25926 | | | |
| CHHATTISGARH | 2253 | 81.5 | 60.6 | 70.3 |
| MADHYA PRADESH | 5997 | 80.5 | 60 | 69.3 |
| UTTAR PRADESH | 15773 | 79.2 | 59.3 | 67.7 |
| UTTARAKHAND | 1903 | 88.3 | 70.7 | 78.8 |
| **WESTERN REGION** | 19821 | | | |
| GOA | 670 | 92.8 | 81.8 | 88.7 |
| GUJARAT | 7241 | 87.2 | 70.7 | 78.0 |

*Continued*

| | | | | |
|---|---|---|---|---|
| MAHARASHTRA | 11810 | 89.8 | 75.5 | 82.3 |
| DADRA & NAGAR HAVELI | 53 | 86.5 | 65.9 | 76.2 |
| DAMAN & DIU | 47 | 91.5 | 79.6 | 87.1 |
| **SOUTHERN REGION** | 36654 | | | |
| ANDHRA PRADESH | 6290 | 75.6 | 59.7 | 67.0 |
| KARNATAKA | 9365 | 82.9 | 68.1 | 75.4 |
| KERALA | 6190 | 96 | 92 | 94.0 |
| TAMIL NADU | 9847 | 86.8 | 73.9 | 80.1 |
| TELANGANA | 4721 | | | |
| LAKSHADWEEP | 13 | 96.1 | 88.3 | 91.9 |
| PUDUCHERRY | 228 | 92.1 | 81.2 | 85.9 |
| **ALL-INDIA** | 130482 | 82.1 | 65.5 | 74.1 |
| Source 1: Reserve Bank of India | | | | |
| 2: Census of India 2011 | | | | |

# ANNEXURE – IX

# BANKS AND HEALTHCARE

| REGION/STATE/UNION TERRITORY | No. of Bank Branches | Infant Mortality Rate | | Hospitals | PHCs | No. of beds |
|---|---|---|---|---|---|---|
| | (No) | Male | Female | (No) | (No) | |
| 1 | 2 | 3 | 4 | 5 | 6 | 7 |
| **NORTHERN REGION** | 23843 | | | | | |
| HARYANA | 4407 | 41 | 48 | 154 | 441 | 7879 |
| HIMACHAL PRADESH | 1466 | 36 | 39 | 151 | 449 | 8485 |
| JAMMU & KASHMIR | 1634 | 40 | 41 | 1969 | 375 | 7318 |
| PUNJAB | 6024 | 28 | 33 | 243 | 446 | 11419 |
| RAJASTHAN | 6426 | 50 | 53 | 2512 | 1504 | 38617 |
| CHANDIGARH | 439 | 21 | 19 | 5 | 0 | 1750 |
| NCT OF DELHI | 3447 | 25 | 31 | 109 | 8 | 22961 |
| **NORTH-EASTERN REGION** | 3345 | | | | | |
| ARUNACHAL PRADESH | 135 | 33 | 31 | 384 | 97 | 5010 |
| ASSAM | 2103 | 55 | 56 | 1020 | 856 | 10179 |
| MANIPUR | 138 | 8 | 15 | 225 | 73 | 1385 |
| MEGHALAYA | 294 | 52 | 52 | 40 | 109 | 2957 |
| MIZORAM | 151 | 31 | 37 | 22 | 57 | 1064 |
| NAGALAND | 145 | 15 | 26 | 53 | 126 | 2427 |
| TRIPURA | 379 | 29 | 29 | 39 | 79 | 3485 |
| **EASTERN REGION** | 20893 | | | | | |
| BIHAR | 6210 | 44 | 45 | 671 | 1863 | 13231 |
| JHARKHAND | 2763 | 36 | 43 | 549 | 330 | 5414 |
| ODISHA | 4410 | 55 | 58 | 1750 | 1279 | 16683 |
| SIKKIM | 122 | 23 | 30 | 33 | 24 | 1560 |
| WEST BENGAL | 7327 | 30 | 34 | 1566 | 909 | 77210 |
| ANDAMAN & NICOBAR ISLANDS | 61 | 19 | 27 | 32 | 19 | 1075 |
| **CENTRAL REGION** | 25926 | | | | | |
| CHHATTISGARH | 2253 | 47 | 50 | 2023 | 716 | 10770 |
| MADHYA PRADESH | 5997 | 57 | 62 | 1539 | 1155 | 30302 |
| UTTAR PRADESH | 15773 | 55 | 59 | 861 | 3692 | 56384 |
| UTTARAKHAND | 1903 | 34 | 38 | 695 | 239 | 7965 |
| **WESTERN REGION** | 19821 | | | | | |
| GOA | 670 | 7 | 14 | 11 | 19 | 2510 |

*Continued*

| | | | | | | |
|---|---|---|---|---|---|---|
| GUJARAT | 7241 | 39 | 42 | 1553 | 1096 | 35470 |
| MAHARASHTRA | 11810 | 24 | 25 | 1173 | 1816 | 47217 |
| DADRA & NAGAR HAVELI | 53 | 35 | 36 | 2 | 60 | 281 |
| DAMAN & DIU | 47 | 17 | 27 | 4 | 3 | 200 |
| **SOUTHERN REGION** | 36654 | | | | | |
| ANDHRA PRADESH | 6290 | 40 | 46 | 460 | 1570 | 37961 |
| KARNATAKA | 9365 | 34 | 35 | 765 | 2193 | 51986 |
| KERALA | 6190 | 11 | 13 | 1255 | 813 | 37021 |
| TAMIL NADU | 9847 | 21 | 23 | 1995 | 1283 | 62229 |
| TELANGANA | 4721 | | | | | |
| LAKSHADWEEP | 13 | 27 | 20 | 3 | 4 | 120 |
| PUDUCHERRY | 228 | 17 | 20 | 50 | 24 | 2103 |
| **ALL-INDIA** | 130482 | 43 | 46 | 35416 | 23673 | 1376013 |
| | | | | | | |

Source: (i) Health Statistics in India;

(ii) Information furnished by the Union Minister of Health & Family Welfare

(Shri Gulam Nabi Azad) on 13/08/2013

(iii) Infant Mortality Rate is published by the Office of the Registrar General, Government of India, Ministry of Home Affairs.

# ANNEXURE – X

## BANKS AND POVERTY RATIO (2011–12)

| REGION/STATE/UNION TERRITORY | No. of Bank Branches | Calorie Intake (Kcal) | | Monthly per capita (₹) | | Below Poverty Line-2011–12 (%) | | |
|---|---|---|---|---|---|---|---|---|
| | | Rural | Urban | Rural | Urban | Rural | Urban | Combined |
| 1 | 2 | 3 | 4 | 5 | 6 | 7 | 8 | 9 |
| **NORTHERN REGION** | 23843 | | | | | | | |
| HARYANA | 4407 | 2441 | 2443 | 1015 | 1169 | 11.6 | 10.3 | 11.2 |
| HIMACHAL PRADESH | 1466 | | | 913 | 1064 | 8.5 | 4.3 | 8.1 |
| JAMMU & KASHMIR | 1634 | | | 891 | 988 | 11.5 | 7.2 | 10.4 |
| PUNJAB | 6024 | 2483 | 2299 | 1054 | 1155 | 7.7 | 9.2 | 8.3 |
| RAJASTHAN | 6426 | 2408 | 2320 | 905 | 1002 | 16.1 | 10.7 | 14.7 |
| CHANDIGARH | 439 | | | | | 1.6 | 22.3 | 21.8 |
| NCT OF DELHI | 3447 | | | 1145 | 1134 | 12.9 | 9.8 | 9.9 |
| **NORTH-EASTERN REGION** | 3345 | | | | | | | |
| ARUNACHAL PRADESH | 135 | | | 930 | 1060 | 38.9 | 20.3 | 34.7 |
| ASSAM | 2103 | 2170 | 2110 | 828 | 1008 | 33.9 | 20.5 | 32 |
| MANIPUR | 138 | | | 1118 | 1170 | 38.8 | 32.6 | 36.9 |
| MEGHALAYA | 294 | | | 888 | 1154 | 12.5 | 9.3 | 11.9 |
| MIZORAM | 151 | | | 1066 | 1155 | 35.4 | 6.4 | 20.4 |
| NAGALAND | 145 | | | 1270 | 1302 | 19.9 | 16.5 | 18.9 |
| TRIPURA | 379 | | | 798 | 920 | 16.5 | 7.4 | 14.1 |
| **EASTERN REGION** | 20893 | | | | | | | |
| BIHAR | 6210 | 2242 | 2170 | 778 | 923 | 34.1 | 31.2 | 33.7 |
| JHARKHAND | 2763 | 2138 | 2175 | 748 | 974 | 40.8 | 24.8 | 37 |
| ODISHA | 4410 | 2215 | 2191 | 695 | 861 | 35.7 | 17.3 | 32.6 |
| SIKKIM | 122 | | | 930 | 1226 | 9.9 | 3.7 | 8.2 |
| WEST BENGAL | 7327 | 2199 | 2130 | 783 | 981 | 22.5 | 14.7 | 20 |
| ANDAMAN & NICOBAR ISLANDS | 61 | | | | | 1.6 | 0 | 1 |
| **CENTRAL REGION** | 25926 | | | | | | | |
| CHHATTISGARH | 2253 | 2162 | 2205 | 738 | 849 | 44.6 | 24.8 | 39.9 |
| MADHYA PRADESH | 5997 | 2234 | 2209 | 771 | 897 | 35.7 | 21 | 31.7 |
| UTTAR PRADESH | 15773 | 2200 | 2144 | 768 | 941 | 30.4 | 26.1 | 29.4 |
| UTTARAKHAND | 1903 | | | 880 | 1082 | 11.6 | 10.5 | 11.3 |
| **WESTERN REGION** | 19821 | | | | | | | |
| GOA | 670 | | | 1090 | 1134 | 6.8 | 4.1 | 5.1 |
| GUJARAT | 7241 | 2024 | 2154 | 932 | 1152 | 21.5 | 10.1 | 16.6 |

*Continued*

| | | | | | | | | |
|---|---|---|---|---|---|---|---|---|
| MAHARASHTRA | 11810 | 2260 | 2227 | 967 | 1126 | 24.2 | 9.1 | 17.4 |
| DADRA & NAGAR HAVELI | 53 | | | | | 62.6 | 15.4 | 39.3 |
| DAMAN & DIU | 47 | | | | | 0 | 12.6 | 9.9 |
| **SOUTHERN REGION** | 36654 | | | | | | | |
| ANDHRA PRADESH | 6290 | 2365 | 2281 | 860 | 1009 | 11 | 5.8 | 9.2 |
| KARNATAKA | 9365 | 2164 | 2245 | 902 | 1089 | 24.5 | 15.3 | 20.9 |
| KERALA | 6190 | 2162 | 2198 | 1018 | 987 | 9.1 | 5 | 7.1 |
| TAMIL NADU | 9847 | 2052 | 2112 | 880 | 937 | 15.8 | 6.5 | 11.2 |
| TELANGANA | 4721 | | | | | | | |
| LAKSHADWEEP | 13 | | | | | 0 | 3.4 | 2.8 |
| PUDUCHERRY | 228 | | | 1301 | 1309 | 17.1 | 6.3 | 9.7 |
| **ALL-INDIA** | 130482 | 2233 | 2206 | 816 | 1000 | 25.7 | 13.7 | 21.9 |

Source: Calorie intake (Kcal) per day per capita has been published by the Ministries of Health & Family Welfare and the Ministry of Woman and Child based on state-wise distribution of nutrient intake as per 68th round of NSSO in 2011–12; poverty line refers to the year 2011–12 published by the Planning Commission, Government of India- computed as per Tendulkar methodology- and published in July 2013.

# ANNEXURE – XI

## DEPOSITS & CREDIT (C-D) RATIO – March 2015

| REGION/STATE/UNION TERRITORY | No. of Bank Branches | Total Deposits Mobilised in the State (₹ Mn) | Total credit utilised in the State (₹ Mn) | C-D Ratio as per utilisation |
|---|---|---|---|---|
| 1 | 2 | 3 | 4 | 5 |
| **NORTHERN REGION** | **23843** | **17935498.0** | **16467382** | **91.8** |
| Haryana | 4407 | 2226845.1 | 1898210 | 85.2 |
| Himachal Pradesh | 1466 | 598764.8 | 219182.4 | 36.6 |
| Jammu & Kashmir | 1634 | 737205.0 | 313648 | 42.5 |
| Punjab | 6024 | 2619723.4 | 2013210.4 | 76.8 |
| Rajasthan | 6426 | 2354794.7 | 2121822.3 | 90.1 |
| Chandigarh | 439 | 554331.3 | 611150.1 | 110.2 |
| Nct Of Delhi | 3447 | 8843833.6 | 9290158.8 | 105.0 |
| **NORTH-EASTERN REGION** | **3345** | **1554802.0** | **547264** | **35.2** |
| Arunachal Pradesh | 135 | 80085.6 | 23335.3 | 29.1 |
| Assam | 2103 | 973814.4 | 361886.1 | 37.2 |
| Manipur | 138 | 57300.7 | 19788.4 | 34.5 |
| Meghalaya | 294 | 166439.4 | 44782 | 26.9 |
| Mizoram | 151 | 53152.5 | 20206.9 | 39.9 |
| Nagaland | 145 | 69382.7 | 23636.5 | 34.1 |
| Tripura | 379 | 154626.7 | 52628.7 | 34.0 |
| **EASTERN REGION** | **20893** | **11113496.6** | **5384329.3** | **48.4** |
| Bihar | 6210 | 2168098.5 | 743700.7 | 34.3 |
| Jharkhand | 2763 | 1421112.8 | 434332.8 | 30.6 |
| Odisha | 4410 | 1900738.8 | 835232.7 | 43.9 |
| Sikkim | 122 | 57144.3 | 21115.4 | 37.0 |
| West Bengal | 7327 | 5536916.1 | 3338365.7 | 60.3 |
| Andaman & Nicobar Islands | 61 | 29486.2 | 11582.1 | 39.3 |
| **CENTRAL REGION** | **25926** | **11396700.1** | **5842505.8** | **51.3** |
| Chhattisgarh | 2253 | 991656.2 | 628768.2 | 63.4 |
| Madhya Pradesh | 5997 | 2793419.1 | 1610041.9 | 57.6 |
| Uttar Pradesh | 15773 | 6725295.6 | 3291402.2 | 48.9 |
| Uttarakhand | 1903 | 886329.2 | 312293.5 | 35.2 |

*Continued*

| | | | |
|---|---|---|---|
| **WESTERN REGION** | **19821** | **26853629.8** | 21717730.4 | 80.9 |
| Goa | 670 | 515442.3 | 145379 | 28.2 |
| Gujarat | 7241 | 4777581.9 | 3774923.3 | 79.0 |
| Maharashtra | 11810 | 21500095.1 | 17776398.9 | 82.7 |
| Dadra & Nagar Haveli | 53 | 27172.8 | 9842.3 | 36.2 |
| Daman & Diu | 47 | 33337.8 | 11186.9 | 33.6 |
| **SOUTHERN REGION** | **36654** | **20366985.5** | 18825513.7 | 92.4 |
| Andhra Pradesh | 6290 | 1933489.3 | 2043338.3 | 108.3 |
| Karnataka | 9365 | 6342916.2 | 4606692.8 | 72.6 |
| Kerala | 6190 | 3283993.6 | 2147499 | 65.4 |
| Tamil Nadu | 9847 | 5453170.4 | 6406311.7 | 117.5 |
| Telangana | 4721 | 3235158.7 | 3538633 | 107.8 |
| Lakshadweep | 13 | 7618.0 | 694 | 9.1 |
| Puducherry | 228 | 110639.3 | 82345 | 74.4 |
| **ALL-INDIA** | **130482** | **89221112.1** | 68784725.2 | 77.1 |
| Source: Reserve Bank of India | | | | |

# ANNEXURE – XII

## Select Banking Variables

| YEAR (Apr.-Mar) | Population (Million) | Branches (Number) | Deposits (₹ Billion) | Credit (₹ Billion) | Investment (₹ Billion) |
|---|---|---|---|---|---|
| 1 | 2 | 3 | 4 | 5 | 6 |
| 1950–51 |  | 2765 | 8.93 | 8.81 |  |
| 1951–52 |  | 2646 | 8.61 | 9.14 |  |
| 1952–53 | 372 | 2671 | 9.71 | 8.92 |  |
| 1953–54 | 379 | 2671 | 8.48 | 9.58 |  |
| 1954–55 | 386 | 2838 | 9.43 | 8.72 |  |
| 1955–56 | 393 | 2953 | 10.43 | 9.26 |  |
| 1956–57 | 401 | 3263 | 11.75 | 10.69 |  |
| 1957–58 | 409 | 3263 | 14.52 | 9.63 |  |
| 1958–59 | 418 | 3922 | 16.35 | 10.14 |  |
| 1959–60 | 426 | 4150 | 19.02 | 11.28 |  |
| 1960–61 | 434 | 4390 | 17.36 | 13.36 |  |
| 1961–62 | 444 | 4608 | 19.17 | 14.08 |  |
| 1962–63 | 454 | 5004 | 20.42 | 15.88 |  |
| 1963–64 | 464 | 5499 | 22.85 | 18.17 |  |
| 1964–65 | 474 | 5902 | 25.83 | 20.35 |  |
| 1965–66 | 485 | 6382 | 29.51 | 22.87 |  |
| 1966–67 | 495 | 6781 | 34.25 | 26.92 |  |
| 1967–68 | 506 | 7446 | 38.56 | 30.32 |  |
| 1968–69 | 518 | 8262 | 43.38 | 33.96 |  |
| 1969–70 | 529 | 10131 | 50.28 | 39.71 | 14.81 |
| 1970–71 | 541 | 12013 | 59.06 | 46.84 | 17.72 |
| 1971–72 | 554 | 13622 | 71.06 | 52.63 | 21.9 |
| 1972–73 | 567 | 15362 | 86.43 | 61.15 | 28.97 |
| 1973–74 | 580 | 16936 | 101.39 | 73.99 | 32.86 |
| 1974–75 | 593 | 18730 | 118.27 | 87.62 | 39.15 |
| 1975–76 | 607 | 21220 | 141.55 | 108.77 | 46.07 |
| 1976–77 | 620 | 24802 | 175.66 | 131.73 | 55.36 |
| 1977–78 | 634 | 28016 | 222.11 | 149.39 | 78.97 |
| 1978–79 | 648 | 30202 | 270.16 | 182.85 | 91.09 |
| 1979–80 | 664 | 32419 | 317.59 | 215.37 | 106.24 |
| 1980–81 | 679 | 35707 | 379.88 | 253.71 | 131.86 |

*Continued*

| 1981–82 | 692 | 39177 | 437.33 | 296.82 | 151.41 |
|---------|-----|-------|--------|--------|--------|
| 1982–83 | 708 | 42079 | 513.58 | 354.93 | 183.34 |
| 1983–84 | 723 | 45332 | 605.96 | 412.94 | 212.46 |
| 1984–85 | 739 | 51385 | 722.44 | 489.53 | 281.38 |
| 1985–86 | 755 | 53287 | 854.04 | 560.67 | 305.53 |
| 1986–87 | 771 | 53859 | 1027.24 | 633.08 | 385.82 |
| 1897–88 | 788 | 55410 | 1180.45 | 705.36 | 465.04 |
| 1988–89 | 805 | 57699 | 1401.51 | 847.19 | 546.62 |
| 1989–90 | 822 | 59752 | 1669.59 | 1014.53 | 643.69 |
| 1990–91 | 839 | 60220 | 1925.41 | 1163.01 | 750.65 |
| 1991–92 | 856 | 60570 | 2307.58 | 1255.92 | 901.96 |
| 1992–93 | 872 | 61169 | 2685.72 | 1519.82 | 1056.56 |
| 1993–94 | 892 | 61803 | 3151.32 | 1644.18 | 1325.23 |
| 1994–95 | 910 | 62367 | 3868.59 | 2115.61 | 1492.53 |
| 1995–96 | 928 | 63026 | 4338.19 | 2540.15 | 1647.82 |
| 1996–97 | 946 | 63550 | 5055.99 | 2784.01 | 1905.14 |
| 1997–98 | 964 | 64218 | 5984.85 | 3240.79 | 2187.05 |
| 1998–99 | 983 | 64939 | 7140.25 | 3688.37 | 2545.95 |
| 1999–2000 | 1001 | 65412 | 8133.45 | 4359.58 | 3089.44 |
| 2000–01 | 1019 | 65919 | 9626.18 | 5114.34 | 3701.59 |
| 2001–02 | 1040 | 66190 | 11033.6 | 5897.23 | 4382.69 |
| 2002–03 | 1056 | 66535 | 12808.53 | 7292.15 | 5475.46 |
| 2003–04 | 1072 | 67188 | 15044.16 | 8407.85 | 6775.88 |
| 2004–05 | 1089 | 68355 | 17001.98 | 11004.28 | 7391.54 |
| 2005–06 | 1106 | 69586 | 21090.49 | 15070.77 | 7174.54 |
| 2006–07 | 1122 | 71946 | 26119.33 | 19311.89 | 7915.16 |
| 2007–08 | 1138 | 75925 | 31969.39 | 23619.14 | 9717.15 |
| 2008–09 | 1154 | 79864 | 38341.11 | 27755.49 | 11664.11 |
| 2009–10 | 1170 | 85156 | 44928.26 | 32447.88 | 13847.52 |
| 2010–11 | 1186 | 90896 | 52079.69 | 39420.83 | 15016.19 |
| 2011–12 | 1202 | 98533 | 59090.82 | 46118.52 | 17377.87 |
| 2012–13 | 1217 | 106389 | 67504.54 | 52604.59 | 20061.05 |
| 2013–14 | 1233 | 117630 | 77055.61 | 59940.96 | 22128.21 |
| 2014–15 | 1267 | 125857 | 85332.85 | 65364.21 | 24918.25 |

# ANNEXURE – XIII

## POPULATION GROUP-WISE NUMBER OF BRANCHES OF SCHEDULED COMMERCIAL BANKS

| YEAR | RURAL | SEMI-URBAN | URBAN | METROPOLITAN | TOTAL |
|------|-------|------------|-------|--------------|-------|
| 1 | 2 | 3 | 4 | 5 | 6 |
| 1975 | 6807 | 5598 | 3489 | 2836 | 18730 |
| 1976 | 7690 | 6421 | 3998 | 3111 | 21220 |
| 1977 | 9537 | 7428 | 4542 | 3475 | 24802 |
| 1978 | 11806 | 7628 | 4843 | 3739 | 28016 |
| 1979 | 13337 | 7889 | 5037 | 3939 | 30202 |
| 1980 | 15105 | 8122 | 5178 | 4014 | 32419 |
| 1981 | 17656 | 8471 | 5454 | 4126 | 35707 |
| 1982 | 20401 | 8809 | 5693 | 4274 | 39177 |
| 1983 | 22686 | 9081 | 5917 | 4395 | 42079 |
| 1984 | 25380 | 9326 | 6116 | 4510 | 45332 |
| 1985 | 30185 | 9816 | 6578 | 4806 | 51385 |
| 1986 | 29703 | 10585 | 7209 | 5790 | 53287 |
| 1987 | 30209 | 10637 | 7218 | 5795 | 53859 |
| 1988 | 31114 | 11132 | 7322 | 5842 | 55410 |
| 1989 | 33014 | 11166 | 7524 | 5995 | 57699 |
| 1990 | 34791 | 11324 | 8042 | 5595 | 59752 |
| 1991 | 35206 | 11344 | 8046 | 5624 | 60220 |
| 1992 | 35269 | 11356 | 8279 | 5666 | 60570 |
| 1993 | 35389 | 11465 | 8562 | 5753 | 61169 |
| 1994 | 35329 | 11890 | 8745 | 5839 | 61803 |
| 1995 | 33004 | 13341 | 8868 | 7154 | 62367 |
| 1996 | 32995 | 13561 | 9086 | 7384 | 63026 |
| 1997 | 32915 | 13766 | 9340 | 7529 | 63550 |
| 1998 | 32878 | 13980 | 9597 | 7763 | 64218 |
| 1999 | 32857 | 14168 | 9898 | 8016 | 64939 |
| 2000 | 32734 | 14407 | 10052 | 8219 | 65412 |
| 2001 | 32562 | 14597 | 10293 | 8467 | 65919 |
| 2002 | 32380 | 14747 | 10477 | 8586 | 66190 |
| 2003 | 32303 | 14859 | 10693 | 8680 | 66535 |
| 2004 | 32121 | 15091 | 11000 | 8976 | 67188 |
| 2005 | 32082 | 15403 | 11500 | 9370 | 68355 |
| 2006 | 30051 | 15773 | 12129 | 11633 | 69586 |

*Continued*

| 2007 | 30184 | 16535 | 12993 | 12234 | 71946 |
| 2008 | 30712 | 17777 | 14245 | 13191 | 75925 |
| 2009 | 31395 | 19065 | 15273 | 14131 | 79864 |
| 2010 | 32430 | 20788 | 16684 | 15254 | 85156 |
| 2011 | 35923 | 23089 | 17629 | 16255 | 90896 |
| 2012 | 36546 | 25834 | 18879 | 17274 | 98533 |
| 2013 | 39816 | 28546 | 19935 | 18092 | 106389 |
| 2014 | 45293 | 31530 | 21532 | 19275 | 117630 |
| 2015 | 48557 | 33766 | 23036 | 20498 | 125857 |

Note: The population group 'Rural' includes centres with population less than 10,000. The population group 'Semi-Urban' includes centres with population of more than 10,000 but less than one lakh. 'Urban' centres are those with population of more than one lakh and less than one million. 'Metropolitan' centres include those with more than one million (10 lakh). The data represent number of bank branches excluding administrative offices of these banks. The data presented is as per the extant geographical boundaries to the extent updated in the latest Ministry of Finance (MOF) database on account of reorganization of States/districts.

Source: RBI Handbook of Statistics on the Indian Economy 2014–15.

# ANNEXURE – XIV

## Advances and NPAs of Domestic Banks by Priority and Non-Priority Sectors *

## (Amount in ₹ Billion)

| Bank Group | Priority Sector | | | Non-Priority Sector | | | Total | | |
|---|---|---|---|---|---|---|---|---|---|
| | Gross Advances | Gross NPAs | Gross NPAs as Per Cent of Total | Gross Advances | Gross NPAs | Gross NPAs as Per Cent of Total | Gross Advances | Gross NPAs | Gross NPAs as Per Cent of Total |
| **Public Sector Banks** | | | | | | | | | |
| 2013 | 12,790 | 669 | 42.9 | 27,769 | 890 | 57.1 | 40,559 | 1,559 | 100.0 |
| 2014 | 15,193 | 792 | 36.5 | 30,712 | 1,375 | 63.5 | 45,905 | 2,167 | 100.0 |
| 2015 | 16,563 | 959 | 35.9 | 32,598 | 1,712 | 64.1 | 49,161 | 2,671 | 100.0 |
| **Nationalised Banks**\*\* | | | | | | | | | |
| 2013 | 8,891 | 405 | 42.2 | 19,170 | 554 | 57.8 | 28,061 | 959 | 100.0 |
| 2014 | 10,711 | 530 | 37.7 | 21,249 | 877 | 62.3 | 31,960 | 1,407 | 100.0 |
| 2015 | 12,182 | 702 | 35.8 | 22,133 | 1,260 | 64.2 | 34,315 | 1,962 | 100.0 |
| **SBI Group** | | | | | | | | | |
| 2013 | 3,899 | 264 | 44.1 | 8,599 | 335 | 55.9 | 12,498 | 600 | 100.0 |
| 2014 | 4,482 | 261 | 34.4 | 9,463 | 499 | 65.6 | 13,944 | 760 | 100.0 |
| 2015 | 4,381 | 257 | 36.2 | 10,465 | 452 | 63.8 | 14,846 | 709 | 100.0 |
| **Private Sector Banks** | | | | | | | | | |
| 2013 | 3,157 | 52 | 26.0 | 7,309 | 148 | 74.0 | 10,467 | 200 | 100.0 |
| 2014 | 3,831 | 61 | 26.6 | 8,287 | 167 | 73.4 | 12,117 | 227 | 100.0 |
| 2015 | 4,444 | 72 | 22.8 | 9,942 | 244 | 77.2 | 14,386 | 316 | 100.0 |
| **All SCBs (Excluding Foreign Banks)** | | | | | | | | | |
| 2013 | 15,947 | 721 | 41.0 | 35,078 | 1,038 | 59.0 | 51,025 | 1,759 | 100.0 |
| 2014 | 19,024 | 852 | 35.6 | 38,998 | 1,542 | 64.4 | 58,022 | 2,395 | 100.0 |
| 2015 | 21,007 | 1,031 | 34.5 | 42,541 | 1,955 | 65.5 | 63,548 | 2,987 | 100.0 |

Notes : 1. * : Excluding foreign banks.
     2. ** : Includes IDBI Bank Ltd.
     3. Constituent items may not add up to the total due to rounding off.

**Source :** Based on off-site returns (Domestic), Reserve Bank of India

| REGION/STATE/UNION TERRITORY | DEN SITY | Rural P.I | Urb. P.I | LITERACY | SEX-RATIO | RURAL BPL | URBAN-BPL | COMBINED BPL | sub-centr | PHCs | CHCs | G. Hosp | Beds | Pop Served | Male Lit | Fem. Lit | URB-ANIS% | unem-R | unem-U | Cal. R | Cal. U | Inf. M.M | Inf. M.F | 2014-15 P.Cap Rs | Housing shortage | Bank Br. (No.) | Bank Dep. | Bank Credit | Credit to Agri. Rs.M | Hous R.M | Credit to C-D Ratio | HDI |
|---|---|---|---|---|---|---|---|---|---|---|---|---|---|---|---|---|---|---|---|---|---|---|---|---|---|---|---|---|---|---|---|---|
| 1 | 2 | 4 | 5 | 6 | 7 | 8 | 9 | 10 | 11 | 12 | 13 | 14 | 15 | 16 | 17 | 18 | 19 | 20 | 21 | 22 | 23 | 24 | 25 | 26 | 27 | 28 | 29 | 30 | 31 | 32 | 33 | 34 |
| **NORTHERN REGION** | | | | | | | | | | | | | | | | | | | | | | | | | | 23843 | 17935498 | 16467382 | 1517200 | 403532 | 91.8 | |
| HARYANA | 573 | 1015 | 1169 | 75.6 | 879 | 11.6 | 10.3 | 11.2 | 2484 | 441 | 107 | 154 | 7879 | 3122 | 85.4 | 66.8 | 24.2 | 18 | 25 | 2441 | 2443 | 41 | 48 | 147076 | 0.42 | 4407 | 2226845 | 1898210 | 319772 | 56868 | 85.2 | 0.641 |
| HIMACHAL PRADESH | 123 | 913 | 1064 | 82.8 | 972 | 8.5 | 4.3 | 8.1 | 2071 | 449 | 73 | 151 | 8485 | 808 | 90.8 | 76.6 | 10 | 16 | 49 | | | 36 | 39 | | 0.04 | 1466 | 598764 | 219182 | 43700 | 17289 | 36.6 | 0.837 |
| JAMMU & KASHMIR | 56 | 891 | 988 | 67.2 | 889 | 11.5 | 7.2 | 10.4 | 1907 | 375 | 75 | | 7318 | 1733 | 78.3 | 58 | 27.2 | | | | | 40 | 41 | 58888 | 0.13 | 1634 | 737205 | 313648 | 61466 | 16644 | 42.5 | 0.626 |
| PUNJAB | 551 | 1054 | 1155 | 75.8 | 895 | 7.7 | 9.2 | 8.3 | 2950 | 446 | 129 | 243 | 11419 | 2426 | 81.5 | 71.3 | 37.5 | 26 | 48 | 2483 | 2299 | 28 | 33 | 99578 | 0.39 | 6024 | 2619723 | 2013210 | 501088 | 60785 | 76.8 | 0.734 |
| RAJASTHAN | 200 | 905 | 1002 | 66.1 | 928 | 16.1 | 10.7 | 14.7 | 11487 | 1504 | 368 | 2512 | 38617 | 1777 | 80.5 | 52.7 | 24.9 | 4 | 22 | 2408 | 2320 | 50 | 53 | 72156 | 1.15 | 6426 | 2354795 | 2121822 | 410409 | 107103 | 90.1 | 0.318 |
| CHANDIGARH | 9258 | | | 86.1 | 818 | 1.6 | 22.3 | 21.8 | 16 | 0 | 2 | 5 | 1750 | 603 | 90.5 | 81.4 | 97.3 | | | | | 21 | 19 | | 0.02 | 439 | 554331 | 611150 | 21969 | 12426 | 110.2 | |
| NCT OF DELHI | 11320 | | 1134 | 86.2 | 868 | 12.9 | 9.8 | 9.9 | 41 | 8 | 0 | 109 | 22961 | 744 | 91 | 80.9 | 97.5 | 25 | | | | 31 | | 240849 | 0.49 | 3447 | 8843834 | 9290159 | 158805 | 132417 | 105 | |
| **NORTH-EASTERN REGION** | | | | | | | | | | | | | | | | | | | | | | | | | | 3345 | 1554802 | 547264 | 74503 | 34741 | 35.2 | |
| ARUNACHAL PRADESH | 17 | 930 | 1060 | 65.4 | 993 | 38.9 | 20.3 | 34.7 | 286 | 97 | 48 | 384 | 5010 | 236 | 73.7 | 59.6 | 22.7 | 39 | 52 | 2170 | 2110 | 33 | 31 | 96199 | 0.03 | 135 | 80085 | 23335 | 1751 | 467 | 29.1 | 0.402 |
| ASSAM | 398 | 828 | 1008 | 72.2 | 958 | 33.9 | 20.5 | 32 | 4604 | 856 | 108 | 1020 | 10179 | 3062 | 78.8 | 67.3 | 14.1 | | | | | 55 | 56 | 49480 | 0.28 | 2103 | 973814 | 361886 | 53728 | 22994 | 37.2 | |
| MANIPUR | 128 | 1118 | 1170 | 76.9 | 985 | 38.8 | 32.6 | 36.9 | 420 | 73 | 16 | 225 | 1385 | 876 | 86.5 | 73.2 | 20.2 | | | | | 8 | 15 | 69516 | 0.08 | 138 | 57301 | 19788 | 3878 | 2386 | 34.5 | |
| MEGHALAYA | 132 | 888 | 1154 | 74.4 | 989 | 12.5 | 9.3 | 11.9 | 405 | 109 | 29 | 40 | 2957 | 1132 | 77.2 | 73.8 | 20.1 | | | | | 52 | 52 | 44782 | 0.03 | 294 | 166439 | 44782 | 3893 | 2023 | 26.9 | |
| MIZORAM | 52 | 1066 | 1155 | 91.3 | 931 | 35.4 | 6.4 | 20.4 | 370 | 57 | 9 | 22 | 1064 | 370 | 93.7 | 89.4 | 51.5 | | | | | 31 | 37 | 85544 | 0.02 | 151 | 53152 | 21207 | 1429 | 3420 | 39.9 | |
| NAGALAND | 119 | 1270 | 1302 | 79.6 | 931 | 19.9 | 16.5 | 18.9 | 396 | 126 | 21 | 53 | 2427 | 905 | 83.3 | 76.7 | 29 | | | | | 15 | 26 | | 0.21 | 145 | 69383 | 23636 | 2853 | 1078 | 34.1 | |
| TRIPURA | 350 | 798 | 920 | 87.2 | 960 | 16.5 | 7.4 | 14.1 | 627 | 79 | 11 | 39 | 3485 | 1026 | 92.2 | 83.2 | 26.2 | | | | | 29 | 29 | | 0.03 | 379 | 154627 | 52629 | 6971 | 2373 | 34 | |
| **EASTERN REGION** | | | | | | | | | | | | | | | | | | | | | | | | | | 20893 | 11113497 | 5384329 | 667244 | 237494 | 48.4 | |
| BIHAR | 1106 | 778 | 923 | 61.8 | 918 | 34.1 | 31.2 | 33.7 | 9696 | 1863 | 70 | 671 | 13231 | 7846 | 73.4 | 53.3 | 11.3 | 20 | 73 | 2242 | 2170 | 44 | 45 | 36143 | 1.19 | 6210 | 2168098 | 743701 | 209425 | 30224 | 34.3 | 0.108 |
| JHARKHAND | 414 | 748 | 974 | 66.4 | 948 | 40.8 | 24.8 | 37 | 3958 | 330 | 188 | 549 | 5414 | 6089 | 78.5 | 56.2 | 24.1 | | | 2138 | 2175 | 36 | 43 | 52147 | 0.63 | 2763 | 1421113 | 434333 | 47307 | 22691 | 30.6 | 0.218 |
| ODISHA | 270 | 695 | 861 | 72.9 | 979 | 35.7 | 17.3 | 32.6 | 6688 | 1279 | 231 | 1750 | 16683 | 2514 | 82.4 | 64.4 | 16.7 | 30 | 42 | 2215 | 2191 | 55 | 58 | 59229 | 0.41 | 4410 | 1900739 | 835233 | 103743 | 41612 | 43.9 | 0.268 |
| SIKKIM | 86 | 930 | 1226 | 81.4 | 890 | 9.9 | 3.7 | 8.2 | 147 | 24 | 0 | 33 | 1560 | 390 | 87.3 | 76.4 | 25 | | | | | 23 | 30 | | 0.01 | 122 | 57144 | 21115 | 1219 | 3813 | 37 | |
| WEST BENGAL | 1028 | 783 | 981 | 76.3 | 950 | 22.5 | 14.7 | 20 | 10356 | 909 | 348 | 1566 | 77210 | 1213 | 82.7 | 71.2 | 31.9 | 40 | | 2199 | 2130 | 30 | 34 | 78903 | 1.33 | 7327 | 5536916 | 3338366 | 304925 | 137913 | 60.3 | 0.483 |
| ANDAMAN & NICOBAR ISLANDS | 46 | | | 86.6 | 876 | 1.6 | 0 | 1 | 114 | 19 | 4 | 32 | 1075 | 353 | 90.1 | 81.8 | 35.7 | 19 | | | | 19 | 27 | 115632 | 0 | 61 | 29486 | 11582 | 625 | 1241 | 39.3 | |
| **CENTRAL REGION** | | | | | | | | | | | | | | | | | | | | | | | | | | 25926 | 11396700 | 5842506 | 1158666 | 326863 | 51.3 | |
| CHHATTISGARH | 189 | 738 | 849 | 70.3 | 991 | 44.6 | 24.8 | 39.9 | 4776 | 716 | 143 | 2023 | 10770 | 1984 | 81.5 | 60.6 | 23.2 | 7 | | 2162 | 2205 | 47 | 50 | 64442 | 0.35 | 2253 | 991656 | 628768 | 59470 | 33990 | 63.4 | 0.291 |
| MADHYA PRADESH | 236 | 771 | 897 | 69.3 | 931 | 35.7 | 21 | 31.7 | 8869 | 1155 | 333 | 1539 | 30302 | 2492 | 80.5 | 60 | 27.6 | 7 | 29 | 2234 | 2209 | 57 | 62 | 59770 | 1.1 | 5997 | 2793419 | 1610042 | 382809 | 105626 | 57.6 | 0.252 |
| UTTAR PRADESH | 829 | 768 | 941 | 67.7 | 912 | 30.4 | 26.1 | 29.4 | 20521 | 3692 | 515 | 861 | 56384 | 3499 | 82.4 | 59.3 | 22.3 | 10 | 29 | 2200 | 2144 | 55 | 59 | 40373 | 3.07 | 15773 | 6725296 | 3291402 | 646562 | 160984 | 48.9 | 0.214 |
| UTTARAKHAND | 189 | 880 | 1082 | 78.8 | 963 | 11.6 | 10.5 | 11.3 | 1765 | 239 | 55 | 695 | 7965 | 1194 | 88.3 | 70.7 | 30.6 | 34 | | | | 34 | 38 | 115632 | 0.16 | 1903 | 886329 | 312294 | 69824 | 26262 | 35.2 | 0.641 |
| **WESTERN REGION** | | | | | | | | | | | | | | | | | | | | | | | | | | 19821 | 26853630 | 21717730 | 2099071 | 1120651 | 80.9 | |
| GOA | 394 | 1090 | 1134 | 88.7 | 973 | 6.8 | 4.1 | 5.1 | 172 | 19 | 5 | 11 | 2510 | 581 | 92.8 | 81.8 | 62.2 | | | | | 7 | 14 | | 0.06 | 670 | 515442 | 145379 | 8101 | 12924 | 28.2 | |
| GUJARAT | 308 | 932 | 1152 | 78 | 919 | 21.5 | 10.1 | 16.6 | 7274 | 1096 | 290 | 1553 | 35470 | 1746 | 87.2 | 70.7 | 42.6 | 7 | 18 | 2024 | 2154 | 39 | 42 | 90517 | 0.99 | 7241 | 4777582 | 3774923 | 340079 | 224722 | 79 | 0.526 |
| MAHARASHTRA | 365 | 967 | 1126 | 82.3 | 929 | 24.2 | 9.1 | 17.4 | 10580 | 1816 | 365 | 1173 | 47217 | 2477 | 89.8 | 75.5 | 45.2 | 6 | 32 | 2260 | 2227 | 24 | 25 | 129235 | 1.94 | 11810 | 21500095 | 17776399 | 1750103 | 880956 | 82.7 | 0.627 |
| DADRA & NAGAR HAVELI | 700 | | | 76.2 | 774 | 62.6 | 15.4 | 39.3 | 50 | 60 | 1 | 2 | 281 | 1221 | 86.5 | 65.9 | 46.6 | | | | | 35 | 36 | | 0.05 | 53 | 27173 | 9842 | 358 | 1126 | 36.2 | |
| DAMAN & DIU | 219 | | | 87.1 | 618 | 0 | 12.6 | 9.9 | 26 | 3 | 2 | 4 | 200 | 1215 | 91.5 | 79.6 | 75.2 | | | | | 17 | 27 | | 0.01 | 47 | 33338 | 11187 | 430 | 923 | 33.6 | |
| **SOUTHERN REGION** | | | | | | | | | | | | | | | | | | | | | | | | | | 36654 | 20366986 | 18825514 | 3397772 | 1030514 | 92.4 | |
| ANDHRA PRADESH | 308 | 860 | 1009 | 67 | 902 | 11 | 5.8 | 9.2 | 12522 | 1570 | 167 | 460 | 37961 | 2230 | 75.6 | 59.7 | | 12 | 31 | 2365 | 2281 | 40 | 46 | 90517 | 1.27 | 6290 | 1886280 | 2043538 | 1121819 | 1034322 | 108.3 | 0.466 |
| KARNATAKA | 329 | 902 | 1089 | 75.4 | 973 | 24.5 | 15.3 | 20.9 | 8143 | 2193 | 325 | 765 | 51986 | 1119 | 82.9 | 68.1 | 38.6 | 5 | 27 | 2164 | 2245 | 34 | 35 | 101594 | 1.02 | 9365 | 6342916 | 4606693 | 687724 | 309045 | 72.6 | 0.507 |
| KERALA | 860 | 1018 | 987 | 94 | 1084 | 9.1 | 5 | 7.1 | 4575 | 813 | 233 | 1255 | 37021 | 910 | 96 | 92 | 47.7 | 76 | 73 | 2162 | 2198 | 11 | 13 | | 0.54 | 6190 | 3283993 | 2147499 | 498049 | 239574 | 65.4 | 0.981 |
| TAMIL NADU | 555 | 880 | 937 | 80.1 | 996 | 15.8 | 6.5 | 11.2 | 8706 | 1283 | 256 | 1995 | 62229 | 1203 | 86.8 | 73.9 | 48.5 | 15 | 32 | 2052 | 2112 | 21 | 23 | 128366 | 1.25 | 9847 | 5453170 | 6406312 | 1075561 | 1888255 | 117.5 | 0.761 |
| TELANGANA | | | | | | | | | | | | | | | | | 38.7 | | | | | 27 | 20 | | | 4721 | 3282367 | 3538633 | | | 107.8 | |
| LAKSHADWEEP | 2149 | | | 91.9 | 946 | 0 | 3.4 | 2.8 | 14 | 4 | 3 | 3 | 120 | 533 | 96.1 | 88.3 | 68.3 | | | | | 20 | | | 0.01 | 13 | 7618 | 694 | 113 | 17 | 9.1 | |
| PUDUCHERRY | 2547 | 1301 | 1309 | 85.9 | 1037 | 17.1 | 6.3 | 9.7 | 53 | 24 | 3 | 50 | 2103 | 571 | 92.1 | 81.2 | 78.1 | | | | | 17 | 20 | 175006 | 0.07 | 228 | 110639 | 82345 | 14506 | 17971 | 74.4 | |
| ALL-INDIA | 382 | 816 | 1000 | 74.1 | 940 | 25.7 | 13.7 | 21.9 | 147069 | 23673 | 4535 | 35416 | 1376013 | 879 | 82.1 | 65.5 | 31.2 | 16 | 34 | 2233 | 2206 | 43 | 46 | | 18.78 | 130482 | 89221112 | 68784725 | 8914465 | 3153795 | 77.1 | 0.411 |

# BIBLIOGRAPHY

**Books**

Abidi, A.I. : (1977) "Commercial Banks and Economic Development" Praeger Publishers, New York.

Adelman, Irma and Morris T. Cynthia: (1967) "Society, Politics and Economic Development. A Quantitative Approach," John Hopkins Press, Baltimore.

Adelman, Irma and Morris T. Cynthia: (1973) "Economic Growth and Social Equity in Developing Countries," Stanford University Press, U.S.A.

Agrwal, B.P.: (1963) "Industrial Estates in India," Asia Publishing House, NewYork.

Bandyopadhyay, R. and Khankhoje, D.P.: (1985) "Finance and Development," National Institute of Bank Management, Bombay.

Basu, S.K. : (1965) "Finance and Practice of Development Banking" Asia Publishing House, Bombay.

Bhagwati P.D. Agrawal: (1962) "Commercial Banking in India After Nationalisation," Classical Publishing Co., New Delhi.

Brahmananda, P.R.: (1982) "Productivity in the Indian Economy" Rising inputs for falling outputs" Himalaya Publishing House, Bombay.

Cameron, R.: (1972) "Banking and Economic Development" Oxford University Press, New York.

Desai, Mutalik, V.R.: (1966) "Savings in a Welfare State," P.C. Manaktala & Sons, Bombay.

Desai, Priya Mutalik (Ed): (1979) "Economic and Political Development of Kenya," Himalaya Publishing House, Bombay.

Desai, Priya Mutalik: (1982) "Development Issues In Africa," Himalaya Publishing House, Bombay.

Desai, S.S.M. (1986) "Rural Banking in India" Himalaya Publishing Co., Bombay.

Desai, Vasant : (1988) "Development Banking In India" Himalaya Publishing House, Bombay.

Friedman, Milton (Ed): (1956) "Studies in the Quantity Theory of Money," University of Chicago Press, Aldina.

Galbraith, John Kenneth : (1965) "Money Whence it Came, Where it Went," Indian Book Company, New Delhi.

Ghosh, D.N.: (1979) "Banking Policy in Indai – An Evaluation," Allied Publishers Pvt. Ltd., New Delhi.

Goldsmith, Raymond, W.: (1969) "Financial Structure and Development," Yale University Press, New Haven.

Gilbert Etienne: (1988) "Food and Poverty – India's Half Won Battle," Sage Publications, New Delhi.

Gunnar Myrdal : (1968) "Asian Drama: An Enquiry into Poverty of Nations," Penguin, Harmondsworth.

Gunnar Myrdal: (1969) "Economic Theory and Underdeveloped Regions," University Paper Back (Reprint).

Gurley, J.G. and Shaw, E.S.: (1960) "Money in a Theory of Finance," Brookings Institution, Washington.

Hawtrey, R.G,: (1950) "Currency and credit," Longmans, Green, London.

Iengar, H.V.R. :(1962) "Monetary Policy and Economic Growth,"Vora& Co., Bombay.

Jain, L.C.: (1929) "Indigenous Banking in India," Macmillan & Co., London.

Joseph A. Schumpeter: (1934) "The Theory of Economic Development – An Enquiry into Profits, Capital, Interest and the Business Cycle," (translated by Opic R.) Harward University Press, Cambridge, Mass.

Joshi, N.C. : (1978) "Indian Banking,"Ashish Publishing House, New Delhi.

Keynes, John Maynard : (1924) "Indian Currency and Finance," Macmillan & Co., London.

Keynes J.M.: (1930) "A Treatise on Money,"Harecourt Brace & Co., Inc., New York.

Kurian, C.T. : (1978) "Poverty, Planning and Social Transformation."

Mahajan, V.S.: (1986) "Studies in Indian Agriculture and Rural Development," Bombay.

Malcolom, S.K. :Adiseshiah: (1985) "Seventh Plan prospective," (Ed) Madras.

Mandal, S.K. : (1987) "Regional Disparities and Imbalances in India's Planned   Economic Development," Deep & Deep Publications, New Delhi.

Marshall, A. : (1923) "Money, Credit and Commerce," Macmillan & Co.,   London.

Mckinnon, R.I.: (1973) "Money and Capital in Economic Development,"  Brookings Institution, Washington, D.C.

Mckinnon, R.I. (Ed): (1976) "Money and Finance in Economic Growth and    Development,"Mancel Dekker Inc. New York.

Mukundan, A.P.: (1987) "From Shylocks to Credit Melas – A Brief History of  the Metamorphosis in the Philosophy of Banking," Pioneer   Printers.

Mongia, J.N.: (1982) "Banking Around the World," Allied Publishers Pvt. Ltd.,   New Delhi.

Muranjan, S.K.: (1952) "Modern Banking in India," Kamala Publishing House,   Bombay.

Nigam, B.M.L.: (1967) "Banking and Economic Growth,"Vora& Co., Bombay.

Pandey, K.L.: (1968) "Development of Banking in India since 1949," Scientific   Book Agency, Calcutta.

Raj, K.N.: (1948) "The Monetary Policy of the RBI," Popular Prakashan,   Bombay.

Rangarajan C.: (1982) "Innovation in Banking," Oxford & IBH Publishing Co.,   Bombay.

Rangaswamy, B. : (1985) "Public Sector Banking in India," Government of  India, New Delhi.

Rao, Hemalatha : (1984) "Regional Disparities and Development in India," Bangalore.

Rao, V.K.R.V.: (1973) "District Planning," Planning Commission, New Delhi.

Saunders, L.S.: (1969) "Technique of Opening a Branch Bank," Bankers  Publishing Co., Boston.

Sayers, R.S.: (1951) "Modern Banking," Oxford.

Sharma, B.P. : (1974) "The Role of Commercial Banks in India's Developing  Economy,"S.CHand& Co., Bombay.

Sharma, S.L.: (1986) "Development: Socio Cultural Dimensions,"Rawat Publications, Jaipur.

Shaw, E.S. (Ed): (1973) "Financial Depending in Economic Development," Oxford University Press, New York.

Shetty, S.L. (Ed) : (1979) "Framework for a National Credit Plan," National  Institute of Bank management, Bombay.

Shrivastava, O.S.: (1984) "Advanced Economics of Development and  Planning."

Simha, S.L.N. : (1970) "History of Reserve Bank of India – 1935-51," RBI,  Bombay.

Simha, S.L.N. (Ed): (1972) "Reforms of the Indian Banking System," Orient  Longman, Madras.

Subrahmanya, S. (Ed) : (1986) "Trends and Progress of Banking in India," Deep & Deep Publications, New Delhi.

U.N.: (1951) "Measures for the Economic Development of Under Developed  Countries," New York.

Vaswani, T.A.: (1974) "Indian Banking System,"Lalvani Publishing House,  Bombay.

Vishnu Datta: (1970) "Bank Nationalisation in Perspectives," Publication Division, New Delhi.

Velayudham, T.K.: (1985) "Human Resources Development in Banking  Industry," Indian Banks Association.

**Websites**

URL http://dbie.rbi.org.in - for database on Indian Economy

URL http://explore.data.gov.i

URL http://www.nass.usda.gov.i

URL http://www.nationalarchives.gov.uk/document

URL http://db.nedfi.com/

**Journals**

Angadi, V.B. and V. John Devaraj: (1983) "Productivity and Profitability of  Banks in India," Economic and Political Weekly, Vol.XVIII, No.48,    Nov. 26.

Agrawal, N.N.: "New Dimensions of Commercial Bank Credit in India," The   Indian Journal of Commerce, Vol.XXXVII, pp.97-109.

Alan J. Fernandes: "Development of Banking in India," The Journal of the Indian Institute of Bankers, Vol.XXXVI, No.2, P.108.

Anthony R. Measham: (1986) "Health and Development – The Bank's Experience, Finance and Development, December, pp. 26-29.

Arvinder Singh Chawla and Prem Kumar: (1986) "Banks for Balanced Regional Development," LokUdhyog, Vol.XIX, No.11, February, pp. 29- 35.

ArunGhosh: (1988) "Banking and Decentralisation," Economic and Polotical Weekly, Vol.XXIII, No.28, July, pp. 1408-1411.

Ashakant: (1978) "Branch Expansion Policy for Commercial Banks," The Journal of the Indian Institute of Bankers, VOl.49, No.4, Oct-Dec, pp.157-166.

Ashok Mitra: (1979) "Integrated Strategies for Economic and Demographic Development," Economic and Political Weekly, p.207. Vol.XIV.

Bandyopadhyay, R.: (1986) "Mass Banking: Management Problems," Economic and political Weekly, Vol.XXI, No.22, May, pp. N.52-N.58.

Bhabatosh Datta: (1976) "Banking Structure - A Re-Appraisal," Economic and Political Weekly, Vol.XI, P.781.

BhabatoshDatta: (1987) "Economic History and Economic Theory," Economic and Political Weekly, Vol. XXII. No. 18, May 2.

Bharadwaj, R. : (1974) "Theorem on Decentralised Decision-Making," Indian Economic Journal.

----------------------: (1988) "Sound Base to Build on ", The Hindu Survey of Indian Industries.

Bhat, N.S.: (1986) "The Banking System as the Financial Infrastructure and the Economy," The Indian Economic Journal, VOl.34, No.1.

Brahmananda, P.R. : (1978) "The Falling Economy and How to Revive it," The Indian Economic Journal, Vol.25, No.3, Jan-Mar.

Central Vigilance Commission : Annual Reports – Various Issues.

Chatterjee, G.S. : (1976) "Disparities in Per Capita House-hold Consumption in India – A Note," Economic and Political Weekly.

Dantwala, M.L.: (1978) "Recommendation of Working Group on Block Level Planning," Economic Intelligence Service, CMIE, July,

----------------------: (1985) "Discussion – 'GaribiHatao' Stratergy Options," Economic and Political Weekly, Vol.XX, No.11, March 16, pp.475-776.

----------------------: (1987) "Integrated Rural Development Programme and Village Structure," Economic and Political Weekly, VOl.XXII, No.22, May 30.

Dasgupta, S.: (1971) "Socio-Economic Classification of Districts: A Statistical Approach," Economic and Political Weekly, VOl.VI, pp.1763-1774.

Douglas D. Evanoff and Diana Fortier : (1986) "The Impact of Geographic Expansion in Banking - Some Axioms to Grind," PRB Chicago Economic Perspectives, Vol.X, No.3, May/June, pp.24-38.

Elangovan, S. : (1987) "social Banking: Achievements and Tasks Ahead," IBA Bulletin, Vol.IX, No.11, Nov.

Francis Cherunilam : "Development of Backward Regions: Policy, Approach and Progress," The Indian Journal of Commerce, Vol.XXXVII, pp.123- 127.

Fry, M.J.: (1978) "Money and Capital or Financial Depending in Economic Development," Journal of Money, Credit and Banking, p.10.

Ghosh, D.N. : (1986) "Poverty Alleviation Programme: Financial Bodies Must be Sound," SBI Monthly Review, Vol. XXI, No.6, June, pp.279-283.

Gurley, J.G. and E.S. Shaw.: (1967) "Financial Structure and Economic Development," Economic Development and Cultural Change, April, p.15.

Hanumantha Rao, C.H.: (1983) "Agricultural Growth and Rural Poverty," Economic and Political Weekly, p.1369.

Hazari, R.K.: (1970) "Commercial Banks and Development, Some Observations on the Indian Experience, "Journal of the Indian Institute of Bankers, Vol.41, No.1, Jan/Mar.

Indira Hirway : (1985) "Discussion - 'GaribiHatao' Can IRDP do it?" Economic and Political Weekly, March 30, pp.561-564.

----------------------: (1987) "Hosuing for Rural Poor," Economic and Political Weekly, Aug.22.

Jha, L.K.: (1970) "Banking and Development," RBI Bulletin, Feb. p.272.

Kannan, R. : (1987) "Banking Development and Regional Disparities," The Indian Economic Journal, (Oct – Dec.) Vol. 35, No.2.

Kanvinde, D.J. : (1978) "Branch Expansion and Lead Bank Scheme-An Exercise in area Planning," SBI Monthly Review, Dec.

Krishna Raj: (1988) Editorial-"Monetarist Blinkers," Economic and Political Weekly, Sep.10.

Majumdar, N.A. : (1979) "Banking Development in Sixth Plan: Some Issues," Economic and political Weekly, p. 2098.

Malcom S. Adiesehiah : 'Mid-Year Review of the Sixth Plan," Economic and Political Weekly, Vol.XIX, No.4, pp. 167-189,

Malhotra, R.N.: (1986) "The Role of Banking In Rural Development," The Journal of the Indian Institute of Bankers, Vol.57, No.3,July-September.

----------------------: (1987) "Financial Structure, Policies and Economic Growth," Commerce, Feb.21-27, pp.17-20.

Manmohan Singh: (1986) "Development Social Justice and Modernisation," The Indian Economic Journal, Vol.33, No.4, (April-June).

MeenakshiTygarajan : (1975) "The Changing Pattern of Commercial Banking of India," Gokhale Endowment Lectures, University of Madras, Oct.

----------------------: (1982) "Deposits with Commercial Banks A Profile," Economic and Political Weekly, Vol.XVII, No.43, Oct.23, pp.1744-1749.

Narasimham, M. : (1989) "Keynote Address Delivered at the 12th Bank Economists' Meet in Bombay on January 20."

Nilakantha Rath : (1985) "'GaribiHatao' : Can IRDP do it?" Economic and Political Weekly, Vol.XX, No.6, Feb.

Noorbasha Abdul and Dakshinamurthy, D. : (1983) "Rich Farmers Grab All Benefits, Leave Poor Farmers in the Lurch," Yojana, July 16-31.

Ojha, P.D. : (1987) "Banking and Economic Development in India: Problems and Prospects, National Bank News Review, January.

Pai, T.A. : (1970) "Banking for the Small Man," Commerce, Feb.17.

Patrick, H.T.: (1966) "Financial Development and Economic Growth in Under-developed Countries," Economic Development and Cultural Change, Jan. p.14.

Pendharkar, V.G. : (1967) "Bank Deposits in the Indian Economy – A Note on Creation and Leakages," Economic and Political Weekly, Special Number, Aug.

Raj, K.N. : (1984) "Some Observations on Economic Growth in India over The period 1952-53 to 1982-83," Economic and political Weekly, p.1801.

Raj Krishna: (1983) "Growth, Investment and Poverty in Mid-Term Appraisal of Sixth Plan," Economic and Political Weekly, p/1972.

Rangarajan, C. : (1974) "Banking Development Since Nationalisation and Reduction in Disparities," Sankhya Vol.36, Series C.

Rao, V.K.R.V., Dandekar, V.M. and Sukhtand : (1981) "measurement of Poverty," Economic and Political Weekly, pp.1241-1440.

Reddy, K.N.: (1976) "Inter-State Differences in Social Consumption in India – A note," Economic and Political Weekly, p.672.

Samuel Paul and Ashok Subramanian : "Development Programmes for the Poor: Do Strategies Make A difference?," Economic and Political Weekly, p.1146.

Samuel Paul : (1984) "Institutional Factors in Development Economic and Political Weekly, p.164.

www.ingramcontent.com/pod-product-compliance
Lightning Source LLC
Chambersburg PA
CBHW081724220526
45468CB00008B/1962